COLD WAR
in the
CONGO

COLD WAR
in the
CONGO

The Confrontation of Cuban Military Forces, 1960-1967

Frank R. Villafaña

Transaction Publishers
New Brunswick (U.S.A.) and London (U.K.)

First paperback printing 2012

Copyright © 2009 by Transaction Publishers, New Brunswick, New Jersey.

This book is printed on acid-free paper that meets the American National Standard for Permanence of Paper for Printed Library Materials.

Library of Congress Catalog Number: 2009016358
ISBN: 978-1-4128-1007-4 (cloth); 978-1-4128-4766-7 (paper)
Printed in the United States of America

Library of Congress Cataloging-in-Publication Data

Villafana, Frank R.
    Cold war in the Congo : the confrontation of Cuban military forces,
    1960-1967 / Frank R. Villafana.
        p. cm.
    Includes bibliographical references and index.
    ISBN 978-1-4128-1007-4
        1. Congo (Democratic Republic)—History—Civil War, 1960-
    1965—Participation, Cuban. 2. Congo (Democratic Republic)— History—Civil War, 1960-1965—Diplomatic history. 3. Cubans--Congo (Democratic Republic)—History—20th century. 4. Mercenary troops—Congo (Democratic Republic)—History—20th century. 5. Exiles—Cuba—History—20th century. 6. United States. Central Intelligence Agency. I. Title.

DT658.22.V55 2009
967.5103'1—dc22

                                                    2009016358

Contents

List of Figures

Acknowledgments

Many people and institutions have assisted me in the research and writing of these historical events.

I am indebted to the surviving Cuban exile combatants who defended freedom in Congo. They gave generously of their time in answering my questions, contacting other veterans of the Congo campaign, and finding documents and photographs. Without their help, this story would not have come alive.

I am very grateful to Ramón Barquín, who in spite of his busy schedule read various versions of the manuscript as it evolved over time. It was Ramón who pointed me in the direction of this incredible story, thought by many as a myth, yet so recondite in its true details.

Lawrence R. Devlin, CIA Chief of Station Congo 1960-1967, patiently answered my many questions about events involving Cubans and Cuban exiles during his tenure in Congo. I thank him for his openness and candor.

My personal thanks go to Jean-Paul Deschamps for his assistance in researching the Revolt of the Mercenaries chapter at the *Albertine* National Library in Brussels, as well as his encouragement. I also thank Roger Presas for his constructive comments on early versions of the manuscript.

Armando González of the *Miami Herald* walked me through important doors in Miami and offered insightful observations on the manuscript, particularly on the early days of the Cuban Revolution. I am grateful for his help and advocacy.

My thanks go to the knowledgeable and helpful staff at the University of Miami Library, Cuban Heritage Collection, particularly to Lesbia Orta Varona. I am also grateful to the library staff at the Universidad de Almería in Spain for their help in obtaining on loan reference books from many libraries around the world.

I appreciate the time and effort devoted by my son David Martin Villafaña, the cartographer, in the preparation of maps included in this book.

And finally, my most emphatic thank you is for my wife Karen for reading the many iterations of the manuscript and continuously offering support and encouragement. During this process, she immersed herself in the evolution of Congo after independence and asked me to answer questions, which were vital to the continuity of the narration.

Frank Villafaña
August 2008

Introduction

The fact that Congo became an East versus West battlefield during the first half of the decade of the 1960s is unquestionable.

Literature on these hostilities is abundant, yet mention of the participation of Cuban exiles in Congo is scant. The purpose of this work is to detail the contribution made by the Cuban exiles to the preservation of democracy in Congo, and wherever possible, to bring a human face to the Cuban exiles involved.

The story covered in this book starts a bit before June 30, 1960, the date Belgium officially granted Congo's independence. The detailed events actually start on January 1, 1959, the date Fidel Castro seized control of the government of Cuba, an island only ninety miles south of U.S. shores, for Castro did not wait long to begin exporting his revolution.

Congo was at war in various degrees from 1960 through 1967, although 1964 and 1965 were the critical years. When Congo was given its independence by Belgium in mid-1960, a significant number of Congolese people believed that their new government had been installed by the West and considered it to be a form of neo-colonialism. A number of anti-colonial, anti-government Congolese patriots soon started fighting against their government. Some of these fighters were pro-communist, some anti-communist, while the majority didn't know the difference. Additionally, there were many countries directly or indirectly involved on both sides of this conflict. Some of these were: Cuba, the Soviet Union, The People's Republic of China (PRC), the U.S. (represented by military advisors, the CIA and Cuban exiles), Belgium, France, the U.K., and several African nations.

The Cold War actions of the U.S., the USSR and to some extent the PRC were generally predictable and not so difficult to understand. The Cuban involvement in Congo was neither predictable nor easy to understand. The answers to some questions about Castro's involvement in Congo will be explored in this work. Why did Castro choose Africa? Did Castro have a master plan? Why did Castro choose Che Guevara to head this ill-fated military expedition? Why did the U.S. allow Castro to freely export his revolution? Why did the U.S. and the CIA choose Cuban exiles to prevent the mineral riches of Congo from falling into the hands of international communism?

While researching this book, I have relied on literature published in Cuba, the U.S., Spain, France, Belgium, and various other countries, as well as interviews with surviving combatants and knowledgeable U.S. personnel. A list of the persons interviewed is presented in Appendix IV. When I quote material not written in the English language, I have translated the words as well as the intended meaning to the best of my abilities.

This is not a book of fiction. When conclusions are supported by historical evidence, I will say so. When I had to go beyond available data to back up my ratiocination, I will state that this is my own deduction.

The main conclusion is clear: CIA-sponsored Miami Cuban exiles played a significant role in preventing Congo from being dragged into the communist orbit and were instrumental in thwarting Castro's African plan, which is believed to have included a confederacy with Tanzania and Congo (Brazzaville), to gain control of Central Africa and its vast resources.

I dedicate this book to the Miami Cuban exiles that fought in Congo under the sponsorship of the Central Intelligence Agency. These same exiles were not permitted to fight to liberate their beloved Cuba from communism, but when their adopted country called for volunteers to help preserve democracy in Congo, they took a step forward, stood in attention, and said: "we're ready."

Some of these brave Cuban-Americans were killed in action in Congo and many have died since 1967 in accidents or of old age. I trust that as freedom-loving people read this book they will develop respect and gratitude for this small group of Cuban exiles who risked their lives for freedom and democracy.

Part I

Congo on the Cross-Hair of Communism

1

Importance of Congo

This book is about a remote and little appreciated but highly significant episode of the Cold War. It involves the country we now know as the Democratic Republic of Congo. Although many sub-Saharan countries would play a role in the Cold War, Congo would be the one taking center stage during the first half of the decade of the 1960s.

In order to minimize confusion, the Democratic Republic of Congo will be simply referred to as Congo. The neighboring country across the river, the former French Congo, now known as Republic of the Congo will be referred to as Congo (Brazzaville), using the name of its capital city within parentheses for differentiation. The current name of the capital of Congo is Kinshasa, then known as Léopoldville, but for the sake of consistency the current geographic names will be used throughout this text. Appendix I contains the current names of Congolese cities mentioned in this book with the corresponding city names from the 1960-1967 timeframe. The geography of Congo is provided in Figure 1.

Which events catapulted Congo into its prominent role in the Cold War in 1960? Many simultaneous events played a role, including: Congo's independence from Belgium on June 30, 1960; Congo's immense mineral wealth, both in terms of economic and strategic value; and the absence of Congolese leadership after independence.

Congo was a Belgian colony for many years, during which time its mineral wealth was controlled by Belgian, British, and American consortia. Although these corporations wielded significant influence, they did not control the policy decisions of their respective governments. The most powerful multinational mining organization operating in Congo was the Belgian/British/U.S. conglomerate *Union Minière du Haut Katanga* (UMHK). UMHK would attempt to change the Congo political landscape to suit its profit motives.

By mid-1959 it became evident that Congo's independence from Belgium was imminent, but the election of Patrice Lumumba as Congo's

3

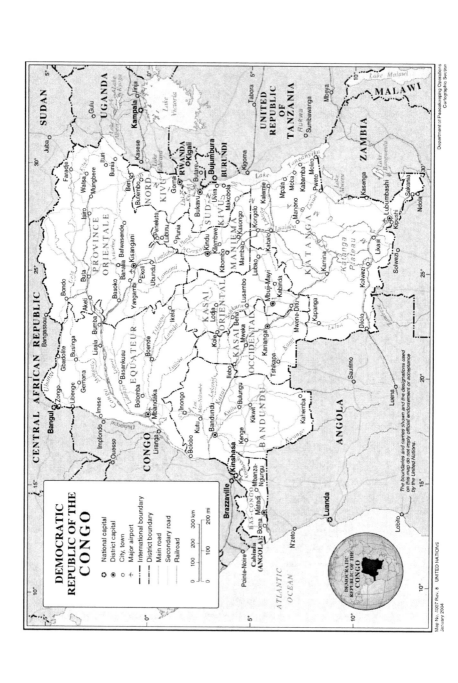

Prime Minister and Congo's independence on June 30, 1960 seemingly took the West by surprise. It is likely that there were other high priority issues capturing the attention of the governments of Britain, Belgium, and the U.S., which prevented them from developing a strategy to secure Congo's critical mineral wealth. In any event, Congo's independence created a major crisis in the West and an immense opportunity for the USSR and the PRC. How important to the West were Congo's minerals?

During the late 1950s and 1960s U.S. military strategy relied heavily on nuclear defense. Additionally, the defense of NATO and the West depended on rocket technology to deliver its war heads. A number of the critical minerals required for both the construction of nuclear devices and the delivery thereof, at the time, were available to the West only in Katanga Province, Congo. Two of these critical minerals were uranium and coltan. Coltan is the colloquial name given to the ore columbo-tantalite, which contains niobium (also known as columbium) and tantalum, two minerals essential for nuclear weapons. Congo is estimated to hold 80 percent of the world's coltan reserves, and at the time it held the largest known deposits of uranium. As a matter of interest, the uranium to build the first U.S. nuclear devices (Hiroshima and Nagasaki) was obtained from the Shinkolobwe mine near the town of Likasi, formerly known as Jadotville, in Katanga Province, Congo.

There were other mineral reserves of immense economic value in Congo, which made walking away from Congo even more difficult. These include, as a percentage of known world reserves, 65 percent of cobalt, 15 percent of copper, 40 percent of germanium, and 78 percent of diamond. Congo also holds large deposits of iron, tin, chromium, manganese, zinc, cadmium, and gold. Cobalt is a strategic mineral for the defense and aerospace industries, and no known substitute has been found. Cobalt also has many uses in civilian industries and medicine.

While many eyes must have been focused on the wealth of resources in Congo prior to its independence from Belgium, the USSR and the PRC had been careful not to antagonize Belgium before Congo's independence. As early as the late 1950s, both the USSR and the PRC had commenced courting left-leaning regimes in the African continent, but kept a low profile when dealing with leftist Congolese politicians. During these years, the USSR and the PRC had limited their territorial expansion to the takeover of neighboring countries. On or about the time of the Korean Police Action, it became clear that the international community would not allow this territorial growth to proceed. Promptly after Belgium announced their intention to grant independence to Congo,

Soviet and Chinese strategists saw an opportunity to not only increase their respective territories in a different manner, but more importantly to gain control of Congo's mineral wealth.

With independence, the lack of strong local leadership to rule Congo became glaringly evident to strategists from both the East and the West. As soon as Belgian administrators were removed from the public sector, the country sank into chaos. As the situation worsened, private sector European managers, fearing for their safety and the safety of their families, started to depart Congo. This combination of events was of concern to the U.S. administration, as the general belief at that time was that chaos led to Communism. Confirming this concern, CIA Director Allen Dulles sent a cable to Congo CIA Station Chief Larry Devlin, stating that: "… if Lumumba continues to hold high office, the inevitable result will at best be chaos and at worst pave the way to Communist takeover of Congo with disastrous consequences for the prestige of the UN and for the interests of the free world generally."[1]

The mineral riches of Congo, coupled with the unstable political situation, centered Congo on the cross-hair of international communism.

In his insightful study of American Foreign Policy in Congo, historian Stephen Weissman states: "Western Europe was almost totally dependent upon Katangan and Rhodesian [now Zimbabwe] mines for its copper imports. This gave America an *indirect* interest in the stability of [Congo] mining operations."[2]

After a thorough analysis of American and Western European economic interests, Weissman concluded that: "… an *access* interest rather than an investment one was perhaps the most important material incentive for American involvement in Congo."[3]

It follows that if Soviet and Chinese analysts did their job well, Communist interest would have been to curtail or better yet to cut off Western access to Congo's mineral wealth.

Notes

1.   Quoted in: Kalb, Madeleine G., *The Congo Cables: The Cold War in Africa from Eisenhower to Kennedy*, Macmillan Publishing Co., Inc., New York, 1982, pp. 64-65.

2.   Weissman, Stephen R., *American Foreign Policy in the Congo 1960-1964*, Cornell University Press, 1974, p. 30.

3.   *Ibid*, p. 28.

2

Castro's Early Interest in Africa

At the time of Congo's independence, President Eisenhower was on the last few months of his second term. The Eisenhower administration, having just lost Cuba to the USSR, would not allow Congo to go the way of Cuba.

The Cuban takeover by international communism was to have long-lasting effects in U.S. foreign policy, even to this day. Congo would be only one of many countries in which the U.S. intervened to save democracy in reaction to the loss of Cuba. A cable sent by Congo CIA station chief Lawrence Devlin to Washington on August 18, 1960 sets the stage for Congo's immediate future: "Embassy and Station believe Congo experiencing classic Communist effort takeover government. Many forces at work here: Soviets, Communist party, etc. Although difficult [to] determine major influencing factors to predict outcome [of] struggle for power, decisive period not far off. Whether or not Lumumba actually commie or just playing commie game to assist his solidifying power, anti-West forces rapidly increasing power [in] Congo and there may be little time left in which to take action [to] avoid another Cuba."[1]

The first true Cuban international military operation under Castro took place on June 14, 1959, when 56 soldiers flew from Manzanillo, Cuba to Constanza, Dominican Republic in an attempt to topple the right-wing Trujillo government. Dominican navy and air force sank two vessels, which were carrying weapons and provisions for the invaders. Most of the Cubans were killed by peasants armed with machetes, thus ending this ill-fated mission.[2]

This initial defeat did not deter Castro from adding his personal dimension to the Cold War. At first, Cuba limited itself to training left-leaning elements in the art of guerrilla warfare and urban terrorism. Cuba concentrated in training revolutionaries from Latin American countries such as Guatemala, Venezuela, Chile, and Colombia, to name a few, but Castro kept his options open to assist revolutions in other continents.

He also continued to tell the world that Cuba was a non-aligned nation, even though his actions clearly demonstrated that at the time, he owed allegiance to the Kremlin.

"In June 1959, Che Guevara visited Egypt, India, Pakistan, Indonesia, Japan, Yugoslavia, and his trip concluded with a secret visit to the USSR."[3] While in Cairo, Guevara established contacts with African liberation movements stationed in that city and supported by Egypt's popular socialist president Gamal Abdel-Nasser. Even though Guevara established a warm relationship with the Egyptian leader, Nasser never attempted to hide his contempt for Fidel Castro, as Nasser did not believe Castro's self-proclamation of being a non-aligned leader.

Then, Castro went African and following a subsequent visit by Raúl Castro and Che Guevara to Cairo and Gaza in late 1959, leftist African leaders from Congo, Ghana, Kenya, Tanganyika, and Zanzibar, among others, were welcomed in Cuba for indoctrination and military training. Castro's first semblance of a developing African strategy surfaced during his address to the UN in September 1960[4] when he urged the UN to intervene in the Algerian independence war. Castro was not only ignored by France and Algeria, but by all African independent nations.

Comparing Castro's actions in Latin America with those in Africa during his first two years in power, it appears that Castro was undecided as to whether it made more sense to join in *liberation* movements in Latin America, in Africa, or in both. It is difficult to ascertain if Castro was reluctant to display a higher profile in Latin America because of fear of U.S. retaliation, or if he confused the nationalistic proclamations of African leaders with their desire to join the communist brotherhood of nations. At a minimum, Castro must have recognized the mineral wealth of Central Africa. Juan Benemelis, one of the original architects of Castro's African strategy and infrastructure during the 1960s, in his book published in 2002 states: "… considering its magnitude, the investment in human and material resources, as well as the strength of determination, it is evident that the African scene was given at least as much attention as Latin America."[5]

In late 1960, in spite of his prior rebuff by the UN, Castro became convinced that Algeria's revolution against French colonialism was worthy of Cuban support. As Castro became bolder, in December 1961 he shipped weapons to Ben Bella's Algerian National Liberation Front (FNL) through the Moroccan port of Casablanca.[6] Nevertheless, the Cuban government was extremely careful to conceal its international revolutionary activities for fear of reprisal from the U.S.

As Cuban exiles landed in the inhospitable area known as Bay of Pigs in April 1961, another American sponsored intervention was underway the full width of the Atlantic Ocean away. The U.S. administration had decided that America's access to the mineral riches of Congo had to be protected, and had instructed its intelligence services accordingly.

The U.S. and Western Europe allies had made all the necessary preparations to remove Prime Minister Lumumba, the only Congolese leader who had had any chance to unite his people after independence, literally before he took office. However, with Lumumba dead, the U.S.'s limited assets in Congo were insufficient to counter any move the Soviet Union and/or the People's Republic of China (at that time, no one would have guessed that Cuba would eventually become a threat to Congo) might initiate. The American embassy in Kinshasa, as well as the small CIA office in that city, was staffed by only a handful of civil servants. They immediately asked for help to weather the upcoming storm.[7]

After denying any communist ties for almost three years, and proclaiming that his revolution was humanist and not communist, Castro publicly declared himself a Marxist-Leninist on December 2, 1961.[8] Taking words into action, in June 1962, Che Guevara and Raúl Castro signed a secret treaty with the USSR to place mid-range rockets with nuclear heads in the island-nation. Castro had hoped that by declaring Cuba a communist country, the Soviet Union would include Cuba in the Warsaw Pact, thus obtaining for Cuba the protection of the entire Soviet Bloc in the event of an invasion. The USSR never did officially cover Cuba under the Warsaw Pact umbrella.

The Cuban Missile Crisis ended when Khrushchev announced the removal of the missiles on October 28, 1962. One of the conditions demanded by the Soviet Union to end the crisis was that the U.S. would enforce a hands-off-Cuba policy.

Not all portions of the Kennedy-Khrushchev agreement have been declassified, but it is known that President Kennedy gave Premier Khrushchev assurances against an invasion of Cuba from the United States at any time in the future, and Kennedy added that he was "confident that other nations in the Western Hemisphere would be prepared to do likewise."[9]

Kennedy and Khrushchev may have also discussed Castro's involvement and support of revolutionary activities in Latin America. If so, it is likely that Khrushchev gave Castro some fatherly advice and asked him to keep a low profile in Latin America, thus making Africa a more attractive target.

Following the resolution of the Missile Crisis, several Latin American nations were concerned that the U.S. had bound them also into a hands-off-Cuba agreement without consulting with them. They further feared that the U.S. had guaranteed a permanent Soviet regime in Cuba.[10]

It is likely that Castro had finalized his African strategy by mid-1963, but he first needed to test Cuba's military strength as well as perform a reality check on leaders who had said they would support liberation movements. His first move was in May 1963, after Algeria's independence, when Cuba provided physicians and other medical assistance to Ben Bella's unstable government.

The opportunity to test Cuba's military as well as Castro's African strategy presented itself in October 1963, during a border dispute between Algeria and Morocco. This situation had been festering since 1845, and for several years prior to 1963 some sort of military action had been predicted.

In August 1963, Castro had sent a military delegation to his Algerian friend Ben Bella, headed by Che Guevara, and composed of Victor Dreke, Harry Villegas and Raúl Suárez, people with whom the reader will become familiar in Chapters Eight and Ten as Dreke and Villegas would serve in Congo under the command of Che Guevara. The first Cuban troops arrived at the Algerian port of Oran on October 21, 1963, in three merchant ships: *Aracelio Iglesias*, *Playa Girón*, and *Sierra Maestra*. The remaining troops arrived on October 28, 1963, in the vessel *González Lines*.

Cuban troop strength was 2,200 soldiers plus around 1,000 men for logistical support. There were 50 heavy T-55 tanks, as well as a number of MiG-17 fighters. Troops were under the command of Efigenio Ameijeiras.[11] In an unusual display of cooperation, Cuban troops fought alongside Egyptian troops. Castro and Nasser were enemies for life, but war does make for strange bedfellows.

The combined Cuban-Algerian-Egyptian forces were too much for the Moroccans, and after frantic negotiations in Mali, a cease fire was agreed on November 2, 1963. It was not until November 4, 1963, that Cuban soldiers stopped fighting. A small portion of the Cuban troops were allowed to return to Cuba, but the majority stayed for some time in Algeria and other African countries to train African revolutionaries. Some troops went on to Congo (Brazzaville), possibly to prepare for future action in Congo. Another large contingent of Cubans was operating in Sudan during the Simba revolt, and was instrumental in supplying the Congolese anti-government rebels. Cuban troops located in Sudan, Rwanda, and Uganda participated from time to time in military operations inside Congo.

Algeria became a Cuban outpost until Ben Bella's ouster on June 19, 1965. Castro must have been aware that Ben Bella's leadership position in Algeria was weakening, for at the end of 1964, two Cuban battalions stationed in Algeria were sent to the Lake Tanganyika area of Tanzania. This move possibly had a two-fold purpose: to get Cuban troops out of Algeria in case a Civil War erupted, and to position these troops for future Congo action. Additional Cuban troops were dispatched to Sudan, Uganda, and Burundi, near the Congo border. The mission of all of these troops was to train Congolese rebels and to assist in the logistics of supplying Simba rebels. Occasionally, these Cuban troops would also join in on the fighting.

Why did Castro not try to help his friend Ben Bella when Colonel Houari Boumedienne conducted a *coup d'etat* and took power in Algeria? After all, Castro had thousands of troops in Africa, as well as armored vehicles, planes, and artillery. Castro would have simplified the logistics of future operations, as he would have been able to maintain his Algerian base of operations and he also would have been protecting a friend. Possibly, Ben Bella had outgrown his usefulness. Additionally, Castro had no interest in North Africa or a potential showdown with militarily powerful France, a country which at that time was a bitter enemy of the Castro regime. Castro's lack of action in Algeria did have a price, for "in July 1965, Boumedienne expelled all Cuban Intelligence officers (DGI) from Algeria, and put an end to training by Cubans at Algerian guerrilla camps."[12]

By the start of 1964, Fidel Castro's recently tested African strategy was ready to be implemented. This is evidenced in Che's speech before the UN as well as Che's declarations in Tanzania in early 1964: "The Cuban embassies in Algeria and Tanzania report directly to Fidel Castro."[13]

Castro's African adventures began to yield fruit. On January 12, 1964, an insurrection led by John Okello, a revolutionary trained in Cuba, overthrew the pro-Western government of Zanzibar and proclaimed the People's Republic of Zanzibar. This new country was promptly recognized by the Soviet Union and Cuba. The Johnson administration asked Britain to send troops to stop the left-wing-inspired takeover in the former British Crown colony of Zanzibar by John Okello, but Britain refused.

While Castro was hard at work developing and testing his Central Africa strategy, the Kennedy administration was devoting their energy to the ever-escalating Vietnam conflict and the civil rights movement. Little time was left for the U.S. administration to develop a strategy to protect Western interests in Congo.

Weissman traces America's failure to produce a coherent Congo policy (1960-1963) directly to President Kennedy. Weissman evidences the President's inclination to compromise internal differences even when these differences were uncompromisable. Weissman further states: "Kennedy made panicky decisions in Congo in response to a minuscule right-wing lobby."[14] Weissman concludes his analysis with the statement: "The Congo was only an instance of Kennedy's most glaring failure: his incapacity as a statesman."[15]

In order to insure the support of African leaders, Castro embarked on a campaign to demonstrate that Cuba was a *non-aligned* nation. An excellent example is provided by Benemelis: "After the African tours by Malcolm X in 1963 and 1964, Castro established an alliance with Malcolm X as a way to raise Cuba's prestige in Africa."[16] This alliance must have continued for some time since Malcolm X blasted the Cuban exiles fighting in Congo, in a speech loaded with sarcasm given in Rochester, New York on February 16, 1965, five days before his death. "... American-trained, that makes them okay. Anti-Castro Cubans, that makes them okay. Castro's a monster, so anybody who's against Castro is all right with us ..."[17]

The political situation in Africa during the first half of the decade of the 1960s should also be examined. North Africa, both in population and territorial extension was under the influence of the Soviet Union, with the exception of the two smaller countries, Morocco and Tunisia, which were decidedly pro-Western. The PRC was concentrating its efforts in Sub-Saharan Africa, and enjoying significant success since virtually all African regimes in this area were suspicious of Soviet motives.

The government of Ben Bella in Algeria depended on Soviet support for its survival. The Soviets also supported Libya in its efforts to control Chad and Sudan. And finally, Egypt (then the United Arab Republic) under Nasser was indeed a non-aligned country even though it received unconditional military support from the Soviet Union in its struggle against Israel. An unusual situation in the Cold War was that because of his hatred of Nasser, Castro maintained close ties with Israel until Nasser's death.

The Soviet Union was also openly supporting Ethiopian encroachment on Somalia. The situation in central and southern Africa was even more violently anti-Western, as the Soviet and Chinese ideologists had managed to convince key African political figures that the West's only aim was to reinstate colonial rule in Africa.

The newly-independent Republic of the Congo (Brazzaville) was receptive to Soviet overtures and welcomed China with open arms. This was unique, as most African nations at the time were either pro-Soviet or pro-Chinese.

Given the political situation in central Africa during this critical Cold War period (1960-1965), as portrayed in Figure 2, Congo's geographic location made it an apparent easy target.

Many African leaders were socialists and left-leaning, but there were two key pro-communist Sub-Saharan African leaders who came to the help of any African nation purporting to struggle for African rule. They were Guinea's President Sekuo Touré and Tanzania's President Julius Nyerere.

During the first half of the decade of the 1960s, the key African support locations for any nationalist armed struggle activity were Cairo, Algiers, Dar Es-Salaam, Bissau, and Brazzaville. It is well-known that any liberation movement in Africa was encouraged by the support of Egypt's Nasser and Algeria's Ben Bella.

Castro's military strategy clearly included using the friendly regimes of Congo (Brazzaville) and Tanzania as bases from which to take over Congo. If Congo were to fall under his control, his friendly territory would reach from coast to coast. This would be important for logistics since ports in the Indian as well as the Atlantic Ocean would be available to resupply his armies. Castro's next moves would likely have been the liberation of the Portuguese colonies, (oil and diamond rich) Angola and (poverty stricken) Mozambique. The priority was clearly Angola, but as a self-declared non-aligned strategist he would have had to show equality. Since these actions would have soon encroached on Namibian territory, logically the next encounter would have been with the powerful South African armed forces. Anti-colonial rebels in the Portuguese colonies of Angola and Mozambique were fighting for independence with a predominance of pro-Soviet leadership. When all of the above is coupled with South Africa's militancy against apartheid and Namibia's struggle for African majority rule, there was a strong likelihood that the southern portion of the African continent could have fallen under Communist rule.

This was possibly the analysis that Cuba's Fidel Castro had done. Why he waited until the spring of 1965 to send troops to Congo is a secret he may take to the grave, but had he taken action a year earlier, perhaps the outcome would have been quite different. The Ben Bella government was toppled in mid-1965, thus depriving Cuban invaders of a vital logistical support point. The key initial country to Castro's apparent African strat-

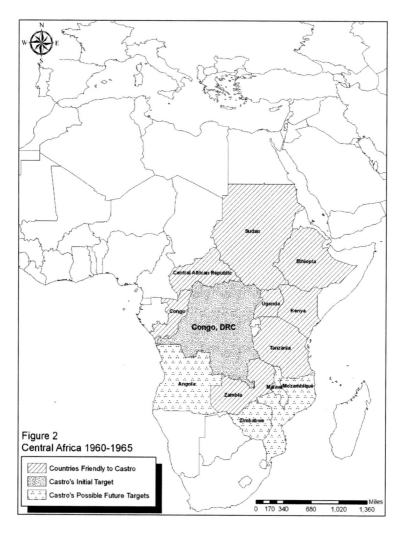

Figure 2
Central Africa 1960-1965

Countries Friendly to Castro
Castro's Initial Target
Castro's Possible Future Targets

egy was Congo. This was so, not only because of its mineral wealth, but because a confederation with Tanzania, Congo (Brazzaville), and Zambia could easily be orchestrated. And with the military support of both the Soviet Union and the PRC, this confederation would have had a good chance to rule the destiny of a good portion of the African continent. Concurrently, Castro would be delivering the mineral riches of Congo to the Soviet Union. The Soviet Union had all the uranium they needed, but the important point to Castro was that Congo's mineral resources would no longer be available to the West.

It is difficult to comprehend, even today, how Cuba, an island in the Caribbean Sea with a population during the year 1960 of around 6 million people, would try to seize Congo, a country 20 times its size, having around 8 times more people, and located almost 11,000 kilometers away. It is even more difficult to comprehend how the U.S. and Western Europe came close to allowing Castro to execute his Congo strategy, when Congo contained an array of mineral deposits, which were strategically critical to the survival of the West at that time.

Castro said many times that to defeat the U.S. all he needed was two, three ... many Vietnams. It is not known for certain when Castro used this expression for the first time. Some people in Castro's inner circle, such as his brother Raúl and Che Guevara openly articulated this slogan as early as 1961.

Vietnam number one was the then existing Asia conflict, and the U.S. had its hands full. Vietnam number two was Latin America (which could, in fact, explode into several Vietnams), where the implementation of Castro's strategy was being handled by a select group of KGB operatives under the direction of Russian/Spanish General Enrique Líster Forján.

The presence of General Líster in Cuba was well-known. However, his role as a strategist of the Cuban Revolution was top secret, as this would have detracted from Castro's claimed non-aligned position. In fact, it was not until a 2003 book by Jaime Costa, that the role of General Líster in exporting the Cuban revolution was revealed.[18] Costa was a close friend and associate of the Castro brothers, who later became a political prisoner, and was released in 2001 on humanitarian grounds.

In late 1959, General Líster joined Cuban Intelligence Chief Ramiro Valdéz in designing and later implementing the Committees for the Defense of the Revolution. Afterwards, Líster became the *éminence grise* in the execution of Castro's Latin America strategy.

Vietnam number three was Africa (which could also expand to include several nations), with Che Guevara nominally in charge, while Castro pulled the strings, secure that he would have the support of Algeria, Ghana, Congo (Brazzaville), and Tanzania. Castro was convinced that the U.S. could be forced to actively participate militarily in all Vietnams. Castro's challenge was clear: control the government of Congo and then the other pieces of the puzzle would follow.

Notes

1.   U.S. Senate Select Committee, *Interim Report: Alleged Assassination Plots Involving Foreign Leaders*, Washington, DC., GPO, November 20, 1975, p. 14.

2. Carbonell, Nestor T., *And the Russians Stayed*, Morrow, New York, 1989, p. 73.
3. Benemelis, Juan F., *Castro, Subversión y Terrorismo en Africa*, Editorial San Martín, Madrid, 1988, pp. 31-32.
4. Benemelis, Juan F., *Las Guerras Secretas de Fidel Castro*, Fundación Elena Maderos, Miami, 2002, p. 79.
5. *Ibid*, p. 75.
6. Carbonell, *op. cit.*, p. 288.
7. Devlin, Larry, *Chief of Station, Congo*, Public Affairs, New York, 2007, pp. 48-49.
8. Carbonell, *op. cit.*, p. 73.
9. Carbonell, *op. cit.*, p. 260.
10. *Ibid*, pp. 234-238.
11. Benemelis, *Las Guerras Secretas de Fidel Castro*, p. 89.
12. Benemelis, Castro, *Subversión y Terrorismo en Africa*, p. 180.
13. *Ibid*, p. 157.
14. Weissman, *op. cit.*, pp. 191-193.
15. *Ibid*, p. 194.
16. Benemelis, Castro, *Subversión y Terrorismo en Africa*, p. 158.
17. From *http://themilitant.com/1997/6110/6116*, downloaded April 6, 2005.
18. Costa, Jaime, *El Clarín Toca al Amanecer*, Ediciones Rondas, Barcelona, 2003, pp. 429-435.

3

Lumumba

The political situation in Congo immediately after independence was certainly in disarray, but with Lumumba's election win and his appointment as Prime Minister, it looked as if circumstances would improve. Lumumba's assassination, six months later, instantly turned disarray into chaos. There were many mistakes made by both the East and the West during the Cold War, but if the mistakes made by the West were to be ranked by order of importance regarding their impact on future events, Lumumba's assassination would rank close to the top of the list.

Patrice Emery Lumumba was born in Onalua, Kasai Oriental Province, Congo on July 2, 1925. Lumumba was tortured and assassinated somewhere in Katanga Province on January 17, 1961, by Belgian mercenaries in the presence of Moïse Tshombé, who was the self-appointed President of Katanga.[1]

Lumumba was a member of Batetela, a small tribe, attended a Catholic mission school, and afterwards went to work at Kindu, where he was active in the club of *évolués,* or French-speaking educated Africans. It was at this time that he began writing poetry and essays, which were published in Congolese journals, and in doing so, his name became known.

After obtaining a job as a postal clerk, Lumumba moved to Kinshasa. He was later promoted to accountant in the post office of Kisangani, then known as Stanleyville, and continued to contribute to the Congolese press, thus increasing his popularity.

In 1955, Lumumba became active in the Belgian Liberal Party in Congo. Lumumba was an eloquent speaker and frequently expressed his anti-colonial and pro-independence ideas during his many speaking engagements. Belgian authorities distrusted anyone harboring pro-independence and anti-colonial sentiments.

Lumumba, along with other Congolese politicians, was invited in 1956 by the Belgian Minister of Colonies to make a study tour of Belgium. Upon his return, he was arrested and charged with embezzlement of post office funds. Some believe this study tour was staged by colonial authorities to allow enough time to fabricate evidence of a crime never committed, and thus remove Lumumba from circulation. After many hearings and various reductions of sentence, he was condemned to a one-year prison term and a fine. He maintained his innocence throughout the process.

After his release from prison, Lumumba became even more active in politics. In October 1958, he founded the Congolese National Movement (*Mouvement National Congolais*, or MNC), which was the first nation-wide Congolese National Party, advocating unification of all Congolese regardless of ethnicity.

In December 1958, Lumumba attended the first All-African People's Conference in Accra, Ghana. There he met nationalists from the entire African continent and was made a member of the permanent organization. Even though his pronouncements were for national unity and pan-African goals, he was labeled a militant nationalist by Belgian colonial authorities.

Also in December 1958, the Belgian government promulgated a program that would lead to independence for Congo in five years, with the first step in this program to be local elections to be held in December 1959. The MNC considered these elections to be a sham, an effort to install puppets before independence, and thus announced a boycott of the elections.

The answer from the Belgian authorities was repression. As restraints became more severe, the riots became increasingly violent. On October 30, 1959, there was a clash in Kisangani that resulted in thirty deaths, and Lumumba was accused of inciting to riot and imprisoned. The Congo uprisings became the most powerful ever against Western rule in Africa. Hundreds of thousands of workers took to the streets to demand freedom and independence from Belgium. Rioting grew to such levels that the Belgians decided they could not hold on to power. In January 1960, the Belgian government called for a Round Table Conference in Brussels of all Congolese parties to discuss political change and the granting of independence within six months time. The MNC refused to attend the Conference without Lumumba. Having run out of options, the Belgian authorities reluctantly released him from prison and flew him to Brussels as part of the preparation for Congolese elections.

The Conference agreed to hold national elections in May 1960, and the transfer of power was set for June 30, 1960. The MNC, with the conviction of its popularity, changed its strategy, entered the elections, and obtained a sweeping victory in the eastern part of Congo, primarily in the provinces of Orientale, Equateur, and Maniema. In the important city of Kisangani, Lumumba obtained 90 percent of the votes. With this landslide victory, the MNC and Lumumba emerged as the leading nationalist political force in Congo. The Belgian government attempted various ploys to prevent Lumumba from forming a coalition and taking power, but they were ultimately unsuccessful. He was asked to form the first government and did so on June 23, 1960.

The new government took office on June 30, 1960 (a date observed in Congo as Independence Day) with the key leaders being Prime Minister Patrice Lumumba and President Joseph Kasavubu.

Joseph Kasavubu was born sometime between 1910 and 1918 in the Mayombe district of Bas Congo Province. He attended Catholic schools and studied for the priesthood at Kasai. For reasons that never were made clear, Kasavubu was dismissed from the seminary, but was given the equivalent of a baccalaureate degree and a teacher's certificate. He entered public life in 1946. In 1955 he became president of ABAKO, a cultural association (cum political party) of the Bakongo people. After independence ABAKO would become an above-board political party and a strong rival of the MNC.

Lumumba appointed his long-term supporter Joseph Mobutu to the position of Secretary of State for Defense. Mobutu would become a key player in Congo politics for the next 37 years.

Joseph-Désiré Mobutu was born in Lisala, Congo in 1930. Of Sudanese ancestry, he grew up among the Bangala people of the Bantu ethnic group. He was educated by Catholic missionaries. In 1949, he joined the *Force Publique* of the Belgian colonial authorities, where he rose to the rank of Sergeant Major. In 1956, Mobutu left the armed forces and worked as a journalist. He traveled to Belgium to study journalism and upon his return to Congo became a newspaper editor. In 1958, he joined the nationalist *Mouvement National Congolais* (MNC) and became a close friend of Lumumba and one of his main collaborators. It was because of Lumumba's gratitude for the excellent work done by Mobutu during the electoral process, that Lumumba appointed him to the post of Secretary of State for Defense. Mobutu's new responsibilities included heading the *Armée Nationale Congolais* (ANC), or National Congolese Army, the successor to *Force Publique*, the Belgian colonial army.

The Belgians had hoped for a calm transfer of power. Several Congolese politicians spoke on Independence Day, but when Lumumba's turn came, Baudouin, King of the Belgians and Gastón Eyskens, Belgium's Prime Minister, squirmed in their seats as they listened to Lumumba:

... Our lot was eighty years of colonial rule. We have known sarcasm and insults, endured blows morning, noon and night because we were "niggers" ... We have seen our lands despoiled under the terms of what was supposedly the law of the land but which only recognized the right of the strongest. We have also seen that this law was quite different for a white man than for a black: accommodating for the former, cruel and inhuman for the latter ...[2]

Upon concluding his declamation, supposedly Lumumba told King Baudouin: "We are no longer your monkeys."[3] Unlike the British, who made a serious effort to train leaders of each colony for a future transition of power, the Belgians did little to prepare Congo for its independence. There was not a single native physician, attorney, trained military officer, or architect. The Belgian educational colonial legacy consisted of 16 university graduates (mostly prepared for the priesthood) and 136 graduates of high school. This lack of native elite was possibly consistent with Belgium's financial interests, for it appears that Brussels intended to maintain its economic grip on Congo's reserves of coltan, copper, uranium, cobalt, and diamonds, independence notwithstanding.

The five-year smooth transition originally envisioned by Belgian politicians became a five-month reluctant and tumultuous transfer of power. Congo had great resources, but almost no infrastructure for nation-building. Western investors were particularly concerned as they were unable to predict what new laws would be enacted by this volatile and inexperienced administration. Not only Belgium, but England, France, and especially the U.S. had no intention of allowing their vast economic resources in Congo to be disturbed by this new democratically-elected Republic. Based primarily on Belgian colonial authorities' opinion, the press in Western countries labeled Lumumba as left-leaning and pro-Soviet, a label that would continue to haunt him until his tragic death. The Lumumba administration had to come to age in a hurry, for it had to handle two major crises within days of independence. These were the secessions of Katanga and South Kasai Provinces, and the mutiny of the ANC.

The Belgian mining companies quickly decided that the Lumumba government at Kinshasa would not protect their interests, and nominated Moïse Tshombé, a wealthy plantation owner, as their man-in-Katanga.

Moïse Kapenda Tshombé was born in 1919 to wealthy parents in Masumba, Katanga Province. Masumba was the ancient capital of the Lunda people, and in fact Tshombé was related to the Lunda royal family. Tshombé received his education from an American mission school and trained as an accountant. In 1951, he took over a chain of department stores in Katanga Province and commenced his involvement in politics, which eventually led to his founding of a political party in 1956. The original name of Tshombé's party was UCOL, or Union for Colonization, but since these were virulent anti-colonial times, he changed the party's name to National Katangan Coalition (CONAKAT). This party was supported by Belgium both before and after independence, and had a platform of a loose federation of independent states in Congo. In early 1960, he attended the Brussels Congo Conference and in the subsequent pre-independence general elections of 1960, CONAKAT won control of the Katanga provincial legislature.

Back to the crisis immediately after independence, on July 11, 1960, the pro-Western Tshombé declared Katanga an independent nation and appointed himself head of the government stating "we are seceding from chaos."[4] In August 1960, he was "elected" president of Katanga and asked the Belgian government to send military officers to recruit and train a Katangan army.

A few days later, following Katanga's lead, another mining province, Kasai Occidental, also declared its secession from Congo. The leader of this secession was Albert Kalonji, a former supporter of Lumumba. Kalonji, a man more concerned with his personal wealth than with Congo's independence, immediately became a fierce enemy of Lumumba.

During the first week of July 1960, the National Congolese Army mutinied against the few remaining white officers and carried out numerous attacks against Europeans. Lumumba responded by removing the Belgian officers, including General Emile Janssens, the Belgian commander in chief of the ANC, and appointing a reluctant Joseph Kasavubu to this post. Additionally, Lumumba raised the wages of the ANC by 30 percent.

These were not sound decisions, for they angered Kasavubu and Mobutu as well as the foreign corporations operating in Congo. Kasavubu felt insulted, for as the President he had a country to run and he should not be distracted with the day-to-day functioning of the army. Mobutu was offended as this move implied that he was not performing his function properly. Once the ANC's wages were raised by 30 percent, all Congolese workers expected the same treatment by their employers, thus further distancing profit-driven Western investors from the Lumumba government.

Regarding the secession of Katanga, while "the UMHK bankrolled the whole military operation,"[5] the Belgian military assisted Tshombé in organizing the insurrection and in hastily assembling a mercenary army initially composed of white Rhodesians and South Africans, and Nazi veterans of World War II.

The army mutiny took away whatever little authority the civilian government had. There were numerous terrorist attacks by Congolese civilians on Europeans, and panic engulfed the European population of Congo, as nearly 100,000 Belgians lived in or around the capital city of Kinshasa. Many old scores were settled with spears, machetes, and weapons left behind by mutinous soldiers. The Belgian government responded by sending paratroopers to protect Belgian citizens in Congo. Under international law, this was an illegal act, for Congo was an independent nation and the government of Congo had not invited the troops. The majority of the Belgian troops, ostensibly sent to protect the Belgians living in Kinshasa, landed in Katanga (more than 1,500 kilometers away) to prop up the secessionist regime of Tshombé. As soon as Belgian troops arrived in Katanga, they tried to disarm the ANC, and thus firefights broke out between Belgian soldiers and ANC units.

The Eisenhower administration openly supported the Belgian military intervention in Katanga. In fact, the American embassy in Kinshasa had requested that military assistance be provided to the Katanga regime. The two primary reasons behind this U.S. posture were Washington's dislike of Lumumba resulting from Belgian colonial propaganda, and the fact that a number of prominent administration (and UN) officials had financial ties to the Katanga wealth. Arthur Dean, U.S. delegate to the Geneva Conference on Disarmament was a Vice President of American Metal Climax, while Adlai Stevenson, former presidential candidate and U.S. ambassador to the UN, was the lawyer for Templesman and Son, both corporations with substantial operations in Katanga Province, Congo. Even after Stevenson was appointed ambassador to the UN by President Kennedy, he continued to lobby for Templesman. "The full details of the Stevenson-Templesman relationship may never be known."[6]

Lumumba was not yet aware that he was disliked by the White House. As a democratically elected head of state, Lumumba traveled to the U.S. in July of 1960 to meet with President Eisenhower and ask for his help. Eisenhower avoided him by escaping to Rhode Island for a short holiday. Lumumba met instead with Secretary of State Christian Herter and his assistant C. Douglas Dillon, and asked for the help of the U.S. in removing the Belgians from his country. Help was denied.

In 1975, during a Congressional investigation into political assassinations, the subject of Lumumba's murder was reviewed. Then Under Secretary of State C. Douglas Dillon told the Senate Select Committee on Intelligence Activities, chaired by Senator Frank Church, a liberal Idaho Democrat, that the Eisenhower administration had concluded that

Lumumba was "a very difficult if not impossible person to deal with, and was dangerous to the peace and safety of the world."[7] This statement would later move author Jonathan Kwitney to observe: "How far beyond the dreams of a barefoot postal clerk in 1956, that in a few short years he would be dangerous to peace and safety of the world! The perception seems insane, particularly coming from the National Security Council, which really has the power to end all human life within hours."[8] Former CIA Angola task force chief John Stockwell, who was raised in Congo, suggested that the reason why Lumumba received the cold-shoulder treatment, was that he offended his hosts when he reacted adversely to the experience of segregated washrooms, during his visit to the nation's capital to ask for Eisenhower's help.[9]

Having failed to secure U.S. help, Lumumba requested assistance from the UN. The U.S. viewed this as an opportunity to extend friendly foreign military control in Congo, without being directly involved. At that time, the U.S. exerted significant influence in the running of the UN and the UN Secretary General, Dag Hammarskjöld, was very responsive to U.S. requests and suggestions.

Behind the scenes, the U.S. pushed the UN to comply with Lumumba's request. UN blue helmet troops (Operation UNOC) arrived on July 14, 1960 but they were no match for the 10,000 troops, which Belgium had built up in Congo.

The UN troops had clear instructions not to take sides between Lumumba's government in Kinshasa and Tshombé's mercenary army in Lumumbashi, formerly known as Élisabethville. The UN Security Council had given the UN troops four tasks: restore law and order and maintain it; stop other nations from getting involved with the crisis; assist in building the nation's economy; and restore political stability.

Lumumba was well-aware of the restrictions placed on UN forces by the Security Council; nevertheless, as soon as the UN forces arrived, Lumumba asked them to attack Tshombé's mercenaries in Katanga and to force the Belgian troops to leave Congo. Although the first request was in conflict with the UN mandate, the request to force Belgian troops out would have been clearly within the scope of the UN Security Council resolution. The UN Secretary General, Dag Hammarskjöld, refused permission for either action. As a matter of interest, Bo Hammarskjöld, Dag's elder brother, was on the Board of Directors of a Swedish mining corporation with interest in Katanga's copper.

Lumumba accused the United Nations of siding with Tshombé and the rich European companies that mined Katanga's wealth. In desperation, after first being rebuffed by the U.S. and then frustrated by the ineffectiveness of the UN, Lumumba appealed to the Soviet Union for military help in late July, 1960. The USSR examined the situation and seeing an opportunity immediately dispatched fifteen Ilyushin II fighter planes and fourteen transport planes, all hastily marked with Congolese colors, as well as 100 military trucks and 200 technicians.[10] Madeleine Kalb in *The Congo Cables,* states that the number of Ilyushin II fighter planes was ten rather than fifteen.[11] Each Ilyushin II transport plane had a crew of eight, and was capable of transporting several hundred Congolese troops at a time. In order to complete the new nation's Air Force, Lumumba appropriated five Air Congo DC-3s which were owned by SABENA, the then Belgian National Airlines.

Fortunately for his opposition, Lumumba was no military strategist. His plan was to transport some 1,000 ANC troops to Kananga, then known as Luluabourg, the capital of Kasai Occidental, gain control of this province and then move on to Katanga. During this operation, Lumumba's forces massacred hundreds of pro-Kalonji Balubas as punishment for seceding from Congo. When Soviet trucks carrying ANC troops with their new Czech officers arrived in Mbuji-Mayi, formerly known as Bakwanga, the capital city of Kasai Oriental, Kalonji escaped and hid in the jungle to avoid capture and certain death.

The situation was quite different as the troops marched in the direction of Katanga Province. Now that the element of surprise was gone, when the ANC forces were only some 32 kilometers from Katanga, Tshombé's mercenaries and Belgian regulars attacked and crushed the force loyal to Lumumba. If Lumumba would have attacked Katanga first, his unanticipated action might have worked.

As these events were unfolding, President Eisenhower was in the last few months of his second term, and he clearly did not want to leave the White House under a cloud of dislocation. Eisenhower was the first president to use the CIA as an instrument of foreign policy. A 1954 CIA-sponsored operation to overthrow the leftist regime of Guatemalan President Jacobo Arbenz was arranged in response to the threat by Arbenz to nationalize the properties of the Boston-based United Fruit Company. The CIA hand-picked Carlos Castillo Armas, a renegade colonel, to lead Guatemala. The key elements of the operation were to discourage the army from fighting and to conceal the origin of the operation in the event of failure. The process lasted for nine days and it was successful, but hardly repeatable. Similarly, when Iranian Prime Minister Mohammed Mossadegh menaced U.S. and British oil interests, the CIA arranged to overthrow his government. These are the best two examples of a U.S. intervention model for the replacement of the leader of a country. A similar model would be later used, albeit unsuccessfully, in operations such as the 1961 Bay of Pigs invasion.

The White House had requested information on Lumumba from the U.S. embassy in Kinshasa prior to Lumumba's visit to New York and Washington and the answer was given on July 26, 1960 by the Deputy Ambassador Robinson McIlvaine: "Lumumba is an opportunist and not a communist."[12] A month later, around August 27, 1960 with Czech officers being present and Soviet equipment being used, dwellers of the White House were seeing red. Eisenhower still smarted from Fidel Castro turning Cuba over to Moscow after a rebuff from Washington. The thought of a Soviet-controlled mineral rich Congo was too much for Washington to accept. Eisenhower promptly reached for his intelligence services and told them to work with the Belgian secret service and plot against Lumumba.

Western collusion soon came to fruition. On September 5, 1960, fearing that Lumumba had made too many enemies too quickly, President Joseph Kasavubu dismissed him as Prime Minister. This was a move of questionable legality, for the Congolese parliament strongly supported Lumumba. Lumumba appealed to the UN, but Secretary General Hammarskjöld publicly endorsed the dismissal before the Security Council.

Lumumba's reaction was to dismiss Kasavubu and insist that he, Lumumba, was still Prime Minister. Lumumba tried to broadcast his case to the Congolese people, but the UN closed the radio station. On his last radio address, on or around September 15, 1960 to the citizens of Congo, Lumumba said: "We know that the U.S. understands us and we are pleased to see the U.S. position in bringing about international peace.... If the Congolese place their confidence in the U.S., which is a good friend, they will find themselves rewarded."[13]

Kasavubu sent his own representatives to the UN, and in October the UN General Assembly recognized the credentials of Kasavubu's government. In November 1960, the UN voted 53 to 24 to disown Lumumba's delegation as the one to represent Congo. These were incredible events for an independent country during the second half of the 20th century.

Kasavubu appointed Colonel Joseph Mobutu, then Secretary of State for Defense, to the newly vacant post of Prime Minister. Mobutu accepted the post, set up his government in Kinshasa, suspended the constitution and expelled the Czechs and Russians. Meanwhile, Lumumba's supporters set up a rival government in Kisangani, Orientale Province.

Clare Timberlake, the American ambassador to Congo, vocally supported the coup culprits, Mobutu and Kasavubu, and urged Larry Devlin, CIA station chief in Kinshasa, to turn against Lumumba. We were indeed living in a strange world in 1960. The communist world was supporting a democratically elected government while the U.S. and Western Europe were on the side of individuals who had seized the government by force.

To further complicate the situation in Congo, Hammarskjöld's deputy on the scene, Rajeshwar Dayal of India, refused to recognize the Kasavubu-Mobutu government. Unilaterally, Dayal decided to offer UN protection and sanctuary to Lumumba and his second-in-command, Antoine Gizenga, from arrest warrants from the new regime.

Antoine Gizenga was born in 1925. He was an exemplary Lumumba supporter and had become his Vice Prime Minister in 1960.

Following Dayal's instructions, Lumumba was kept safe in the Prime Minister's villa in Kinshasa by UN troops. In reality, Lumumba's situation can be better described as being under house arrest. He was safe, but he could not run the affairs of Congo. Despite enormous risks, Lumumba decided to escape and join his government in far away Kisangani. He nearly made it, but he was constantly being delayed by supportive crowds demanding he speak to them.

Mobutu's army, with the help of Devlin's informants and the Belgians, closely followed Lumumba and captured him in Kasai Oriental Province on December 1, beat him savagely and placed him in a prison camp in Mbanza-Ngungu, formerly known as Thysville. Mobutu and Kasavubu debated what to do with him. They likely concluded that an imprisoned Lumumba was more dangerous than a dead former Prime Minister, and hence, they decided to deliver him and two aides to Albert Kalonji, Lumumba's former supporter, and now bitter enemy.

Mike Hoare, a mercenary who would become a key player in future events in Congo, provides the most generally accepted version of Lumumba's assassination. "On January 17, 1961, Patrice Lumumba, Joseph Okito [former Deputy Speaker of the Congolese Parliament] and Maurice Mpolo [former Minister for Youth and Sports] were sent by plane from Kinshasa to Kalonji's capital of Bakwanga. During the flight, all three prisoners were brutally beaten by their Congolese guards. When the DC-3 arrived at Bakwanga, the pilot could not land since the landing strip had been obstructed with 55-gallon drums. The pilot then headed to Élisabethville [now known as Lumumbashi], and when the plane landed, Lumumba was near death. The three prisoners were taken to a villa outside town, where they were killed by two Belgian mercenaries, Carlos Huyghe and Captain Gat. Lumumba was 35."[14]

As pointed out by Monteagle Stearn, in the foreword to Michael Hoyt's 2000 book *Captive in Congo*: "For the Kennedy administration, the Congo was the first battlefield in the struggle for the hearts and minds of the Third World ... After winning the presidency in 1960, he announced the selection of his assistant secretary of state for African affairs, the former governor of Michigan, G. Mennen Williams, before he had selected his secretary of state."[15] During the final days of campaigning for the 1960 elections, candidate John F. Kennedy began to quote Ghana's President Kwame Nkrumah, Lumumba's chief African ally. This indicated Kennedy's departure from Eisenhower's Congo policy. In a major address shortly before the 1960 presidential election, Kennedy: "... warned of rising Soviet influence in Africa and castigated the Republicans for yielding to French pressure in Guinea, leaving President Touré no recourse but to seek aid from the Communists."[16]

Author John Morton Blum in *Years of Discord* [17] analyzed the cable traffic between Larry Devlin, CIA station chief in Kinshasa, and CIA Director Allen W. Dulles, and concluded that both Dulles and Devlin feared what Kennedy might do if he took office before Lumumba was killed. Lumumba was killed on January 17, 1961. Kennedy's inauguration was on January 20, 1961, and the news of Lumumba's assassination did not reach Washington until February 13, 1961.

Kennedy may have been kept in the dark by the U.S. intelligence services; Castro was also apparently unaware of the situation in Congo. The January 19, 1961 issue of the newspaper *Revolución*, the then official Cuban government publication, states that Lumumba, Okito and Mpolo were delivered to Lumumbashi and "viciously beaten."[18] In the January 24, 1961 issue of *Revolución,* only the death of Joseph Okito is confirmed.[19] The January 25, 1961 issue contains a copy of a petition by the UN, requesting that Lumumba be delivered to an international court to be tried. No indication was given as to what the charges may have been.[20]

Revolución was the official newspaper of the Castro government until the formation of the PCC (Cuban Communist Party) in mid-1965, at which time the newspaper *Granma* replaced *Revolución*.

The murder of Lumumba was officially announced in Havana on February 14, 1961, one day after President Kennedy was informed. The article goes on to name the murderers: "Belgian imperialism, Yankee imperialism, Dag Hammarskjöld [Secretary General of the UN], Tshombé, Mobutu, and 'other traitors.'"[21]

The *Revolución* issues of February 15-17, 1961 go to great lengths to describe the so-called spontaneous protests of Cuban people throughout the island-nation asking for justice and revenge. According to Cuban newspapers, all of Cuba was up in arms.[22]

The most interesting issue of the days following Lumumba's assassination is the one of February 18, 1961. The headline states, in one inch letters:

"FIDEL CASTRO DOES NOT ONLY BELONG TO CUBA, BUT IS A SYMBOL TODAY FOR ALL AFRICAN COUNTRIES"

The article goes on to say that African countries have a great deal of admiration for Cuba's anti-imperialist movements, and that Cuba is sending diplomatic missions to Ghana and Guinea, which are "the first steps to organize our collaboration and open the way to the final victory."[23] This article provided a preview of Cuba's future political and military involvement in Africa.

The assassination of Lumumba had worldwide repercussions. In addition to the aforementioned widespread demonstrations in Cuba, there were explosions of popular anger in London, Belgrade, Warsaw, Vienna, Moscow, Tel Aviv, Oslo, New Delhi and most of Africa.

It is difficult to understand why Lumumba's name provokes such intense emotions. His viewpoint was not exceptional. He was for a united Congo and against division of the country along tribal or regional lines. He was against colonialism. He proclaimed his regime's policy to be one of positive neutralism, which he defined as acceptance of African values and rejection of imported ideology, including that of the Soviet Union.

For many years, Lumumba's death was blamed on the CIA. We now know that the CIA did not kill him.[24]

The world continues to praise the barefoot postal clerk who became Prime Minister. In Moscow, the Patrice Lumumba Free University trains students from developing nations in various professions. Abdulah Kassem Hanga, the first African to graduate from Moscow's Patrice Lumumba Free University was one of the leaders of the Zanzibar communist revolt. There are countless streets, parks, and squares around the world named after Lumumba.

In December 2001, a Belgian parliamentary commission of inquiry concluded that "Belgium bears a moral responsibility for the killing of Lumumba." Mr. Geert Versnick, the commission chairman said: "We lecture them about human rights and good government and the rule of law. And they ask us: 'What did you do here?'" The commission concluded that there was no documentary evidence that any member of the Belgian government "gave the orders to physically eliminate Lumumba." However, it did find that King Baudouin knew of plans by Mr. Lumumba's opponents to assassinate him and that some Belgian officers had witnessed the killing.[25]

The Unites States government remains silent on Lumumba's death.

Notes

1. Hoare, Mike. *The Road to Kalamata*, Lexington Books, Toronto, 1989, p. 95.
2. De Witte, Ludo, *The Assassination of Lumumba*, Verso Publishers, Amsterdam, The Netherlands, 2001, p. 2.
3. "Annan's Congo Burden: déjà vu," *Washington Times*, August 23, 2004.
4. *http://en.wikipedia.org/wiki/Congo_Crisis*, Section 2.4, Downloaded February 4, 2008.
5. Hoare, *op. cit.*, p. 11.
6. Gibbs, David N., *The Political Economy of Third World Intervention: Mines, Money and U.S. Policy in the Congo*, University of Chicago Press, 1991, p. 110.
7. Quoted by William Blum in Killing Hope, taken from *www.thirdworldtraveler.com/Blum/Congo_KH.html*, downloaded September 17, 2004.
8. *Ibid.*
9. Meldon, Jerry, The Consortium, *www.consortiumnews.com/archive/story31.html*, downloaded September 4, 2004.
10. Quoted by Enrique Ros in *Cubanos Combatientes Peleando en Distintos Frentes*, Ediciones Universal, Miami, 1998, p. 85, taken from Colin Legum, Congo Disaster.
11. Kalb, Madeleine G., *The Congo Cables*, Macmillan, New York, 1982, p. 69.
12. Ibid, p. 36.
13. Mahoney, Richard D., *JFK: Ordeal in Africa*, Oxford University Press, 1983, p. 44.
14. Hoare, *op. cit.*, p. 95.
15. Hoyt, Michael P. E., *Captive in the Congo*, Naval Institute Press, Annapolis, Maryland, 2000, p. xii.
16. Quoted by Weissman, *op. cit.*, pp. 115-116.
17. John Morton Blum, *Years of Discord: American Politics and Society, 1961-1974*, Norton, 1991, p. 23.
18. *Revolución*, Havana, Cuba, January 19, 1961, p. 2.
19. *Revolución*, Havana, Cuba, January 24, 1961, p. 2
20. *Ibid*, January 25, 1961, p. 3.
21. *Ibid*, February 14, 1961, Front Page.
22. *Ibid*, February 15-17, 1961, various pages.
23. *Ibid*, February 18, 1961, p.5.
24. Devlin, Larry, *Chief of Station, Congo: A Memoir of 1960-1967*, Public Affairs, New York, 2007, pp. 94-99.
25. Africa Recovery, United Nations, Vol. 15, #4, December 2001.

.

Part II

Cuban Exiles Defend Congo

4

Why Send Cuban Exiles to Defend Congo?

Why did the U.S. government choose Cuban exiles to help ensure that the strategic mineral resources of Congo would continue to be available to the West? This is a question, which could have only been categorically answered either by President John Kennedy or his brother, Attorney General Robert Kennedy. Since this definitive answer cannot be obtained, the reasoning and events that may have led to this decision have been reconstructed through interviews and research.

There are no exact numbers available of the Cuban exiles that trained for and assisted in the April 1961 Bay of Pigs invasion. We do know that a total of approximately 1,300 Cuban exiles landed. Of these, some 120 were killed in action and 1,180 were taken prisoner.

There were at least another 1,000 Cuban exiles that had been involved in the Bay of Pigs invasion but that somehow did not land in Cuba. Included in this number would be pilots and support personnel for air operations, as well as men who were supposed to land at the Bay of Pigs or at a second landing spot in the eastern part of Cuba and were instructed to return to base when it became clear that the invasion was heading for disaster. Approximately 130 men of the 7th Battalion had been trained to spearhead a second landing, which never took place. These men were left in Guatemala and then taken to Miami after the failure of the invasion. There was another group of about 100 men that had been infiltrated in various points in Cuba prior to the invasion. These men were to work with the local resistance to organize revolts, which were to take place simultaneously with the invasion.

After the failure of the invasion, most of these men returned to the U.S. and many of them put their military training to use conducting attacks against Castro's Cuba infrastructure. There were groups trained and supported by the CIA carrying out acts of infiltration and sabotage in Cuba. There were also groups that would have nothing to do with the

CIA, who were waging war against Castro with money collected from anti-Castro exiles. U.S. authorities looked the other way while freelance Cuban exiles were conducting military operations against the Havana regime, even though U.S. neutrality laws were being broken.

A few days after Castro paraded the Cuban exile prisoners on Cuban national TV, the Kennedy administration, perhaps embarrassed by its failure to follow through on the invasion plans, started negotiations with Castro aimed at securing the release of the imprisoned Cuban exiles. These negotiations went on for nearly two years. While the negotiations were taking place, select prisoners were summarily executed by Castro, some died in Cuban prisons, and nine were given lengthy prison terms. Regarding this last small group (the final prisoner was released in 1986) Castro made it clear to the U.S. negotiators that these men could not be ransomed.

While conducting negotiations to liberate the prisoners, President Kennedy in late 1961 instructed Air Force General Edward Lansdale to develop and execute a plan to help overthrow the Castro regime. The secret project was called *Operation Mongoose* and it encompassed political, psychological, military, and intelligence operations. The group was also authorized to arrange the assassination of key political leaders. General Lansdale was an expert in psychological operations, and many plans were devised, but few executed. A number of Cuban exiles participated in the more traditional military, sabotage and intelligence actions under the sponsorship of Operation Mongoose. For reasons that were never made clear, this project was suspended on October 30, 1962.

Although no tangible results can be attributed to Operation Mongoose, the negotiations to liberate the prisoners were ultimately successful. There were 1,113 Cuban exile patriots flown to freedom on the day before Christmas 1962 after the Kennedy administration paid some $53 million for their release.

With the release of the Bay of Pigs veterans at the end of 1962, not only had the number of Cuban exiles willing and able to fight communism doubled, but these men, along with the Cuban Revolutionary Council (CRC) were given assurances by President Kennedy (his agreement with Khrushchev notwithstanding) at Miami's Orange Bowl on December 29, 1962 that Cuba would soon be free with the help of the U.S.

The CRC was a small group of well-known Cuban exiles who had been selected by various Cuban exile organizations and had the approval of the Kennedy administration. The CRC was a shadow Cuban government to that of Castro's and was supposed to be accepted and supported as the true Cuban government by a number of countries, had the Bay of Pigs invasion succeeded.

President Kennedy and the U.S. military offered the Bay of Pigs veterans the opportunity to join the American armed forces and be given special training, within the armed forces, for the next battle to liberate Cuba. Several hundred men accepted the White House offer and joined the Air Force, Navy, Marines, and Army and commenced training at various military bases. The largest concentration of Cuban exiles was at the U.S. Army base at Fort Benning, Georgia.

It did not take long for the Kennedy administration to change its mind regarding offering assistance for the liberation of Cuba. Sometime around mid-March 1963, freelance Cuban exiles had attacked two Russian vessels bringing supplies to Cuba. These attacks were conducted in international waters, and were not supported by the U.S. Nevertheless, the U.S. was severely castigated by international public opinion for allowing these operations to take place.

Secretary of State Dean Rusk wrote a memorandum to President Kennedy on March 28, 1963. In this communication[1] Rusk expressed concern that U.S.-Soviet relations could be damaged by the Cuban exiles' actions, and proposed to criminalize any action carried out by Cuban exiles against Cuba or vessels calling on Cuban ports.

A few days later, the CRC was notified that the specialized military training of Cuban exiles at various U.S. military bases would be terminated immediately and that these men could either stay in the U.S. military or would be given the opportunity to attend U.S. universities under a program similar to the GI Bill. To the Cuban exile community, this was betrayal number two by the White House.

The CRC attempted to meet with President Kennedy, but he was unavailable. Instead, on April 6, 1963 a meeting took place between Dr. José Miró Cardona, CRC's President and the U.S. Attorney General Robert Kennedy. During this meeting, personal insults were traded, thus creating an unfortunate situation, which to a large extent sealed the fate of anti-Castro movements in the U.S. By mid-April 1963 the recommendations of Secretary of State Dean Rusk had been implemented. Cuban exiles paid little attention to these new regulations and continued carrying out operations against Castro's Cuba, some of which were surprisingly still under the sponsorship of the CIA.

Sometime around mid-April of 1963, the Kennedy administration started a highly successful smear campaign to discredit the Cuban exile leadership. Cuban exile training camps were raided by federal agents, their weapons confiscated, and several prominent Cuban exiles were imprisoned. The message was loud and clear: actions against the Castro government were illegal, and punishment for perpetrators would be incarceration. The Kennedy administration meant business, as they did not want the Cuban issue to cloud the 1964 presidential campaign[2] and/or arouse the anger of the Soviet Union.

The state of mind of the Kennedy administration regarding the elimination of the Castro regime was undergoing a transformation as world events unfolded. The Bay of Pigs invasion in April 1961 had been a resounding failure. The Cuban Missile Crisis in October 1962 had brought the world close to a nuclear confrontation. President Kennedy was aware that the Kremlin was taking steps to replace Khrushchev, since the politically powerful Soviet army did not think he was tough enough, and Khrushchev naturally was trying to keep his job. President Kennedy had made a commitment to Khrushchev that aggression against Cuba would stop. Since Khrushchev was in a desperate situation, and desperate men tend to take extreme steps, Kennedy had to succeed in stopping the Cuban exiles from continuing to harass Castro. With all these factors taken together, Kennedy's elimination strategy of Fidel Castro was quickly changed to one of accommodation.

The political situation in Congo was becoming a more serious problem to the Kennedy administration. The U.S. was painfully aware that Tanzania, Zambia, Sudan, Uganda, Burundi, and Congo (Brazzaville) had installed either leftist administrations, or had governments that were pro-Communist. These countries covered all of Congo's borders with the exception of the Portuguese colony of Angola, which at that time, had several Soviet- and Chinese-supported guerrilla movements trying to gain control of the government. American and West European companies had invested heavily in Congo's mineral industry, and Kennedy believed he had to prevent Congo from falling under either Soviet or Chinese protection.

To further complicate matters, the Vietnam War was undergoing a rapid escalation and the Pentagon could ill-afford conducting warfare simultaneously in two distant countries. Even if the Pentagon would have decided they could handle wars both in Congo and Vietnam, the State Department would have opposed direct U.S. military action in Congo for fear that the Soviet Union would send Soviet soldiers to support the Congolese rebels. It was difficult enough to fight the North Vietnamese who were being directly supported by the PRC with troops and weapons.

Secretary of State Dean Rusk and President Kennedy had to find a way to protect Congo's riches without involving the U.S. directly.

President Kennedy's accommodation policy of Castro created a sad state of affairs for the fight to return democratic rule to Cuba. But for Congo and central Africa, there was a ray of hope.

On or around November 1961, approximately six months after the Bay of Pigs invasion, the CIA had commenced training a cadre of Cuban exile pilots with the objective of developing a general-purpose Emergency Response Team. The original intent was that this team could be used anywhere in the world. The training center was located at the Embry Riddle School of Aviation in Miami. A few months later in mid-1962, as the situation in Congo heated up, the CIA approached Roberto Medell, a veteran of the Bay of Pigs invasion, and asked him to take charge of the recruitment and training of additional pilots for Congo service. By late 1962, the first group of pilots was sent to Congo. In spite of the Cuban exiles' belief that they had been betrayed by the White House during the Bay of Pigs invasion, when Medell and other CIA operatives approached these men with the idea of fighting communism in Congo, they agreed without hesitation.

The Cuban exile pilots were from quite divergent backgrounds. There were pilots with military background: Cuban Air Force and Cuban Naval Aviation. There were also former commercial pilots from: Cubana Airlines, Aerovías Q, Cubana Aeropostal, and Expreso Aéro-Interamericano. There were even a few who had been crop dusters or simply were weekend leisure pilots. The youngest member of this Cuban exile air force was 20 and the oldest was 59.

The majority of Cuban exiles have always been staunch anti-communists, but this sentiment was significantly stronger in the years immediately following the Bay of Pigs debacle. Cuban exiles wanted to free Cuba from communism, but would willingly travel anywhere to prevent the communist takeover of any country.

The CIA qualified Caribbean Aero-Marine Company, a Florida corporation with a Post Office address at the Miami International Airport, to handle the selection, training, payroll and transportation of personnel to Congo. The CIA also arranged with the Congolese Consulate in New York to expeditiously issue visas to the Cuban exiles.

The recruiting effort for Cuban exile pilots was carried out by Medell from a rented office in an unremarkable green building located on Miami's NW 36th Street, facing the north fence of the Miami International Airport. There were no radio, TV or newspaper advertisements. Word of mouth was sufficient. Roberto Medell stated: "I personally interviewed every qualified Cuban exile interested in Congo service. I had hired a young man from Puerto Rico to answer the telephone and schedule interviews. He was trained that unless someone asked for me, specifically by name, he was to answer: 'I'm sorry, but I don't know what you are talking about.' The pilots who had already been hired found this situation humorous, for if they asked the young man what time it was, he would reply: 'Sorry, but I don't know what you are talking about.'"[3]

The selection, hiring, and training of Cuban exile pilots was an ongoing process, which lasted for approximately five years, 1962-1967. In contrast, the Cuban exile infantry men were hired all at once, during the summer of 1964. The Cuban exile navy men were also interviewed and hired as a group, during the late summer of 1965.

The selected pilots were checked out in an AT-6 Trainer aircraft at the now defunct Tamiami Airport in Miami. These grounds are now occupied by the main campus of Florida International University. Reginaldo Blanco joined the Cuban exile air force and fought in Congo from August 1964 through February 1965. Blanco recalls the hiring process: "We were not supposed to tell our families where we were going, and certainly not what we were going to do. I told my family that I had a job out of the country and was required to go right away. We were sworn to secrecy by the CIA for thirty years."[4]

The program of having Cuban exile pilots assisting the Congolese armed forces against Soviet- and Chinese- supported guerrillas helped solve two problems for the Kennedy administration. Cuban exiles would be given an opportunity to fight against communism (no one could have imagined at that time that the Cuban exiles would be fighting against Cuban soldiers under the command of Che Guevara) while at the same time preventing Congo's strategic minerals from falling into Soviet or Chinese hands, without obvious direct U.S. involvement.

As the Cuban exiles were not yet naturalized American citizens, if necessary the U.S. government could disavow any knowledge of their actions and claim they were there of their own choosing. An additional side benefit for the Kennedy administration was that Cuban exiles fighting in Congo would have difficulty simultaneously conducting raids against Castro in Cuba.

Therefore, the program of utilizing Cuban exile pilots in Congo was accepted and implemented by President Kennedy and the CIA. President Johnson would later expand the program during the summer of 1964 to include infantry troops to assist in the Kisangani rescue and advise

Congolese forces. Approximately a year later, as a result of political events during the late summer of 1965, a Cuban exile navy was created, primarily to patrol Lake Tanganyika.

The Cuban exile infantrymen, hired for a specific secret operation, only learned the identities of the other members of their unit when they departed for Congo duty. This is in contrast to their counterparts in the air force, for these men had fought together during the Bay of Pigs invasion and in subsequent anti-Castro activities, and trained together for Congo duty.

For the infantry, the CIA and U.S. military made a careful selection of eighteen Cuban exiles. They were looking for dedicated soldiers with significant military experience and top physical conditioning. Additionally, they only hired men that had been involved in conducting sabotage operations against the Castro regime and were skilled in the use of explosives and a multitude of weapons. For instance, Guillermo Lazo had served both in the Cuban Constitutional (before Castro) Army and in the U.S. Army. José González Castro was a Bay of Pigs veteran, and after Congo served three tours of duty in Vietnam. This special operations group did not have such age differences as the navy and air force. The Cuban exile infantrymen ranged in age from twenty-four to forty.

The commanding officer of this Cuban exile elite ground force was William (Rip) Robertson, a former Marine officer turned CIA operative. Many of the infantrymen knew Robertson prior to and during the Bay of Pigs invasion and from additional anti-Castro operations. Even though Robertson was an American, the Cuban exiles thought of him as one of their own.

During the Bay of Pigs invasion, instructions from the White House were that no U.S. citizens would be allowed to land in Cuba. Rip Robertson is believed to have been the first to land. He stayed with his men, assisted in resupplying his troops, and went back several times to try to rescue as many of his men as possible. After the captured exiles were ransomed by the Kennedy administration, Robertson was instrumental in training and planning subversive actions against the Castro regime.

The Congo veterans that have been interviewed for this book agree that the Cuban exile infantry was a well-oiled fighting machine.

These men were flown to a U.S. Army base in the U.S. northeast and then flown to Congo the next day. They traveled from the U.S. together and arrived at the Kamina, Katanga Province military base in early September 1964. After a few weeks of additional training and acclimating to the tropical conditions, the Cuban exile army was ready to join the struggle against the anti-government Simbas.

The Cuban exile navy personnel were selected from *Movimiento de Recuperación Revolucionaria* (MRR), the CIA-supported group led by Bay of Pigs veteran Manuel Artime. These men were conducting ongoing sabotage operations against Castro's Cuba from bases in Central America and the Caribbean. In order to provide an accurate picture of the motivation of the Johnson administration in recruiting these Cuban exiles, an incident, which became a turning point in the anti-Castro campaign by Cuban exiles, must be described.

Said incident occurred on September 13, 1964, approximately 120 miles north of Cape Maisí, Cuba's easternmost point. At the time, Cuba was heavily involved in supporting worldwide left-leaning revolutions. In Chapter Two, the names of the three Cuban merchant vessels, which had been utilized to deliver troops and military equipment to Algeria in October 1963, were given. One of these vessels was the *Sierra Maestra* and she was therefore considered a fair military target by the CIA and the various Cuban exile groups operating in the area.

In direct contravention of U.S. law, two Cuban exile SWIFT boats were patrolling the shipping lanes around the Bahamas in the late afternoon when they sighted a vessel matching the profile of the *Sierra Maestra*. As they came closer to the presumed target they could pick up radio chatter in Spanish. With their powerful binoculars they saw men wearing berets and green fatigues. Approaching from starboard, they could see half of the ship's name and the word was *Sierra*. They concluded it had to be the *Sierra Maestra* and commenced shelling the vessel.

Later, they learned that they had attacked a Spanish merchant vessel named the *Sierra Aránzazu*, on her way to Cuba to deliver toys, blankets, food, and spare parts. They also learned that the ship's captain and two crewmen had been killed in the attack. The Dutch vessel *P. G. Thulin* rescued the surviving Spaniards. Castro made sure the world learned every detail of this incident. A picture of a teary-eyed Cuban girl cuddling a burned-up doll with the caption: "Why would they want to burn my doll?" was printed in newspapers around the world.[5] The diplomatic fallout was severe and the Johnson administration quickly arranged for the formation of the Cuban exile navy and targeted them for Congo duty.

Generoso Bringas has a clear recollection of the recruiting process for the Cuban exile navy. "There were around 16 of us, ranging in age from 20 to 62, and we were individually interviewed in a Miami hotel. We assumed the interviewers were CIA operatives. We were told that Congo had mineral reserves that were critical to the defense of Western democracy. We asked: 'What about Cuba?' and they replied: 'Cuba is next.' Lies! We asked what would happen if a revolution would take place in Cuba while we were in Congo, and they replied: 'We would send a plane and take you to Cuba right away.' More lies!"[6]

All sixteen men signed up. Talking to the Cuban exile navy veterans, a sense of their complete dedication to fighting communism comes across. Also a level of frustration is detected, as well a shared belief that they were betrayed by the U.S. when they were prevented from continuing to fight for Cuba's freedom. These men further believe that the Castro regime has been protected by the U.S.

Félix Toledo, a very articulate Congo Navy veteran, provides further elucidation. "We were part of MRR [Artime Group]. After the sinking of the *Sierra Aránzazu* we met with CIA operatives in Miami. We were told: 'We need your help and expertise in another part of the world. When this mission is completed, you will have our unconditional help in the fight against the Castro regime.' We believed this to be an ideological deal and hence we accepted. When we returned from Congo, our leaders were told by the same CIA operatives that conditions had changed, and that they were no longer in a position to help. The rug was pulled out from under us. They later offered us a 'consolation prize' to man an oceanographic vessel which would actually do spy work for them. We refused."[7]

Generoso Bringas provides additional information on the frustration of the Cuban exile navy veterans. "There will always be malicious people who would say we were mercenaries and we were there for the money. I had a job in Miami making $1,000 per month which I gave up to defend freedom in Congo. We were paid $800 per month and we were promised a per diem of $10, which turned out to be in Congolese money, which was practically worthless. The only bonus we got at the end of our tour of duty was a large disappointment."[8]

No training was required for these combat-hardened Cuban exiles. They were flown in groups of 2 or 3 from Miami to New York and then on to Kinshasa, where they waited for 3 or 4 days before the whole group was flown to Kalemie, then known as Albertville. The crates containing the SWIFT boat parts arrived in Kalemie almost at the same time the men arrived. By mid-August 1965, the Cuban exile navy was ready to commence patrolling Lake Tanganyika.

At the request of the American Embassy in Kinshasa, the U.S. military agreed to send a number of advisors to Congo to assist in the planning and execution of missions, particularly air operations. But the true driver of the Congo operation was the Central Intelligence Agency. The White House knew that only in Langley could they find the expertise required to prevent a communist takeover of Congo. The CIA knew they could trust the Cuban exiles to get the job done. It is understandable that the Cuban exiles did not trust the White House; however, they did trust the CIA.

U.S. policy vis-à-vis Congo changed little during the Johnson administration following the assassination of President Kennedy. This was predictable as the Kennedy cabinet stayed intact. An insightful article by George Lardner, Jr. published in the June 6, 1978 issue of *The Washington Post*[9] provided the American public with then recently declassified information, which had been placed at the LBJ Library in Austin, Texas. With the publication of this article, the machinations that had taken place behind the scenes began to emerge, and it became possible to start piecing together what had gone on in Congo during the mid 1960s.

Said article quotes an August 27, 1964 cable from G. McMurtrie Godley II, then-U.S. Ambassador to Congo, addressed to the State Department, the CIA and the White House. Godley expresses concern that the Congolese government would need to keep the Cuban exile pilots in the fighting for at least another year. The article quotes Godley: "Although a lot will be said about Cubans being U.S. mercenaries, we will continue to say as little as possible and refer all inquiries to the Government of Congo with whom the pilots have contracts."[10] The article reaffirms the White House's position that the Congo strategy was to be kept from the American public.

The Lardner article quotes an August 15, 1964 cable from the then-Secretary of State Dean Rusk, who provided a Chinese menu to State Department officials on how to answer questions "only if asked by the press" about U.S. involvement in Congo. Some elements of the Rusk-provided answers:[11]

- Q. Will Americans fly the B-26s?

U.S. citizens would not in the future be called upon to engage in operational missions in the police action within Congo.

- Q. Will these aircraft be under the control of the U.S. embassy?

The B-26 aircraft will be under the control of the Congolese government and will be flown by personnel engaged by that government.

- On any other subject, just say: We are not prepared to discuss that.

Lardner closes his article quoting an exchange of cables, which commenced on August 15, 1964 between then-Assistant Secretary of State for African Affairs G. Mennen Williams and Dean Rusk. Tshombé had asked for three U.S. parachute battalions, to "save Congo from communist rebels."[12] Rusk was furious at Tshombé for asking and at his people for allowing the question to be asked. After stressful and intense negotiations, on August 16, 1964 the rapid delivery of seven additional B-26 aircraft was promised. On August 17, 1964 the National Security Council advised President Johnson that "We are knocking down any 'Vietnam' talk of U.S. combat involvement in the Congo,"[13] and at the same time the White House was assured that things were looking up in Congo. Apparently, by the late summer of 1964, the U.S. intelligence services appeared to have been listening to Castro and were aware of his many Vietnams strategy.

The Cuban exiles that participated in the fight to maintain democracy in Congo deserve a lot more than a list of names in one of the appendices at the end of this book. It would be impractical to include biographical sketches of each of the combatants, as the central theme of this book would be obscured. Instead, five men have been selected, and through their actions the Cuban exiles of the generation of the 1960s will be exemplified.

* * *

Generoso Bringas served in Congo in the Cuban exile navy. He was born in 1933 in Jovellanos, Matanzas Province, Cuba, and is fit and energetic and appears much younger than his seventy-five years of age.

Bringas started to work in the sugar cane fields as soon as he was old enough to swing a machete. His father did not allow him to go to school as his work in the fields was required to help support his family. When he was twelve or thirteen, he helped an American Methodist missionary who later tried to convince Bringas' father to allow him to go to school. The father refused.

When Bringas became eighteen, he got a job in the mornings and the missionary arranged for a private tutor for the rest of the day plus weekends. In approximately one year, Bringas completed the first through the sixth grades. He then studied for the exam to enter high school, which he passed and then registered at the Instituto de Cárdenas to commence secondary school in the 1956-57 school year.

The war against Batista was raging and instead of school, he took to the mountains of Pinar del Rio. After Batista left, Bringas was given a post in the rebel army, but quickly realized that the communists were taking all the key jobs. By early February 1959, Bringas was already conspiring against Castro.

It was about this time that Bringas had a chance encounter with Fidel Castro. He was wearing his *miliciano* uniform and asked Castro why it was that all the key government posts were going to the communists, and Castro replied: "I am surprised that a brave combatant like you is seeing ghosts everywhere."[14] Bringas knew it was once again time to take to the mountains.

Sometime in early 1960 he was taken prisoner and kept incommunicado for fifteen days. He escaped and swore he would never be taken alive.

From his hideout in the mountains, he organized receiving and hiding weapons intended for local rebels to support the Bay of Pigs invasion. Prior to the Cuban Missile Crisis, he was asked by the CIA to travel to the U.S. for additional training, which he did in March 1962.

There must have been a traitor in his group, as Castro's soldiers were waiting for them on their return to Cuba. Bringas and his companions returned fire and were able to escape back to the U.S., leaving few or no enemy combatants in their wake.

Bringas continued fighting against Castro and then spent a year fighting in Congo as part of the Cuban exile navy. He was surprised at the significant level of support given by the PRC and the USSR to the Simba rebels. He adds: "We confiscated a shipment of Chinese weapons to Congo which was valued at $2 million in 1965."[15]

Bringas is currently Secretary-General of the MRR, also known as the Artime Group in honor of its late founder. The MRR is a Catholic anti-Castro organization founded in Cuba on February 28, 1959. It has a large membership in the U.S., Latin America, and Europe, although hundreds of its members have been killed by Castro's soldiers.

Bringas has never stopped fighting against Castro and communism. He adds: "It is my duty to continue to try to return freedom to the Cuban people. As long as there is any blood left in my body, I will continue to fight Castro-communism."[16]

Bringas lives in Florida with his family.

* * *

Juan (El Negro) Tamayo served in the Cuban exile infantry in Congo. He has a long and proud history of fighting for freedom and democracy. Born in 1939 in Marianao, near Havana, he left Cuba shortly after Castro took over, because, as he told me: "… after the first 3 or 4 weeks of Castro's rule, I had all the evidence I needed that the country was being turned over to international communism."[17]

Tamayo traveled to Mexico and started conspiring against the Castro regime. As soon as the CIA started recruiting for the Bay of Pigs invasion, in the middle of 1960, Tamayo signed up. He was trained as a paratrooper and was dropped over Matanzas Province about 2 months prior to the planned invasion date. He helped organize the various resistance groups that would support the invaders.

After the invasion failed, his only option was to try to find a way to leave the country. Anti-communist farmers in the area provided food and shelter for Tamayo, but he needed Cuban-looking clothing in order to travel. This proved to be a problem, since he is a tall gentleman. They managed to find clothing, but there were no size 14 shoes to be found. Finally, someone came up with what looked like "ballet-dancing slippers"[18] and he was on his way.

He went from safe house to safe house and ended up in the town of Colón, Matanzas Province. Someone arranged a bus ticket to Havana and walked with him to the bus station. Tamayo was told to act as if he was mentally retarded. His contact told the bus driver: "this is my nephew and he is slightly retarded, please make sure that he gets off the bus in Havana at a certain stop."[19]

Timing was nefarious, as the prisoners from the failed invasion were being transported to the Sports Center in Havana, not far from Tamayo's bus stop. The traffic congestion was such that all bus passengers were forced to get off by the Sports Center. Tamayo thought some of the prisoners recognized him and waved, but he just looked the other way and kept on walking. Not knowing what else to do, he walked in the direction of Marianao, and the place where he had grown up. He ran into an old neighbor who took him to the Baldor School, an important safe house at that time.

Eventually, plans were drawn to travel the full length of the island with two other men who had also been infiltrated in Cuba (one was José Basulto, who would later create the organization Brothers to the Rescue). After many vicissitudes, they managed to enter the Guantánamo Naval base and were returned to Miami. Other infiltrators trying to exit Cuba after the failure of the Bay of Pigs invasion were not so lucky, as they were arrested and executed.

Following President Kennedy's promise to help liberate Cuba, Tamayo joined the U.S. Army and was sent to Fort Knox, Kentucky. There, he met

Andrés Romero and Manuel Rivero, with whom he would later fight in Congo. After eight months in the U.S. Army, these three men were given honorable discharges and recruited for special operations, at a place to be later determined. Tamayo fought in Congo for less than a year and played an instrumental part in the Kisangani rescue.

Tamayo has a sharp sense of humor and says he would still love to land in Havana with the survivors of the Kisangani rescue, but recognizes that he and his fellow combatants are too old. "If we were to prepare an operation, someone would have to arrange for canes, walkers and wheelchairs before they worried about weapons."[20]

Tamayo lives in Florida with his family.

* * *

Jorge (El Puma) Navarro served in Congo in the Cuban exile Makasi air force. It only takes a few minutes conversing with him to appreciate his deep love for Cuba and his strong desire to see his country of birth free from communist rule.

Navarro was born in 1938 in Las Cañas, a small town in Pinar del Rio, Cuba's westernmost province, but his family moved to Havana when he was a young boy. He completed secondary education at the Instituto de la Víbora, and joined the Cuban Air Force Academy as his love for flying was stronger than that for academic pursuits.

When Batista escaped Cuba on January 1, 1959, Navarro then in his last year at the Academy, was instructed to report to the airport. He remembers seeing new cars with the keys in the ignition, left by the officers who fled with Batista.

It did not take long for Navarro to start conspiring against Castro. His car license was recorded by the G-2 (Castro's secret police) during a meeting at the residence of Toledo, Ohio native *Comandante* William Morgan, later executed by Castro. Since Navarro was not at home, the G-2 detained his father and left the message that his father would be released when his son surrendered.

Following his family's prudent advice, Navarro went underground and managed to leave Cuba in October 1959, hidden in the engine room of a freighter. His father was released after spending three months in Castro's jail.

Shortly after arriving in Miami, Navarro signed up for the Bay of Pigs invasion. He and a few others were taken to Useppa, a small island off the coast of Fort Myers, Florida. They were tested and classified by the CIA and U.S. military personnel. Those with prior military experience were sent to train in the hills near Fort Gullick, at the then Panama Canal Zone.

Navarro explains: "As there were many pilots much more experienced than I, I accepted to be infiltrated into Cuba to train the resistance prior to the invasion. My group of infiltrators was dropped at a remote area in the southern coast of Pinar del Rio Province by the CIA's Rip Robertson. This was February 1961, and we were carrying weapons, explosives and ammunition to be used at the time of the invasion. Similarly, there were groups of Cuban exiles infiltrated in all areas of Cuba."[21]

Navarro continues: "After the failure of the invasion, our priority was to exit the country and to wrestle with the incredulity that the most powerful nation in the world would leave us stranded to be captured, tortured and executed."[22] Navarro was in various safe houses in Havana for about six weeks until he was taken, hidden in the trunk of a car, to the Brazilian Embassy. Brazilian diplomats finally obtained his safe-conduct and he exited Cuba in late September 1961. As soon as he arrived in Miami, he was recruited by Rip Robertson to conduct sabotage raids against Castro's Cuba.

Following President Kennedy's Orange Bowl speech, Navarro joined the U.S. Army and trained at Ft. Benning, Georgia. In August 1963, he joined the Artime group after obtaining an honorable discharge from the U.S. military. He was one of the pilots of a CIA C-47 aircraft, which transported weapons and supplies to anti-Castro units in Costa Rica, Nicaragua, Panama, and the Dominican Republic.

After the sinking of the Spanish vessel *Sierra Aránzazu* in September 1964, operations were shut down and the men returned to Miami. But Navarro was not through fighting communism. He joined the Congo operation as a pilot and returned to Miami in August 1966.

No more war for Navarro. He moved to Louisiana in 1972, where he lives with his wife. But Cuba is ever-present in his mind. The message on his telephone answering machine says: "Cuba will be free. Please leave your message...."

* * *

Gustavo C. Ponzoa also served in Congo as a pilot in the Cuban exile Makasi air force. At age eighty-four, he still displays the energy and determination that allowed him to convert from a Cubana Airlines commercial pilot to a fearless special operations military pilot. Ponzoa was born in Pinar del Rio Province in 1924, but his family moved to Havana when he was a small boy.

He completed his secondary education at the Baldor School and entered Havana University's School of Architecture. He tried to balance his love of flying with the study of mathematics, but flying won, and he became a pilot with Cubana Airlines in 1948.

He left Cuba in 1960 due to the deteriorating political climate, thus commencing an illustrious career defending freedom and democracy. Soon after his arrival in Miami, he signed up as a pilot for the Bay of Pigs invasion.

The carefully engineered invasion plan called for the destruction of Castro's air force prior to the landing of troops. Cuban planes were kept at two locations: San Antonio de los Baños, near Havana, and Santiago de Cuba, with a distance between these two locations of about 950 kilometers. These two locations were to be attacked simultaneously at 06:15 if the plan was to succeed. Further, the pilots were to fly at the dangerously low altitude of 50 feet above sea level to avoid radar detection.

Ponzoa and his wing man Gonzalo Herrera departed the Puerto Cabezas, Nicaragua airport at 02:15 since they were to hit the farthest away target at Santiago de Cuba. The pilots were instructed to make two runs and then head home. Ponzoa and Herrera made five runs and were hit on the last two runs. They never bothered to count the number of bullet holes in their aircraft. The Havana attack was carried out by a separate group of pilots and took place within five minutes of the Santiago attack. Both raids were successful and a significant portion of Castro's air force was destroyed. Ponzoa adds: "I believe that we damaged or destroyed about 60% of the aircrafts at Santiago de Cuba."[23]

The next attack was scheduled for the following morning and was intended to take out the remaining Cuban aircrafts, which could have been flying or hidden by Castro the previous day. When Ponzoa reported the next morning, the U.S. Air Force officer in charge informed him that President Kennedy had ordered a 48-hour cessation in combat missions, to which Ponzoa replied: "What the President has really ordered is the failure of the invasion."[24] The invasion indeed failed and the pilots were brought back to Miami on April 24, 1961. Ponzoa immediately joined a group conducting sabotage operations against Castro's Cuba.

In mid-1962, Pepín Bosch, the then head of the Bacardi Company purchased a surplus U.S. Air Force B-26 Marauder medium bomber and developed a plan to bomb Cuba's oil refineries. The idea was to push Cuba into an energy blackout, thus creating a condition suitable for national subversion.

Ponzoa was to be the pilot of this much-publicized aircraft, which would later be known as the Bacardi Bomber. After several failed attempts to obtain bombs, including entertaining the thought of homemade devices, a representative of the U.S. government showed up at their Costa Rica location and told them the U.S. could not allow this mission to proceed. The Bacardi Bomber is on display in the museum at Kelly Air Force Base in Texas.

Like many Cuban exiles, Ponzoa joined the U.S. Air Force after Kennedy's Orange Bowl speech. As soon as it became clear that Cuba's liberation was a dead issue, Ponzoa requested and obtained an honorable discharge from the U.S. Air Force.

Ponzoa signed up for Congo duty in early 1964 and spent a few months in Miami training Cuban exile pilots to fly the T-28 aircraft. He flew combat missions in Congo from May 1964 through December 1964. Ponzoa was involved in the liberation of Kalemie, battles to control Gamena, Lisala, Bumba, and Bukavu and was instrumental in the rescue of European hostages in Kindu.

After returning to the U.S. from Congo, Ponzoa joined Southern Air, a CIA-controlled airline, where he worked for fifteen years. He flew weapons to Iran, to prop up the Shah's government, and was involved in rescue operations in Iran and Asia.

Ponzoa lives in Florida with his family, and wishes that he can live long enough to see Cuba free. I hope he can attain his wish.

* * *

Fausto I. Gómez served in Congo as a pilot in the Makasi Cuban exile air force. He made the ultimate sacrifice for freedom and democracy as he was killed in action near Bunia, close to Lake Albert, eastern Congo on December 17, 1964. He was thirty-eight.

One would think that it would be difficult to compile the data for the profile of someone who has been dead for forty-three years. It was not difficult at all. His son, Fausto B. Gómez who was ten at the time of his father's death provided significant insight[25] into his late father's personality, as did a number of pilots who fought alongside this brave man.

Gómez was born in Havana in 1926, and after finishing his secondary education, chose to go to Miami to study flying. He could have attended college or joined the family business, but either of these two alternatives required obeying rules and self-discipline, traits that Gómez admired as long as they applied to others.

He flew for Expreso Aéro-Interamericano, a freight airline operating primarily from Havana to Miami and New York. Physically, he was tall and strong, usually sported a large moustache, and always had a smile on his face.

Most people that knew Gómez claim that he was largely apolitical; nevertheless, his pronouncements during the Batista dictatorship and his refusal to fly weapons from the Dominican Republic to Cuba[26] landed him in prison. As Batista's military was refusing to fight the rebels, Batista drafted all Cuban commercial pilots into the Cuban Air Force. One of the charges against Gómez was insubordination. Through the good offices of his family's friends and the Cuban Pilots Association, the Batista regime agreed to release him provided he would leave the country. He did, as well as did ten other Cuban pilots, asking for political asylum in the U.S. and subsequently landing jobs as pilots of the newly created Air Pakistan.

Gómez returned to Cuba after Batista's departure, but it did not take long before he was at odds with the Castro regime. He knew the way to Miami and once again became an exile.

He signed up as a pilot for the Bay of Pigs invasion, where his experience as a freight pilot was put to good use flying weapons and supplies to the troops. While at the training camps, he earned the nickname *Felo Bemba* that would stay with him forever. Loosely translated from the Cuban dialect, it means big-mouth Ralph, a tribute to his loquaciousness. It is said that he could entertain people for hours with stories.[27]

Gómez was a believer in Santería, but the people that did not know him well thought it was another of his many tales. Santería is a syncretic religion originated by the African slaves in the Caribbean. As the slaves were not allowed to practice their religion by their masters, the slaves made their African Orisha deities look like Catholic saints.

His close friends were convinced that he was a Santería practitioner and he always flew with a large red handkerchief, which was his contact with the various deities.

After the failure of the Bay of Pigs invasion, Gómez was involved in sabotage operations against the Castro regime. Like many other Cuban exiles, he joined the U.S. Air Force after Kennedy's Orange Bowl speech and trained at Fort Benning, Georgia and an Air Force base near San Antonio, Texas.

He was recruited by the CIA for Congo and, after obtaining an honorable discharge from the U.S. military, arrived in Kinshasa in early 1964. He flew many combat missions at the height of the Simba revolt, including search and destroy operations after the Kisangani rescue, covered in Chapter Seven.

When pilots arrived in Congo, they were issued a side arm and told that if they were captured, they could expect torture, dismemberment, and execution. They were further admonished to keep a bullet for themselves in case of imminent capture.

Gómez was flying combat missions during operation White Giant, also covered in Chapter Seven, when his plane was shot down. Fellow pilot Raúl Cross told José Hernández, his son-in-law, many years later that he thought Gómez may have survived the crash.[28] If Cross was correct, I do hope Gómez kept a bullet for himself.

A group of South African mercenaries led by Mike Hoare found Gomez's remains, which they buried by a large tree in the jungle. His watch and ID bracelet were returned to his son in Miami.

* * *

This chapter has dealt with the reasons why the administrations of Presidents Kennedy and Johnson chose Cuban exiles to prevent a communist takeover in Congo. A summary of the reasons which have been explored follows.

1.   Cuban exiles had demonstrated to be highly skilled pilots and brave soldiers who had proven their mettle during the Bay of Pigs invasion.
2.   Cuban exiles were devout anti-communists and were prepared to fight international communism anywhere.
3.   At the time, Cuban exiles were neither U.S. citizens nor permanent U.S. residents. Hence, in the event of an international crisis, the U.S. administration could claim that Cuban exiles were in Congo on their own initiative.
4.   Considering the strength of international reaction to anti-Castro activities by Cuban exiles (e.g.: Spanish vessel *Sierra Aránzazu*), it made sense to have these Bay of Pigs veterans just as far away from Cuba as possible.

Notes

1.   Quoted by Ros, Enrique, *Cubanos Combatientes: Peleando en Distintos Frentes*, Ediciones Universal, Miami, 1998, pp. 17-19.
2.   *Ibid*, p. 34. First paragraph of William Atwood memorandum dated September 18, 1963, declassified on July 22, 1996.
3.   Medell, Roberto, Conversations with the author, Madrid, May 29, 2006.
4.   Blanco, Reginaldo, Conversations with the author, Madrid, October 29, 2005.
5.   *El Pais*, September 15, 1964, p. 2.
6.   Bringas, Generoso, Conversations with the author, Miami, July 25, 2006.
7.   Toledo, Félix, Conversations with the author, Miami, October 20, 2007.
8.   Bringas, Generoso, Telephone conversation with the author, October 31, 2007.
9.   Lardner, George Jr., Cuban Surrogates in Africa: An Old Issue, *The Washington Post*, June 6, 1978, page A14.
10. *Ibid*.
11. *Ibid*.

12.   *Ibid.*
13.   *Ibid.*
14.   Bringas, Generoso, Conversations with the author, Miami, July 24, 2006.
15.   *Ibid.*
16.   *Ibid.*
17.   Tamayo, Juan, Conversations with the author, Miami, July 30, 2006.
18.   *Ibid.*
19.   *Ibid.*
20.   *Ibid.*
21.   Navarro, Jorge, Conversations with the author, New Orleans, August 5, 2006.
22.   *Ibid.*
23.   Ponzoa, Gustavo C., Conversations with the author, Miami, July 24, 2006.
24.   *Ibid.*
25.   Gómez, Fausto B., Conversations with the author, Miami, July 27, 2006.
26.   "Eleven Cuban Pilots Quit, Ask Asylum in Miami," *The New York Times*, April 4, 1958.
27.   Gómez, *op. cit.*
28.   Hernández, José M., son-in-law of the late Raúl Cross, Conversations with the author, Miami, August 22, 2005.

5

Katanga Secession

After Lumumba's military defeat at the hands of Tshombé's army, President Kasavubu appointed Colonel Mobutu to the post of Prime Minister. Mobutu, a powerful man within the Congolese army, had been a strong supporter of Lumumba. Kasavubu, recognizing the need for military support, was pulling the strings behind the scenes with the objective of having his (and Mobutu's) government gain control of the country.

As soon as the Congolese learned of Lumumba's death, the country sank into chaos. The few shreds of national unity, which were created by Lumumba and his followers, vanished. The country split into four elements, each of which claimed all or part of the territory of Congo.

Colonel Mobutu was in nominal control of the legitimate (at least, according to the UN) central government and its army. In reality, his power did not extend beyond the city of Kinshasa and parts of the Province of Bas-Congo and the army units stationed there.

Antoine Gizenga, a Soviet-backed MNC leader, ruled the east as the successor of the martyred Lumumba. He proclaimed Kisangani as the capital of the Free Republic of Congo, centered in Orientale Province. General Victor Landula, former army chief under Lumumba, and his troops supported him. In addition to the Soviet-bloc countries, his government was recognized by Egypt's Nasser and Cuba.

Moïse Tshombé, a man called Africa's most unpopular African, had ruled Katanga Province since mid-July 1960, at which time he declared Katanga to be an independent country. He had the financial backing of the U.K., the ill-disguised support of Belgium, the better-disguised support of a mercenary army mostly arranged for by mining corporations and the CIA, as well as his private army called the Katangan *gendarmes*.

Finally, Albert Kalonji, also a left-leaning leader, emerged from the bush (after Lumumba's troops invaded his province, following his secession) and proclaimed himself King Albert Kalonji, ruler of diamond-rich Kasai Oriental and Kasai Occidental Provinces.

Gizenga and his followers had weapons supplied by the USSR. Mobutu was supported by the UN and somewhat by the U.S., while Tshombé had Belgian and British support as well as covert CIA assistance. Kalonji's weapons were supplied by the mining companies operating in the area. The country seemed ready to explode into a massive civil war by the summer of 1961.

In addition to the four groups involved in the power struggle, there were hundreds or perhaps thousands of small organizations scattered throughout Congo, which believed in the principles espoused by Lumumba. These groups came to be known initially as Lumumbists and later as Simbas.

The different factions wasted no time to commence the killing. Tshombé's supporters killed a number of local MNC leaders in Lumumbashi. Following this precedent, Kalonji arrested and murdered six prominent Lumumbists who had the misfortune of transiting through Kasai Oriental. Soon the conflict escalated to ethnic cleansing.

Tshombé was an ingenious leader who was often able to predict the moves of his enemies in advance. Logically, he knew that he could not count on the support of the Belgian army for long. Since he firmly believed that white officers were required to command black troops, he engaged the services of approximately 250 former Belgian *Force Publique* officers as well as some 35 Belgian army officers on loan, who had stayed behind after most Belgian troops had left the province in late August 1960. He now also had 50 to 100 white mercenaries, from several countries, which had been integrated into the Katangan *Gendarmerie*.[1]

Additionally, Tshombé developed a recruiting campaign aimed at Europeans, North Americans, and white Africans, in which he promised high pay and portrayed Katanga as "a bastion of European civilization against communism."[2] He was able to assemble some 250 English-speaking mercenaries, primarily from the U.S., South Africa, and Rhodesia. He also recruited several hundred French speaking soldiers, primarily from Belgium and France (veterans from the Algeria debacle). Although the term mercenary has evolved to have a negative connotation, the original meaning of this word, coming from the Latin noun *mercenarius,* simply means a warrior at the service of a foreign government for a salary. In the literal sense, this definition did not apply to these men, as Katanga was not a country and thus could not have a government. These men were, in fact, hired and paid for by the various multi-national companies operating in Katanga, striving to have their interests protected. The mercenaries that responded to Tshombé's advertisements were not in very good company, as they were fighting alongside Nazis that had fled Germany after World War II, white South African and Rhodesian separatists and former European *Force Publique* officers who had chosen to stay in Congo rather than return to their countries of origin where they were wanted by the authorities for assorted offenses. The new European recruits were integrated into mixed European-African units of the *Gendarmerie*.[3] The English-speaking mercenaries were placed into the *Compagnie Internationale*, a unit without African troops, and not integrated with the rest of the *Gendarmerie*.

By the end of 1960, Tshombé had recruited 500 men in Brussels and Paris and flown them to Katanga. Another 200 men came from Zimbabwe and South Africa. The Katangan *gendarmes'* strength was then about 1,500 men plus some 600 officers loaned by the Belgian Army.[4] This unusual army of Katangan *gendarmes* and imported white mercenaries would soon be fighting against blue helmet UN troops, which had been sent to Katanga to restore peace and to protect the territorial integrity of Congo. In the meantime, their principal task was to subdue ethnic groups resisting Tshombé's independent government.

In addition to providing the funds for hiring the mercenaries, *Union Minière du Haut Katanga* (UMHK) also arranged to give an intimidating character to the Katangan Air Force. UMHK provided three armed Fouga Magisters, which were delivered by air from the factory in Toulouse, France in February 1961. The Magisters joined two South African supplied DH Vampire jet fighter-bombers, Alouette helicopters, and other aircraft at Katanga Province airstrips in Kisengi, Kabongo, Likasi, and Kolwezi.[5]

Mineral-rich Katanga Province had two primary ethnic organizations: CONAKAT (National Katangan Coalition), and BALUBAKAT (Baluba Association of Katanga).

CONAKAT included people of Lunda and Yeke origin, who constituted the majority of the population. This was the party of Moïse Tshombé, which was fighting for the secession of Katanga. Tshombé himself was an ethnic Lunda. The other significant ethnic group in Katanga was the Luba (sometimes referred to as Ba-Luba) people. The Luba people were originally from the Kasai Provinces and had been moved to Katanga in the 1940s by the Belgians to work in the mines. In a period of only a few years, the Luba people controlled the administration and commerce within the region. The Lunda and Yeke people were resentful of the power that the imported Luba people had in Katanga.

The Luba people, who felt threatened by CONAKAT, created a rival political organization, BALUBAKAT, which entered into an alliance with the national MNC organization, now headed by Antoine Gizenga. This was a logical choice for BALUBAKAT, as their ancestors, the Kasai Luba people had supported the local MNC branch directed by Kalonji. All these events took place prior to Lumumba's death and before Kalonji self-proclaimed himself King. Kalonji was also an ethnic Luba. Tshombé seized the opportunity and set out to exterminate the BALUBAKAT opposition. Katangan *gendarmes* and white mercenaries poured into northern Katanga. Thousands of Luba people died under often horrific circumstances.

When word of the killings in Katanga hit the press, world opinion turned sharply against Tshombé and his Belgian and British financial backers. To non-aligned nations, and former colonies, such as India and Ghana, the actions in Katanga represented a resurgence of colonialism. The term neo-colonialism was coined to describe the intention of multi-national corporations to continue to operate as if they owned the country. Significant pressure was exerted on the UN to bring a quick end to the crisis and arrange for a negotiated integration of Katanga back into Congo.

Presidential elections in the U.S. had brought the John F. Kennedy administration into power in January 1961, within days of Lumumba's assassination. Kennedy's foreign policy, contrary to his predecessors Truman and Eisenhower, was less sympathetic to European economic interests. The U.S. publicly broke with Belgium and maneuvered the UN to demand an end to Katanga secession. Kennedy was hopeful that throwing his support with non-aligned nations would counter the widening Soviet influence.[6]

U.S. and UN diplomats started organizing meetings between Katanga's Tshombé and the Kinshasa government headed by Colonel Mobutu. The blue helmet UN military units were finally allowed to actively defend law and order.

Tshombé would privately agree to the terms of agreement after agreement, only to rebuke them once they were made public. With the knowledge that Belgian and British business interests were behind him, Tshombé was fully aware that any delay would work to his advantage. Additionally, Portugal, South Africa, and Zimbabwe had shown their support of Katanga's secession.

To further complicate matters, a powerful group of U.S. senators from the southern states publicly proclaimed their readiness to block any U.S. action against Tshombé, whom they referred to as an anticommunist hero, for this, after all, was the post-McCarthy era. They were not alone in this line of thinking, since Belgian and British newspapers at the time also portrayed Tshombé as a hero, single-handedly fighting communists such as Lumumba, Kalonji, and Gizenga. Kennedy's support of the non-aligned nations, which was his strategy to counter USSR and PRC influence in central Africa, was erroneously interpreted by the international community as a double message from the U.S.

There were also American inconsistencies in the military aspects of the 1960-1963 Katanga secession conflict. For instance, U.S. Air Force transports carried UN troops to support the Congolese government headed by Colonel Mobutu against the secession of Tshombé's Katanga Province. Concurrently, the CIA and American companies were providing air power and mercenary forces to assist Tshombé and the recently-arrived Belgian paratroopers.

Tshombé instructed his *gendarmes* to assault and provoke UN troops at every opportunity. After each incident, Tshombé would denounce UN aggression, and would appeal to his friends in the U.S. Congress to put an end to UN occupation. He did this so well that at one point he came close to uniting Kasavubu and Kalonji against UN foreign intervention in Congo. When these three leaders, Tshombé, Kasavubu, and Kalonji, met at Mbandaka, then known as Coquilhatville, Tshombé was confronted on his smoke screen to hide Katanga's secession, and stormed out. Mobutu, weary of Tshombé's antics and double-dealings, arrested him.

The U.S. and Western Europe had continuously mentored Tshombé as a future leader of Congo; therefore, they were quite concerned about the future of their investment. It took significant negotiating on the part of the U.S. and UN to convince Kasavubu to force Mobutu to release Tshombé. Tshombé agreed to send delegates to a new session of parliament intended to settle the nation's future peacefully. As soon as Tshombé arrived in the safety of Lumumbashi, he renounced the agreement and reasserted the independence of Katanga.

The U.S. and UN, undeterred by Tshombé's actions, pressed on for parliamentary negotiations, which took place with delegates from Kinshasa, Kisangani and both Kasai Oriental and Kasai Occidental Provinces in attendance. Katanga was unrepresented. Parliament asked Cyrille Adoula, a moderate statesman who was acceptable to most of the opposing leaders, to head a new government. Mobutu was still the chairman of the ANC and in agreement with this parliamentary move. Adoula's coalition united all Congolese factions except Tshombé's. The first priority of Adoula's government was the reintegration of Katanga into the Congo territory, as called for in one of the numerous UN Security Council resolutions.

The U.S. had a difficult decision to make during the summer of 1961. On the one hand, the secession of Katanga had immense economic potential for U.S. companies operating in the area. On the other hand, the U.S. wanted to keep tight reins on the pro-Soviet Lumumbist regime of Gizenga, which was based in Kisangani.

Gizenga was convinced that without Katanga's wealth, Congo could not independently survive, and thus a foreign supporter would be a necessity. The U.S. needed to keep Gizenga within the coalition and without time to flirt with the Soviet Union. Hence, the U.S. agreed with Adoula's plan and promised the UN its full support in order to enforce the Security Council resolutions.

What the UN intended to do was to remove all foreign forces and foreign-supplied heavy weapons from Congo. UN officials hoped that once Tshombé's mercenaries were removed, he would become reasonable. Dag Hammarskjöld, the UN Secretary General, assigned his Irish deputy Conor Cruise O'Brien, to the task of enforcing the Security Council resolution in any manner that he saw fit.

The UN military commanders in the field were frustrated with the UN regulations under which they had been expected to subdue Tshombé, and demanded from O'Brien the freedom of action to defeat the white leadership of the Katangan military. O'Brien gave his consent and an operation codenamed *Rum Punch* was carefully formulated.

Rum Punch was a surprise attack on the Katangan military establishment. On August 28, 1961, at dawn, Ghurkas, attached to the Indian UN force, seized the *Gendarmerie* HQ, the radio station and telephone exchange in Lumumbashi. Simultaneously, UN troops from Sweden, India, and Ireland captured military posts throughout the remainder of Katanga, destroying most of the Katangan Air Force. UN forces began to disarm Katangan *gendarmes* and to arrange for the repatriation of foreign mercenaries and political advisers. Tshombé, having run out of options, agreed to the expulsion of the captured white leadership of the Katangan military.

Surprisingly, Tshombé was able to negotiate with the UN a stay to total disarmament, effective until September 9, 1961. This provided enough time for a group of resolute Frenchmen, veterans of the Algeria war, to mount a counter offensive. They took control of the Katangan *Gendarmerie* and prepared to resist the UN.

O'Brien asked his military chief, General Prem Chand of India, to put a stop to this nonsense. An operation codenamed *Morthor*, Hindi for Smash, was organized. UN troops were to seize the same objectives as in operation Rum Punch, except that they were also to surround Tshombé's house and capture his ministers and key associates in a series of raids.

UN troops underestimated the hardcore French veterans of the Algeria war. Katangan paratroopers fiercely resisted the attack. Even though forces loyal to Tshombé were outnumbered, they created enough dislocation that Tshombé and most of his officials were able to escape to the relative safety of the Katanga Province mining stronghold city of Kolwezi. In spite of this questionable victory, O'Brien prematurely announced that Katanga had been reunited with the rest of Congo.

From Kolwezi, Tshombé ordered desperate counterattacks on UN troops. The once formidable Katangan Air Force had only one surviving aircraft, a Fouga Magister. Belgian mercenary Joseph Deulin bombed and machine-gunned UN positions, unopposed by UN aircraft or anti-aircraft fire. Casualties among UN troops were heavy and Irish units in Likasi were overrun and taken prisoner.

UN Secretary General Hammarskjöld reacted to these setbacks in a most surprising manner. Instead of authorizing reinforcement troops for the UN forces in Congo, he decided to personally negotiate a ceasefire with Tshombé. Hammarskjöld secretly flew to Ndola, Zambia (formerly Northern Rhodesia) to meet with Tshombé, but never made it. His DC-4 crashed under questionable circumstances sixteen kilometers short of the runway on September 17, 1961. There were no survivors.

The new UN Secretary General, U Thant of Myanmar (formerly Burma), in order to secure the release of Irish troops, negotiated a humiliating ceasefire, which surrendered all the ground gained during operation Morthor. Tshombé was convinced that soon Katanga would be recognized as an independent country. When Congolese troops from Adoula's government tried to invade Katanga from Kasai Oriental Province, Tshombé's army destroyed them. With plenty of money in his coffers and his recent military successes, recruitment of mercenaries was never better and Tshombé's army strength swelled to about 13,000 men.

The concern of both the U.S. and UN was that the recent defeat of the Congolese army would bring down the Adoula government. Thus, the U.S. quickly requested and obtained a new UN Security Council resolution, which authorized the use of all force necessary to subdue Katanga's mercenary army.

The UN commanders did not want a replay of the disaster caused to their ground troops by the Fouga Magister aircraft. The plans for this new operation, therefore, included air support. The U.S. offered jet fighters, but this offer was politely refused based on the argument that UN neutrality needed to be preserved. In response, the Kennedy administration hinted that the U.S. Air Force might unilaterally remove the Katangan air force.

In order to prevent the U.S. action threatened by Kennedy, the UN immediately requested assistance to assemble an air force. UN Air Commander Morrison from the Royal Canadian Air Force quickly organized his assets, which consisted of: six Saab J-29B fighters from the Royal Swedish Air Force; six F-86 Sabre fighters from the Ethiopian Air Force; six Canberra B(I) Mk.58 bomber-fighters from the Indian Air Force; sixteen Fairchild C-119 transports from the Italian Air Force; and the UN Dakota squadron crewed by various air forces, primarily Brazil and Argentina.

The selection of the Canberra aircraft supplied by the Indian Air force was controversial. The primary mission of the Indian Air Force was to support the ground troops. The Hunter aircraft was the first alternative, but for reasons yet unknown, Canberra was the final choice.[7] Indeed, the Canberra aircraft were armed with four 20mm cannons with 535 rounds each, had a significant operational range, and were equipped with state-of-the-art navigational aids to operate in the poor weather of Congo and without ground personnel assistance. But in the final analysis, Canberra aircraft are primarily bombers capable of dropping 1,000 pound blockbusters, yet the UN had decreed that no bombs would be carried or dropped.

"London agreed 'with strong encouragement from Washington' to supply twenty-four 1,000 pound bombs for UN's jet force (provided the bombs were used only in 'preventive action against pirate aircraft on the ground')."[8] It is not known how strongly the U.S. influenced the decision to use Canberra aircraft; however, it would have been in the U.S.'s economic interest to inflict severe damage on the mining infrastructure in Congo. If the damaged mines remained in European hands, U.S. corporations outside Congo would have a strategic advantage. If the mines instead fell into communist hands, it would be better for the West if there was no infrastructure. At the time, Belgian and British newspapers exposed the use of 1,000 pound blockbusters against Katangan industrial centers, civilians, and hospitals. Members of Britain's House of Commons pointed out that 1,000 pound bombs were "well suited for destroying large industry (perhaps competitors), but hardly applicable to do battle against Tshombé's small mercenary forces."[9]

UN military commanders prepared a meticulous plan for a full scale attack against Katanga's military and political infrastructure. This operation was called *Grand Slam* and it covered details at levels previously missed in Rum Punch and Morthor. The UN requested and obtained an open-ended commitment from the U.S. Air Force to provide transport aircraft to handle the logistics of a major operation.

With the planning completed, the UN waited for an excuse (the new ceasefire negotiated by U Thant was still in effect) to proceed into Kolwezi and clean house.

It did not take long for Tshombé to provide the required pretext for an attack. In early December 1962, his mercenaries began a new series of deliberate provocations, including setting road blocks, shooting UN positions and finally kidnapping UN personnel. Tshombé was convinced that this constant provocation would wear down the UN. He continued to threaten to destroy the Kolwezi mines thinking that his American and European friends would prevent the imminent UN attack.

In late December 1962, Tshombé's forces shot down a UN helicopter, killing all on board. UN commander General Prem Chand of India, able to launch an attack with only a few hours notice, requested permission to take offensive action against Tshombé from Secretary General U Thant and it was granted. A full scale attack on the Katangan military was launched on December 28, 1962.

On the ground, UN troops in Lumumbashi cleared the roadblocks, captured the radio station and telephone exchange, and seized the *Gendarmerie* HQ, almost without casualties.

From the air, Indian Canberras and Swedish J-29Bs simultaneously attacked Tshombé's airfields destroying the recently replaced aircrafts as well as rendering the runways useless.

UN ground forces rapidly moved southward across Katanga before U.S. and European interests could pressure the UN into stopping the offensive action. As before, Tshombé retreated to the *Union Minière* strongholds around Kolwezi and Likasi. The battle was far from over, for Tshombé, at that time, still commanded approximately 18,000 *gendarmes* as well as 750 mercenaries, and still had vast sums of money.

Tshombé's mercenaries had earlier severely damaged a bridge 24 kilometers from Likasi, which they thought would impede the advance of UN ground troops.

Tshombé had predicted that U.S. and European mining interests would request from the UN Secretary General an immediate cease fire. General

Chand, a brilliant strategist, instructed his troops to forget to turn on their radios. Simultaneously, Chand's radio was also not working.

Indian troops were able to cross the damaged bridge without loss and charged into Likasi. Not surprisingly, the UN troops never received the cease fire orders from the UN civilian leadership.[10]

The UN J-29Bs, by constant patrolling, had severed the air corridor to South Africa and Mozambique, previously known as Portuguese East Africa, thus preventing the supply of replacement aircraft to Tshombé's air force.

The Katanga secession was coming to an end. Tshombé held out in Kolwezi for approximately three weeks of fierce fighting. Secretary General U Thant decided that it was wiser to listen to his military commanders than to Western diplomats in order to put an end to the Katanga secession. Tshombé shuttled between Kolwezi and Ndola, Zambia, threatening to destroy the mines and trying to cut a deal. This time, Tshombé's negotiations failed, at least for the moment.

The UN installed Congolese government officials throughout Katanga, repaired roads and bridges, and transported ANC troops to Katanga. With most of his *gendarmes* having been killed or having deserted, Tshombé capitulated. He renounced secession and demobilized his troops. In return, he was granted amnesty.

Belgium and the U.S. attempted to integrate Tshombé into the Kasavubu-Adoula government, but they failed. Tshombé was then forced into exile in Spain. His mercenaries were to be deported to their countries of origin, but a number of them simply crossed the border into Angola. Katanga's secession ended in January 1963 and became just another ugly episode in Congo's history. The UN troops, who had performed admirably in spite of UN diplomats, went home ahead of schedule, as the Congolese people were concerned that they had been invaded by the UN.

Operation UNOC, the reintegration of Katanga Province into the map of Congo, was the first genuine peacekeeping operation undertaken by the United Nations. UNOC also has the distinction of being the single largest military operation ever undertaken by the UN. "The defense of South Korea in 1950 had nominally been conducted under the UN flag, but it was essentially an American military operation."[11] At the peak of the revolt, there were 30,000 blue helmet troops. This action cost the UN $400 million in 1960. France, Russia, and Belgium refused to pay their portion of the $400 million cost of UNOC, nearly pushing the UN into bankruptcy.[12]

On the political side, the Congolese people remained staunch Lumumbists throughout. In mid-1962, while UN troops were fighting

Tshombé, Gizenga reached a peace agreement with Kasavubu. In return, Kasavubu had Gizenga arrested and thrown into prison, where he remained until June 1964.

Even though the country had been divided into the four factions described at the beginning of this chapter, the Kasavubu-Adoula government, with U.S. and UN help, had managed to reintegrate Katanga Province into the map of Congo. Unfortunately, they had neglected to keep an eye on Lumumba followers, who had instigated guerrilla struggles in several parts of the country. By mid-1964, almost half of Congo's territory was in the hands of rebels of varied persuasions. There were disorganized groups of Congolese nationalists, anti-colonialists, tribalists, and unemployed opportunists, mostly directed by left-leaning leaders. A new bloody war, known as the *Simba* (Swahili for Lion) rebellion, was about to commence.

Notes

1. Hoskyns, Catherine, *The Congo Since Independence, January 1960-December 1961*, London, Oxford University Press, 1965, p. 385.
2. *Ibid*, p. 393.
3. *Ibid*, p. 388.
4. Mike Hoare, *The Road to Kalamata*, Lexington Books, Toronto, 1989, p. 3.
5. Johnson, Robert Craig, *Heart of Darkness*, 1997, *http://worldatwar.net/chandelle/v2/v2n3/congo.html*, downloaded September 17, 2004.
6. Kalb, Madeleine G., *The Congo Cables*, Macmillan, New York, 1982, pp. 201-215.
7. Quoted by Bharat Rakshak in *Canberras in the Congo*, *www.bharat-rakshak.com/IAF/History/Congo/*, downloaded October 10, 2004.
8. Lefever, Ernest W., *Crisis in the Congo: A United Nations Force in Action*, Washington, The Brookings Institution, 1965, p. 167.
9. Quoted in *The Militant*, Vol. 65/No. 28, July 23, 2001, *www.themilitant.com/2001/6258/652850.html*, downloaded September 7, 2004.
10. Bharat Rakshak, *op. cit.*
11. Hoyt, Michael P. E., *Captive in the Congo*, Naval Institute Press, Annapolis, Maryland, 2000, p. xii.
12. United Nations Index, *www.historylearningsite.co.uk*, downloaded September 4, 2004.

6

Simba Rebellion

The three-year struggle against Tshombé's army to defeat the secession of Katanga had taken its toll on the Congolese economy. Unemployment was very high as was inflation. Peasant masses, unable to work the land, poured into cities looking for work. Congo was a ripe fruit waiting to fall into the hands of international communism.

In addition to inflation and unemployment, the majority of Congolese were dissatisfied with the widening gap of wealth between the political elite and the peasant masses. Adding the inefficient and corrupt government and the abuses of Mobutu's National Congolese Army (ANC), the young grew increasingly disappointed with the Kasavubu-Adoula administration and believed that nothing short of a second independence would bring them salvation.

Even though Lumumba had been dead for nearly three years, the Congolese remained staunch Lumumbists. There were portraits of him in virtually every hut in Congo, and his statues adorned hundreds of parks scattered throughout the country. It seemed as if full employment was reserved only for those who made portraits and statues of Lumumba.

The rebellion had been brewing for some time. Congolese people were looking to avenge Lumumba's assassination and were further offended that mostly white UN soldiers had invaded their country. The population looked for leadership from former Lumumba left-wing followers such as Pierre Mulele, Christophe Gbenye, Antoine Gizenga, Gaston Soumialot, and Thomas Kanza.

Pierre Mulele was born in 1929 in Kulu-Matenda, Bandundu Province. He studied in a Catholic mission in Kinzambi and later at a Jesuit school in Kikwit. He spent two years in the ANC at Kananga, serving at the same time as Mobutu. After completing military service, Mulele worked at the Ministry of Public Works in Kinshasa, and in 1959 participated in the creation of the Party of African Solidarity (PSA), of which he was elected Secretary General. In 1959 and 1960 he traveled to Guinea,

Ghana, the United Arab Republic, and Morocco representing the PSA. In 1960, after Congo's independence, he was named Minister of Education and Fine Arts in the Lumumba administration. After Lumumba's assassination, he resigned his cabinet post and traveled widely within the Eastern Bloc, receiving training in guerrilla warfare in China. Regarding Pierre Mulele, the euphemism left-leaning is not needed. Mulele was a full-blown, take-the-government-by-force communist.

Thomas Kanza, a less significant member of the Simba leadership, was born in 1933 and graduated from Louvain University in Belgium in 1956. He became the first Congolese to obtain a degree from a Belgian university, even though the Belgians had ruled Congo for seventy-two years. He was the Congo representative before the UN in New York until the fall of Lumumba. In 1962 he became *chargé d'affaires* in London for the Adoula government. Kanza was more of a diplomat than a rebel strategist.

Even before the departure of the largest bulk of UN blue helmet peacekeeping troops from Congo in January 1963, isolated acts of insurgency were taking place, but the one step, which facilitated the large scale armed struggle in eastern Congo, was the dissolution of parliament in September 1963 by the Kasavubu-Adoula administration. The excuse given was that parliament had become ineffective due to the constant conflict and altercations among deputies. The opposition was thus deprived of its only legitimate forum in which to vent frustrations. In reaction to the dissolution of parliament, several members of parliament affiliated with the MNC, among them the left-leaning Christophe Gbenye and Bocheley Davidson, moved across the river to Congo (Brazzaville).

Christophe Gbenye was born in 1927 in Orientale Province. He was one of the original leaders in the MNC and Lumumba appointed him Interior Minister in the first Congolese Parliament. He was dismissed in September 1960, concurrently with the dismissal of Lumumba, and returned to Kisangani. He was again appointed Interior Minister by Cyrille Adoula during his coalition administration.

Little is known about Bocheley Davidson's life.

In Brazzaville in October 1963[1] Gbenye and Davidson organized the National Liberation Council (CNL), which would become the ideological force behind the eastern Congo rebellion. Additional former members of parliament including Gaston Soumialot and Antoine Gizenga moved to eastern Congo to organize Simba units to fight the Congo government.

Gaston Soumialot was born in 1919 in Nord Kivu Province. He was elected to Parliament during Lumumba's administration. He went into exile at the time of Lumumba's dismissal.

A timetable containing the date of the formation of the CNL and the dates of other critical events during the Simba Rebellion can be found at the end of this book.

The American embassy and CIA Station in Kinshasa had asked for military support to assist the feeble efforts of the ANC against the Simbas. "Washington dispatched a military advisory team to the Congo in July 1962, led by Colonel Michael J. L. Greene."[2] As the Simba rebellion gathered strength, the United States Military Mission, Congo (COMISH) was created in July 1963 under Colonel Frank Williams. COMISH coordinated all operations carried out by the CIA-recruited Cuban exiles. It was not until late 1963, early 1964 that the Simba rebellion became anti-American as the Simba leadership became convinced that American aid permitted the Kinshasa government to resist.

The Kasavubu-Adoula administration had also asked the U.S. for help, and through the good offices of the CIA, Caribbean Aero-Marine was qualified in Miami. The actual birth date of Caribbean Aero-Marine is difficult to determine. Swedish historian Leif Hellström, based on a telegram dated November 15, 1962 from the U.S. Congo ambassador to Washington, which refers to "Adoula's 6 Cuban [exile] pilots from Caribbean Aero-Marine,"[3] determined that the company was chartered within a two-week period prior to the date of the telegram.

Caribbean Aero-Marine's charter included hiring experienced pilots to train non-existing Congolese pilots. This training was to be provided with six AT-6 jet fighter trainers belonging to the Congolese Air Force, which also did not exist.[4] In the Western hemisphere, these planes were called Texan, and in the rest of the world they were known as Harvard.

The first group of Cuban exile pilots arrived in late 1962, and it was composed of seven pilots rather than the six stated in the November 15, 1962 telegram. The pilots were: Mario Ginebra, Rafael García Pujol, Eduardo Herrera, Luis Cosme Toribio, Antonio Soto Vázquez, César Luaices and Alfredo de la Maza. Segisberto Fernández was in charge of aircraft maintenance. The group was under the command of Mario Ginebra, and operated out of the Kinshasa military airport. These pilots were hired for six-month tours.

Segisberto Fernández recalls: "I arrived in Congo a couple of days after the pilots since I had been sent by a different route. The pilots took me to the hangar and told me that they were concerned about the safety of the aircrafts. I looked for manuals, maintenance records, etc and found nothing. There were five AT-6s and only two were in flying condition. We found spare parts in the warehouse, and in five days all five planes could be flown. These planes were not armed."[5]

During the first half of 1963, new pilots arrived: Nildo Batista, Raúl Solís, Ernesto Peynó Inclán, and César Luaices Sotelo. Aviation gunner (Chiqui) Ginebra, radio operator (Toto) Quintero and other support personnel arrived at the same time as the new pilots. Raúl Solís was particularly well-qualified, as he had been a pilot in Cuba's Naval Aviation and had flown a TBM Avenger, an aircraft very similar to the AT-6. The new commander was Joaquín Varela, as Mario Ginebra had completed his contract and returned home. The initial job of these Cuban exile pilots for the first few weeks of their tour was "to fly over the capital [city] in order for the Congolese to trust the military might of its government."[6]

This Cuban Exile Air Force was initially known as *Grupo Voluntario Cubano* (GVC), or Cuban Volunteer Group. The Congolese army, impressed with the high level of success of the missions carried out by these men, gave them the name *Makasi*, which is a Lingala word meaning strong and powerful. This Cuban Exile Air Force will be referred to hereinafter as Makasi.

At the request of the U.S. State Department, and following the personal recommendation of Secretary of State Dean Rusk, the Makasi aircraft were not armed. For the first few months, Cuban exile pilots were instructed to fly low to scare Simba warriors who were carrying out isolated acts of violence against Europeans. While Simbas were on the run, UN helicopters, crewed by Swedes, would rescue missionaries and European plantation owners before they could be massacred by the *jeunesse,* young Congolese men ranging from 12 to 20 years of age with instructions to kill whites.

In addition to scaring Simbas, Makasi's initial job was also to help stabilize the shaky Congolese government. In early May 1963 approximately 2,000 Congolese policemen demanding higher pay, mutinied and seized key posts in Kinshasa. Then Army chief General Joseph Mobutu, in a show of temerity, walked alone into their camp and demanded that they surrender. Some of the policemen refused to surrender, and they were attacked and badly beaten by tough paratroopers and infantrymen. In an article entitled *Congo Police Mutiny Put Down by Mobutu* appearing in the May 4, 1963 *The Washington Post*, it was stated that "During the operation an American-built AT-6 fighter-trainer of the Congolese Air Force, flown by a Cuban exile pilot, swept over the police camp but did not attack."[7] Perhaps the article should have read "could not attack," as these planes were not armed at the time.

The idea of scaring the enemy does not sound preposterous given that the war was being waged in Africa. Mike Hoare comments in one of his books: "... great noise is associated with great power in the African mind and serves to intimidate the enemy."[8] The same technique had been successfully employed during the last few months prior to the May 1960 elections, when *Force Publique* had been instructed by their Belgian officers to fire blanks when breaking down disturbances.

The Cuban exile pilots flying the unarmed AT-6 indicate that these aircraft made a "noise of final judgement,"[9] and thus nicknamed these planes "*El Enano que le ronca*"[10] partially for the noise they made. It is possible that the intent of the Cuban exile pilots was to call the AT-6 *the midget who snores loudly*, but it is even more likely, as the Cuban slang expression goes, that the real nickname of these aircraft was *Midget with large testicles*.

Mugangas (witch doctors) performed incantations on the *jeunesse* and convinced them that while they were under this powerful spell, the bullets fired at them would turn into water. When Simbas approached a battle situation, they would chant *Mai Mulele*, which means Mulele's water. The witch doctors were correct only at that time, as *Force Publique* had been using blanks and the *Enanos que le ronca* could shoot no bullets.

In August 1963, Pierre Mulele arrived in the Kwilu River area, Bandundu Province, western Congo. Mulele's arrival in Kwilu, coupled with the imminent start of the eastern revolts, marked the starting point of the Simba rebellion. Initial leaders of the disjointed Simba rebellion were: Pierre Mulele, Christophe Gbenye, Gaston Soumialot, Antoine Gizenga, and Thomas Kanza.

Upon his arrival in the Kwilu River area, Mulele commenced recruiting warriors among members of his own ethnic group, the Mbunda, as well as among Antoine Gizenga's tribe, the Pende. Both Mbunda and Pende people had been targets of repression by the ANC.

The Kwilu rebellion quickly spread to other parts of Congo. At the same time and over 1,600 kilometers away, the eastern rebellion was organized by Gaston Soumialot, who was sent to Burundi by the CNL. Soumialot successfully negotiated an agreement with Tutsi exiles from Rwanda with the backing of Burundi authorities, and he was able to recruit thousands of dedicated troops in Sud-Kivu Province, along the border with Burundi.

By September 1963, the rebels were no longer scared by the noise made by Makasi aircraft. The Cuban exile pilots were being shot at with real bullets, and they could not return fire. For a while, the Makasi improvised artillery was limited to hand grenades taken from ANC warehouses, which they placed inside drinking glasses and threw from the plane's passenger door.

But by the end of October 1963, Commander Luis Cosme Toribio (Joaquín Varela had been flown to Miami for an emergency appendectomy) of Makasi pilots gave an ultimatum that they would no longer fly unarmed. In fact, a few days before a bullet had missed Cosme's face by only a few inches. When his demand was not met, Cosme resigned. Joaquín Varela, fully recovered after his surgery, returned to Congo to retake command of the Makasi units, now flying out of Kikwit as well as Kinshasa. In November 1963, Makasi pilots began also flying out of the ANC-controlled airport at Kamina, an important military installation in Katanga Province.

The followers of Mulele, in the Kwilu River area, attacked anything Western, including mission stations, foreign company installations, and government outposts. On January 21, 1964 the Kasavubu-Adoula government declared a state of emergency in the Kwilu River area due to Mulele's revolt, and immediately sent troops to the region. On January 22 and 23, 1964, four European missionaries were killed, and on February 5, the Chief of Staff of the ANC was ambushed and killed.

Around April 1964, the Simba rebellion was growing stronger, and the CIA and COMISH military advisors decided that Cosme had been right. Segisberto Fernández remembers arming the AT-6s: "A U.S. technician was flown to Congo with all the necessary equipment to install two .303-calibre machine guns, 2,500 rounds each, and two 2.75-inch rocket tubes, 6 rockets each, on each AT-6. I did all the electrical circuitry while the U.S. technician installed the artillery."[11] Now that the planes were armed, Makasi became a real fighting force, but only operating in the Provinces of Bandundu, Bas-Congo, Kasai Occidental, and the western portion of Katanga.

Larry Devlin, Congo CIA Station Chief at the time recalls: "We had been requesting planes and pilots for quite some time. When we were offered unarmed planes, we accepted, as it was the only deal we could make. The [Cuban exile piloted] planes were a psychological symbol of the strength of the Congolese government. Once the planes were armed, they became an invaluable aid to support the government. Without them [the Makasi pilots], the [Congo] government would have fallen."[12]

The CIA and Department of Defense provided the Congolese army with what *The New York Times* called "an instant air force."[13] The meaning of secrecy, within the context of the Congo effort, was a rather academic concept, even though the U.S. did not admit to the media until October 1964 that it was militarily supporting the Congo administration. The Cuban exiles were sworn by the CIA to not admit any participation for thirty years, while the U.S. government was denying any involvement in Congo. Yet, according to the Cuban exiles interviewed for this book, there were journalists from many countries in the area. There were reporters from France's *Paris Match*, Spain's *ABC*, and both *The New York Times* and *Life* from the U.S., just to name a few. From time to time, journalists were even allowed to accompany Makasi pilots on missions.

By early summer 1964, the CIA had obtained additional T-28 fighters to supplement the growing Makasi. New pilots joined the operation: Gustavo Ponzoa and René García. Meanwhile, in the easternmost part of Congo, troops loyal to Gaston Soumialot attacked and gained control of the town of Uvira on May 15, and a few days later, took control of Fizi. At that time, followers of Soumialot controlled the entire Province of Sud-Kivu. In June 1964, Soumialot's forces took Kalemie, a city of approximately 100,000 inhabitants, and a key port on Lake Tanganyika. It would be near this city, about one year later, where the Cuban troops of Che Guevara would suffer a humiliating defeat. The fall of Kalemie to the troops of the sanguinary General Olenga provided a catalyst to the West to accelerate preparations to take on the Simba rebels.

By June 1964, the forces of Christophe Gbenye, commanded by the infamous Nicholas Olenga, had taken control of most of Nord-Kivu Province and the southern portion of Orientale Province. Olenga had been a booking clerk for the local railroad company and had never served in any armed forces. Olenga's qualifications included belonging to the Batetela tribe (Lumumba's people) and being a loyal follower of Gbenye. As Olenga's troops advanced, Olenga increased his military rank for each major city taken. Gbenye did not complain, as Olenga was a devoted socialist. In late July 1964, Olenga and his People's Army of Simbas marched north in the direction of Kisangani. By the time Olenga arrived in Kisangani, he had awarded himself the rank of General of the People's Army of Liberation.

As the Simba second independence rebellion grew stronger and Chinese and Eastern-bloc support to the rebels increased, the CIA and the U.S. Department of Defense agreed to provide six additional T-28 fighters, ten C-47 transports, six H-21 heavy duty helicopters, spare parts, 100 technicians, as well as several counter insurgency advisors. Said agreement prompted *The New York Times* to write an article on June 18, 1964, entitled "Whose War in the Congo?,"[14] which questioned why the technicians, who were not supposed to take part in combat themselves, did so.

A third front in eastern Congo (independent of Soumialot, and the Gbenye-Olenga duo) appeared in northern Katanga in early June, headed by Idelphonse Massengo and Laurent Kabila. By late June, the Kabila-Massengo binomial controlled the entire west shore of Lake Tanganyika and had captured Moba. They then moved into Maniema Province and on July 22, 1964 captured the strategically important city of Kindu.

The logistics of the insurrection had radically changed. The original uprising, which started in August 1963, had been limited to the Kwilu River valley and around its capital Kikwit. This theater of operations was covered by a circle of approximately 300 kilometers in diameter, with Kikwit being only a short 400-kilometer flight from the ANC air base at Kinshasa. By July 1964, the Simba rebellion had extended to the eastern half of Congo, and an additional Makasi unit was moved closer to the action. This new unit, operating out of the Kabinda airport in Kasai-Oriental Province, would assist Makasi units operating out of Kinshasa, Kikwit, and Kamina airports. The expanded second independence rebellion was taking over Congo from east to west. The support of the Makasi was vital to maintaining a government presence in the eastern part of Congo, for the ANC was on the run at that time. The Cuban exile pilots never stayed longer than several days at any Congolese airport. They were moved around in accordance to battle requirements. All former Makasi pilots interviewed agree that the Kamina airport was their favorite. It had two quality parallel runways of 10,000 feet (more than 3 kilometers) in length.

The three eastern front rebel armies were supplied, other than when ANC troops were there to hand over their weapons before fleeing, by neighboring nationalistic governments. The Soviet Union had promised these governments that they would replace any weapons given to the rebels. To a large extent these were empty promises. In July 1964, Kasavubu expelled all personnel from the Soviet embassy in Kinshasa for their support of the insurgents. The Soviet Union, angry with the expulsion of its diplomats, stepped up supplying the rebels overland from Sudan. Unfortunately for the Lumumbists, Christian rebels in southern Sudan stole several truckloads of weapons, which they turned against the Muslim

Khartoum government. The supply route to the Congolese fighting for a second independence was temporarily cut off by Sudan.

In spite of the rebel military successes, the individual fighting groups did not communicate with each other and did not share a common strategy. The only common denominator among the Simba leadership was their desire to turn Congo into the country Lumumba envisioned. Gbenye's group did receive support and perhaps strategic suggestions from the CNL in Brazzaville. Soumialot had a mistrustful alliance with Gbenye and the CNL. Both Gbenye and Soumialot enjoyed the support of the Soviet Union. Massengo and Kabila were true communist long-term revolutionaries, not connected with any of the other groups, and had the support of Cuba and China. Mulele was also not formally linked to any of the other rebel groups, and had support from China, the Soviet Union, Cuba, and some east European countries, with most of his weapons and supplies flowing across the Congo River through Congo (Brazzaville).

Even though the USSR, the PRC, and Cuba were making an investment in the Simba revolt, and further considering that the key leaders of the movement had been trained in Moscow and Beijing, the ideology of the movement had an autochthonous nature. Monteagle Stearns, a distinguished U.S. career diplomat, stated in the Foreword of Michael Hoyt's book: "To the extent that the [Simba] movement had an ideology, it was a mixture of nationalism, village Marxism, and magic."[15]

Even though these various Simba groups did not communicate, and probably did not know the meaning of the word strategy, they had an unusual yet effective way of subduing cities. The rebels would approach a target city, find a telephone and ask to speak with the highest ranking ANC officer. The Simbas would start by exaggerating the size of their army and the quantity and quality of their weapons. Then they would give the ANC the opportunity to abandon the city, together with their families without having to fight. This may help explain how easily Simbas controlled such a large percentage of Congolese territory.

By late July 1964, approximately one half of Congo was in rebel hands. To put this in perspective, the leftist rebels occupied and terrorized an area larger than the combined sizes of France and Spain, while Mobutu's army was in continual retreat. It is generally believed that ANC soldiers were convinced that Simbas had been rendered invincible by the witch doctors' anti-bullet concoctions. There are many reports of ANC refusing to fight their brothers and surrendering their weapons to the rebels.

The installation of a communist regime in Congo appeared more imminent this time than ever before, and U.S. President Johnson and Secretary of State Dean Rusk, through the U.S. Ambassador to Congo and the CIA Station Chief, joined in the political machinations of Kinshasa. Kasavubu was pressured into dismissing Adoula and appointing no less than silver tongue Tshombé to the post of Prime Minister.

This was not a completely surprising move. During his brief exile in Spain (Tshombé apparently liked Spain as he was reputed to have spoken Spanish fluently and had a Spanish mistress), Tshombé made multiple trips to Brussels and was being groomed for a new role in Congo politics. Belgium's Chancellor Paul-Henri Spaak and U.S. Ambassador W. Averell Harriman conferred with Tshombé several times in Brussels as early as the late spring and early summer of 1963. Belgium and the U.S. had joined forces to make sure that Congo made decisions that would ultimately benefit Belgium, the U.S., and their respective industrial establishments.

On June 30, 1964, exactly four years after independence, as the last of the UN troops who had resoundingly defeated him pulled out of Congo, Tshombé returned to Congo to suffocate the Simba rebellion. He replaced Adoula and even though the ANC was surrendering territory by telephone without a shot being fired, Tshombé publicly announced that he had no doubts that the ANC would defeat the rebels. As a measure of good faith, Tshombé proceeded to release 600 political prisoners, which included Antoine Gizenga. This move greatly angered Kasavubu, for it was he who had thrown Gizenga in prison.

Two days later, in spite of his earlier proclamation, Tshombé asked the U.S. for additional military assistance. Mobutu was the chief of the army, and asking for military assistance without consulting with him was an insult. Additionally, Tshombé arranged for the return of his Katangan *gendarmes* and white mercenary army from Angola, and immediately sent them to fight the Simba rebels.

Tshombé's mercenaries arrived in Congo during July and August 1964; they were fit and ready to fight. Three Commandos were hastily assembled: 5 Commando, under the leadership of South African (Mad) Mike Hoare, was an English-speaking unit; 6 Commando, headed by Frenchman Bob Denard, was a French-speaking outfit; and 10 Commando, under the control of Belgian Jean (Black Jack) Schramme, was a bilingual (French- and Flemish-speaking) unit.

Thomas Michael Hoare, better known as Mad Mike Hoare, was born in 1920 in India to Irish parents. He spent his early days in Ireland and was educated in England. Hoare served in the British Army in the U.K., India, and Burma and was discharged with the rank of major. He moved to South Africa after World War II, where he ran his own safari business. His first mercenary assignment was during the Katanga secession in 1961.

Black Jack Schramme was born in Brugge, Belgium in 1929. He joined the Belgian army at an early age, and at age twenty-four purchased and ran a plantation in the then Belgian Congo. At the time of the Katanga secession in 1960, Schramme became a trusted employee of Moïse Tshombé, becoming the Chief of Police in Katanga. When Tshombé went into exile, Schramme took refuge in Angola.

Bob Denard, born Gilbert Bouregard in Bordeaux, France in 1929, was also known in Arabic as Said Mustapha Mahdjoub. Denard served with the French armed forces in Indochina and later in Morocco. He became a mercenary in the early 1960s during the Katanga secession war.

Contrary to what Lumumba had advocated, the rebellion was organized along ethnic lines. The fighting units were primarily Tetela and Kusu in the east and Pende and Mbunda in the Kwilu River area. And as such, they reverted to ancient animist religious patterns. Each of the ethnic groups believed that magic water provided by a *muganga* would make a warrior immune to government bullets, as long as the witch doctor was from its own ethnic group. Just to insure and/or amplify the power of the magic water, warriors were supposed to be high on hemp before doing battle. Simbas would not fight at night or during a rain storm, for they believed that their magic powers would vanish.[16] The mercenaries were aware of these restrictions and used this knowledge to their military advantage.

On August 5, 1964, a Simba force of only forty warriors, accompanied by several witch doctors frantically waving palm branches, charged the government garrison in Kisangani. The Kisangani force consisted of 1,500 men, heavily armed with machine guns, mortars, and armored vehicles, under the able leadership of Colonel Leonard Mulamba. The national troops, overcome with fear of the witch doctors, ran away and the Simbas took over without a single shot being fired. It must be pointed out that on that date Colonel Mulamba was not present in Kisangani, for at Mobutu's direction, he was in Bukavu.

The ANC troops left behind large quantities of weapons and ammunition, including automatic assault rifles, mortars, and armored cars, as they assumed that carrying a weapon would slow down their run. This act of cowardice of the Congolese army gave the Simbas new strength, for the ANC weapons were light years ahead of machetes and spears.

Emboldened by their effortless victory over the ANC at Kisangani, and controlling a significant percentage of the country, the leftist CNL declared their independence shortly after the takeover of Kisangani. They claimed to be the legitimate government of Congo, changed the name of the country to People's Republic of Congo, and began a reign of terror against counter revolutionaries. Simba's definition of counter revolutionaries included civil servants, Westerners (and Westernized Africans), and anyone wearing glasses.[17] Thousands were massacred and stacked at the feet of Lumumba's many statues.

The People's Republic of Congo was ruled by an Executive Committee composed of Christophe Gbenye, Gaston Soumialot, Antoine Gizenga, and Thomas Kanza, with Gbenye as the Chairman of the Committee. Soumialot was appointed Minister of Defense and Governor of a large portion of the new Republic, with his seat in Kalemie. Nicholas Olenga became General-in-Chief of the Army of Liberation. Cuba, the Soviet Union, and the People's Republic of China immediately recognized the People's Republic of Congo as the true government of Congo and offered aid to the precariously enacted nation.

Kisangani, the capital city of the ephemeral People's Republic of Congo, was a handsome, modern city of around 300,000 inhabitants. It became known that the Simba assault on Kisangani had the planning assistance of Chinese personnel from nearby Burundi and Congo (Brazzaville), including Colonel Kan Mai. The PRC Embassy in Burundi was an important anti-West bastion. Its Ambassador, Liu Yu-Feng was a respected Africa expert while his military attaché Colonel Kan Mai channeled weapons and provided training to insurrection groups. Kan Mai had earlier been expelled from Nepal and later resurfaced in Congo (Brazzaville).[18]

President Johnson instructed the CIA to provide whatever assistance Tshombé required. Some of the equipment rushed by the U.S. to Congo included four C-130 transports, three or four B-26 bombers (there would be a total of seven or eight by January 1965), and fast patrol boats to suppress enemy movement of weapons and personnel across Lake Tanganyika.

On August 6, 1964, one day after the fall of Kisangani, Belgian Colonel Frédéric Vandewalle, a brilliant military strategist based in Brussels, with deep knowledge of Congo, was summoned by Belgium's Chancellor Paul-Henri Spaak. Vandewalle had served as the Belgian consul in Katanga during Tshombé's secession. The next evening, Vandewalle was on his way to Congo, and so was Belgium's Fifth Mechanized Brigade, as well as six Belgian Army logistics units. Shortly after his arrival in Congo, Vandewalle called for an emergency meeting with Tshombé and representatives from the governments of Belgium and the U.S. During this meeting, Vandewalle explained that this was a military operation and that political interference would not be tolerated. He further asked and obtained the authority to work directly with COMISH, the Cuban exile forces and Hoare's mercenaries. The total fighting force of Belgian military, CIA-sponsored Cuban exiles and Hoare's mercenaries was approximately 2,100 men. This number does not include any ANC troops.

A few days after taking Kisangani, the victorious rebels took more than 1,300 Europeans hostage, placed them in detention at the Victoria Hotel and other nearby inns, and announced that any attempt to retake the city would result in the death of the hostages. At this point, the Simba rebellion officially became an international crisis, as the 1,300 hostages included some 500 Belgians and approximately 50 Americans who lived and worked in the Kisangani area. U.S. Foreign Secretary W. Averell Harriman and his Belgian counterpart Chancellor Paul-Henri Spaak initiated frantic negotiations to free the hostages with the Organization for African Unity (OAU), as well as with anyone else who might help. Spaak was in daily contact with rebel leader Thomas Kanza. In the middle of this major crisis, and against the advice of the U.S. military, Secretary of State Dean Rusk prohibited the use of force.

On August 11, 1964 a band of Simbas took five officials from the U.S. Consulate in Kisangani to Camp Ketele, a military installation on the outskirts of this city. The Americans were savagely beaten and forced to chew on American flags.

On August 12, 1964, General Olenga, feeling very secure in Kisangani, summoned Soumialot to Kisangani. This was unusual, for Soumialot was the Minister of Defense, which would have made him Olenga's boss. Soumialot arrived in Kisangani the following day, assumed control of the city, and Olenga marched his army toward Bukavu, an important city of about 200,000 inhabitants located on the southwest shore of Lake Kivu. Olenga attacked Bukavu on August 19, 1964, but this time Lieutenant Colonel Leonard Mulamba of the ANC was present, and with the air power support of the Makasi T-28s, Congolese loyal forces inflicted a crushing defeat on Olenga's Simbas. Segisberto Fernández recalls this battle. "COMISH, the CIA and the ANC believed that holding Bukavu was vital for crushing the Simba rebellion and the eventual rescue of the Kisangani hostages. The U.S. government obtained permission from the government of Rwanda to use the Kamembe airport, on the other side of Lake Kivu, but quite close to Bukavu. We used five T-28s and the battle lasted for twelve long days, as the Simbas kept trying to re-take Bukavu.

As usual, when things got rough, the Simba bosses left Bukavu and went elsewhere."[19] The successful defense of Bukavu provided a much needed victory for the ANC, for it proved that Simba rebels could be defeated, Mai Mulele and witch doctors notwithstanding.

Somehow it became known by the Simba leadership that three Americans had participated in the defense of Bukavu, Colonel William A. Dodds (representative of the Joint Chiefs of Staff in Congo), U.S. Army Lieutenant Colonel Donald V. Rattan, and Lewis R. MacFarlane (from the Bukavu U.S. consulate). Olenga attributed his defeat at Bukavu to American aircraft and hinted to the media that American hostages in Kisangani were now at increased risk. On August 21, 1964 Olenga ordered trials without mercy of American diplomats at Kisangani. On August 29, 1964 Secretary of State Dean Rusk officially recognized the Congo (Kisangani) situation as an American crisis.

Makasi pilots had politely refused to fly the B-26 aircraft that the U.S. had recently provided for them. A number of the Cuban exiles had served in Vietnam and were aware that B-26 planes had a problem with maneuverability and the strength of the wings. They knew that numerous accidents had occurred in Vietnam as a result of a wing falling off. Segisberto Fernández discussed the various aircrafts used during the Congo campaign. "It was like a process of evolution. The AT-6s were okay, but the enemy was starting to use anti-aircraft weapons, and its range was short. The T-28s were originally designed for the U.S. Navy and were a significant improvement over the AT-6s, not only in maneuverability, but also in range and fire power. The normal B-26s were not suitable for the Congo war, and for that matter, were not liked in Vietnam. In fact, our pilots preferred the T-28s over the standard B-26s. Then, faced with criticism, Douglas, which I believe was the manufacturer of the B-26s, went back to the drawing board and produced the B-26Ks. This was a great aircraft! Douglas added air-conditioning and pressurization to the cabin and installed stronger engines with retro-jets. The normal B-26s used brakes.... [Douglas] reinforced the wings in order to hang the heavier engines. With the stronger wings, Douglas was able to place additional fuel tanks on the tips of the wings for extra range. I think that the first three B-26Ks had just been shipped to Turkey, but the U.S. negotiated a deal and had these aircrafts diverted to Congo. Eventually we had a total of seven B-26Ks. We were trained for the maintenance of the B-26Ks by three men from Pensacola, Florida who said they were retired from the Navy. I believe they were CIA."[20]

On August 21, 1964 Makasi pilots flew the first B-26K combat mission in Congo from the Kamina air base. These light bombers would become critical in the war against the rebel Simbas, for they were better armed, had a much longer range, and an improved maneuverability over the T-28 aircraft. The fire power of the B-26K was much superior to that of the T-28 aircraft. The T-28 had four 50-caliber machine guns and two pods of fourteen rockets each, for a total of twenty-eight rockets. The B-26K, on the other hand, had eight 50-caliber machine guns and four pods of nineteen rockets each, for a total of seventy-six rockets, or almost three times as many as the T-28.

Around August 20, 1964 Hoare was asked by Mobutu to assemble his troops, march in the direction of Kisangani and be prepared to assist in liberating the hostages and the city. Hoare, working with COMISH personnel, determined that before initiating the march to Kisangani, the liberation of Kalemie was a requirement, for the following reasons:

- It was the headquarters of Gastón Soumialot, Minister of Defense for the rebels.
- It was a strategic port city for the domination of Lake Tanganyika.
- Its airport was needed for Makasi to be able to operate in this area.
- A revolutionary court had been set up in Kalemie, and many people were being given the death penalty for petty crimes.
- There were about 120 Belgians in Kalemie, as well as a number of other Europeans who feared for their lives.
- A number of priests were being held in the oldest Catholic Mission in Congo.

The battle plan for Kalemie was called operation *Watch Chain*. The main ANC ground force would approach Kalemie from Kabalo on the west, along the Lukuga River, while a diversionary ANC force would approach the city from Kapona, south of Kalemie.

In the meantime, Makasi Cuban exile pilots René García and Jack Varela, flying from their base in Kamina, would bomb rebel strongholds in and around Kalemie, while the real attack force under Hoare's command would approach the city from Lake Tanganyika, coming from the south near the town of Boma.

In advance of the battle for Kalemie, Reginaldo Blanco recalls an interesting experience in Kabalo. "I had arrived in Kamina in early August 1964, and someone asked me if I wanted to go to Kabalo, and I said yes. Gonzalo Herrera was the pilot of the DC-3, I was the co-pilot and Colonel Mulamba was a passenger [later Mulamba would become Prime Minister in Mobutu's administration]. We arrived at the Kabalo airport, at about the same time as two Belgian helicopters 'flying bananas' arrived.

The Belgians were there to install a telecommunications system. We decided to go into town and grab some lunch. While we were eating, about 200 people came running down the street saying the Simbas were entering town. Two Belgian soldiers and I were ordered to protect the bridge, while the remaining men headed to the airport to protect the aircraft. I was carrying 800 rounds of ammunition, and could hardly walk due to the weight of the ammunition. We then found out that the Simbas had already crossed the bridge and were in town, negotiating with the ANC by phone. There were about 25 of us and we all took refuge in a hospital. The rebels set up a machine gun near the hospital front entrance and set the other three sides of the hospital on fire. Fortunately, the Simbas manning the machine gun were so high on hemp that they never saw us flee the hospital. We headed to the airport, but while crossing town, were engaged in hand-to-hand combat by Simbas armed with machetes and spears. There is a definite advantage when you have to fight someone high on hemp, as they move in slow motion. We made it to the airport, got in our respective aircraft and left. The next day, ANC Colonel Kakuji came in and cleaned house at Kabalo."[21]

The battle for Kalemie commenced on August 24, 1964. By August 28, after suffering several casualties, Hoare had to retreat. The battle was saved by Congolese Colonel Kakuji and the battalion of ANC soldiers who had attacked Kalemie from the west. The city was taken on August 30, 1964, thus saving the lives of 135 Westerners.[22] As soon as a continuous perimeter around Kalemie was secured, a Makasi unit was moved to this strategically important airport.

Even with the defeats in Kalemie and Bukavu, the army of the short-lived People's Republic of Congo still controlled about one-half of Congolese territory during late August, early September of 1964. Soumialot, Gbenye, and General Olenga were thinking final victory by taking the capital city of Kinshasa. Two Simba columns were headed for Kinshasa from Equateur Province, one from Mbandaka and the second one from further north in Gemena. Schramme's 10 Commando rapidly attacked and defeated the Simbas at Gemena thus stopping their advance on the capital city.

Meanwhile, in addition to the equipment being provided, the CIA and the U.S. Department of Defense felt compelled to meet the increasing personnel needs of their Congo Air Force. More than twenty Cuban exile pilots were now flying in Congo, supported by Cuban exile aircraft maintenance crews. Since the U.S. had not yet gone public with this operation, in the early fall of 1964, the CIA formed a new Liechtenstein-registered shell company to recruit new forces with the absurd name of *Anstalt Wigmo*, where the WIGMO was an acronym for Western International Ground Maintenance Organization. This company entered into a contract with the Congolese air force.

Cuban exile Oscar A. Carol, payroll officer for WIGMO, stated: "Pilots had a base salary of $550 per month if they flew out of the Kinshasa airport. If they flew from other airports, the salary was $850 per month, the additional $300 per month was considered hazard pay. Flight time was paid at $10 per hour for reconnaissance flights and $20 per hour when flying in a combat zone. Congo was broken down into combat and non-combat zones, and these zones were updated monthly. There was also a CIA-provided life insurance policy, which paid $40,000 if killed in action in a combat zone and $20,000 if killed in a non-combat zone."[23]

It has been suggested that Makasi pilots were paid per round expended and that they therefore never returned with any ammunition. However, the truth is that the pilots were paid even if they returned without having fired a single shot. These wages were not excessive, for at that time, a cargo plane pilot out of Miami made the same wages without any risk to his life. These individuals were not in Congo for monetary gain.

New pilots arriving in the August 1964 timeframe were: Fausto Gómez, Tristán García, Tony Blázquez, Castor Cereceda, Reginaldo Blanco, and others. The U.S. did not admit military support of the Tshombé Congo administration until October 1, 1964.

The Kisangani hostage crisis had become a military and a diplomatic priority for the U.S. as well as for Belgium. The U.S. military and the CIA were developing strategies to extricate the hostages. Belgium had shipped elite ground troops to Congo. The Belgian ground operation was codenamed *L'Ommegang* after a Belgian carnival festivity, and it was to be conducted by the Fifth Mechanized Brigade under the command of Colonel Frédéric Vandewalle, who was working with COMISH and Mike Hoare planning a ground campaign.

The Congo CIA Station and COMISH were actively developing a separate strategy to rescue the U.S. diplomats and CIA operatives being held captive in Kisangani. The job was to be entrusted to a unit, yet to be recruited, of Cuban exiles. Rip Robertson was given the job to select, recruit, and train this group of what would be eighteen experienced Cuban exiles. The U.S. military and the CIA were building up troops and equipment in nearby friendly countries, as they believed the diplomatic efforts were failing. A CIA officer later described this buildup as "bringing in our own animals."[24]

Robertson's Spanish-speaking unit would later be called the 58th Company and it was composed of: José (Pepito) González Castro, Alberto (Dr. Kildare) Pérez, Juan (El Negro) Tamayo, Jorge (Fotingo) Silva, Ricardo Morales, Alicio Calas, Conrado Fernández, José (Juan Roque) Hernández, and ten others. A list of the anti-Castro Cuban exiles that fought against communism in Congo is provided in Appendix II.

The recruiting, training, and transportation to Congo of the Cuban exile infantrymen could be out of a James Bond movie, with some elements of humor added. Three of the Cuban exile infantry veterans, Alicio Calas, Conrado Fernández, and José Hernández recall the events of the time.

The recruiting was personally done by Rip Robertson, and he clearly only interviewed men he fully trusted and that he knew were capable of carrying out the rescue of the American diplomats being held by Simbas in Kisangani. Since the potential recruits knew one another from prior anti-Castro operations, Robertson tried to make sure that the men did not communicate with each other prior to their departure for their mission. He told them that this was a highly secret special mission, that their services were required by the U.S. government, that they would fight against communism and that it would not be in the western hemisphere. Robertson asked each man to keep the information to himself. Conrado Fernández states: "I met Rip at a house in Miami, he told me I was needed by America and that the Cuba situation was on hold but that I would be fighting for freedom and democracy. I said yes."[25]

Alicio Calas relates a similar experience: "I met Rip at a motel near the University of Miami. He told me the special mission was not for Cuba, but it was to defend U.S. interest, and that it would be outside this hemisphere. I accepted, and Rip asked me not to discuss the subject with anyone, and that he would call me."[26]

José Hernández continues explaining the process. "I got a call and was told to report to an airport near Miami. When I arrived, all my friends were there. There were 18 of us. We were loaded on a plane that had all the windows blackened. After two or three hours flight, we landed in what we thought was a U.S. Army base. The name of the base was covered up. And all the car license plates were also covered. We all thought this was funny. What difference did it make if we knew where we were? We boarded a different airplane, a C-47, I think, and took off. On the drive within the airport, we did see some cars that did not have the license plates covered, they all had Virginia plates. We assumed we were in

Virginia. When the sun came out, I told Rip we were flying east, probably to northern England or Scandinavia. He asked me how I knew, and I told him by the position of the sun and the heading of the plane. He just looked puzzled and said: 'I'll be damned.' I am pretty sure we landed and refueled at Glasgow, Scotland and then flew on to a U.S. military base in Weisbaden, Germany. They took us to a safe house and told us not to talk to any servicemen, for they were not aware of any covert operations. We ate well, slept, and were again flying early the next morning."[27]

Continues Alicio Calas: "We all knew we had crossed the Mediterranean Sea. Our next stop was in a place where there were Arabs speaking perfect Castilian Spanish. Clearly, we were in the former Spanish Sahara. By this time, Rip gave up on keeping our destination secret. Our next stop was in a horrible place in Nigeria, where the natives fueled our aircraft out of 55-gallon drums with hand pumps. We then crossed the Sahara for what seemed hours and hours. We arrived at Kamina Air Base in Katanga in the late afternoon, and we were wasted. In addition to Rip, there were two American officers with our group, U.S. Army Lieutenant Colonel Arthur Garza and a USAF/CIA operative we knew only as Mitch."[28]

José Hernández continues the narration: "We really just wanted to have a drink and go to sleep, but Rip told us that our cover was that of Airport Police. We were further advised that we were on alert, were instructed to take our weapons, go to the roofs of the various large buildings and be prepared to defend the airport, because some mercenaries had not been paid their wages by the ANC and were coming from Angola to attack the Airport and collect their money. It was a Friday night, and all the ANC soldiers were drunk, playing their drums, dancing and yelling. We were jet-lagged and scared and probably would have shot at anything that looked suspicious, except that we didn't know what suspicious looked like. If there really were angry mercenaries, they didn't show up. The next morning, and for the next several days, we rehearsed a rescue operation by parachute and helicopter, which we later found out was intended for kidnapped Stanleyville [Kisangani] American diplomats, but which was cancelled the last minute. Once the operation to rescue the diplomats was cancelled, COMISH decided that the Cuban exile infantry special force would join the march to Stanleyville and try to rescue the American diplomats after entering the city."[29]

Alicio Calas remarks: "I know that sometime after the Stanleyville rescue, Fidel [Castro] made a four hour speech where he blasted the mercenary Cuban exile worms who had sold their souls to the imperialists.

I resent being called a mercenary since we were welcomed in the U.S. when we left Cuba, and we had a large debt of gratitude to America. We were asked to go and we volunteered. Our pay was $260 per month for married men and $240 per month for single guys. If we sold our souls, they went for a low price. We did each get a $1,000 bonus upon our return to Miami for what we were told was a job well done."[30]

On September 5, 1964 the OAU called an extraordinary session of all African nations in an attempt to resolve the Kisangani crisis. The highly popular President of Kenya Jomo Kenyatta was appointed to act as mediator.

Congo instantly became a major Cold War theater. The Simba rebels were supplied by transport planes from three nations: The Soviet Union, Egypt (under Abdel Gamal Nasser), and Algeria (under Ahmed Ben Bella). Delivery of weapons was a complex logistical problem. Soviet aircraft carried the weapons to military airfields in Ghana, Algeria, and the United Arab Republic (mostly in present-day Egypt). Then, Algerian Antonov An-12 and Ghanian Il-18 transports flew the arms into Orientale Province, using Brazzaville as a staging point. Egyptian An-12s did the same to Orientale and Nord- and Sud-Kivu from a base in Sudan. Cuban soldiers stationed in neighboring Sudan, Uganda, and Tanzania provided military training for Congolese Simbas.

The U.S. Army, wanting to be helpful, had commissioned in late 1962 one of the most unbelievable strategy papers ever conceived in the history of unconventional warfare. Published in August 1964, its title *Witchcraft, Sorcery, Magic, and Other Psychological Phenomena and Their Implications on Military and Paramilitary Operations in the Congo* must have raised quite a few eyebrows in Washington. It appears that the U.S. Army wanted to be on a firm footing when dealing with palm branch waving witch doctors. A large number of possible counter insurgency methods, including the concoction of medicines to neutralize and overpower the spells cast by insurgency witch-doctors were tested. It is comforting to note that the study's final conclusion was to use traditional means, i.e. brute force, to suppress the witchcraft warriors.[31]

The strategy developed by COMISH, Vandewalle, and Hoare was simple, yet brilliant. Initially, four columns would advance following four different routes in the direction of Kisangani, which had fallen to the insurgents on August 5, 1964. On the way to Kisangani, these four columns would liberate as many towns as possible, similarly to what had been done in Kalemie, thus reducing the size of the territory occupied by rebels, before simultaneously converging on Kisangani. Assuming the plan would work as intended, Kisangani would be assaulted from four directions as follows: from Opala in the west; from Lubutu in the south; from Mambasa from the east; and from the north, coming from Isiro.

In addition, the forces from Denard's 6 Commando and Schramme's 10 Commando would prevent Simba reinforcements from reaching Kisangani, primarily from the rebel strongholds in Equateur Province and the northwest portion of Orientale Province. The down side of this strategy was that many Simbas, when faced with superior fire power, were likely to run in the direction of Kisangani, their perceived stronghold. This would further endanger the lives of Western hostages, but this was a calculated risk they chose to take.

The ground forces that would eventually be used to assault Kisangani, depending on the source material utilized, contained a total of between 2,800 and 3,500 men, including:

- Hoare's 5 Commando, which was further broken down into seven companies, numbered 51 through 57 (a total of about 400 mercenaries),
- The 58th Company of Cuban exiles under the command of Rip Robertson,
- Colonel Vandewalle and Belgium's Fifth Mechanized Brigade, and
- About 2,000 ANC (primarily Katangan) troops, divided into two columns, Lima I and Lima II.

In addition to the above troops, there were six Belgian Army logistics teams. These men would supply weapons, ammunition and rations to the advancing soldiers. The logistics teams were not intended to engage the enemy.

A summary of the military plan by Vandewalle, Rattan, and Hoare follows. All ground forces would assemble at Kamina air base, Katanga before setting the operation in motion. The offensive against Simbas commenced from Kamina in mid-September 1964.

Company 51 would be flown to Gemena via Mbandaka, where nine men from Cuban exile 58th Company under Rip Robertson's command and units from Denard's 6 Commando would join Company 51 in the fighting. Then on to Lisala and Bumba; afterwards, Company 51 and the nine men from Cuban exile 58th Company would be flown to Kindu to join the Punia-Lubutu-Kisangani assault. Denard's 6 Commando would continue north to Gemena and Yokoma.

Company 52 would also go by air to Mbandaka, where they would join up with Schramme's 10 Commando and the ANC Lima II and Company

54. Together they would march through Ingende, Bikili, and Boende, fighting continuously along the way, arriving in Ikela. Company 52 would then be flown from Ikela to Bumba, where they would relieve Company 51 (before Company 51 moved to Kindu), then continue to Aketi and Isiro, where they would wait for orders to move into Kisangani.

Company 53, with the other nine men from the Cuban exile infantry under Lieutenant Colonel Garza would be flown to Uvira, then would move to liberate Bukavu, Goma, and Beni, and would wait at Mambasa for the order to assault Kisangani.

Company 54 would also be flown to Mbandaka. After the liberation of Bukavu, the Cuban exile one-half force would be flown to Kindu to be reunited with the other nine Cuban exiles who had assisted in liberating Lisala. Schramme's 10 Commando, ANC Lima II and Company 52, would march through the rebel strongholds of Ingende, Bikili and Boende and end in Ikela. Company 54 would go on to liberate Opala, where they would wait for orders for the Kisangani assault. Schramme's 10 Commando would move back in the direction of the Congo River to prevent rebel reinforcements from reaching Kisangani.

What was known as the *Stan Column* was initially composed of: Hoare and Companies 55, 56, and 57, Vandewalle and the Fifth Mechanized Brigade, and the ANC Lima I. They would be flown to Kongolo, then move through Kibombo and Kindu, where they would join with Company 51 and Rip Robertson's 58th Company of anti-Castro Cuban exiles. This reinforced Stan Column would assault and take Kindu and then move on to Punia and wait at Lubutu for instructions to move into Kisangani.

"American vehicles and communications provided necessary mobility for the practically autonomous columns, and their advance was very well protected by [Cuban exile piloted] rocket and machine-gun firing B-26Ks and T-28s."[32]

Segisberto Fernández elaborates: "Makasi pilots were always ahead of the infantry. They scouted the enemy as well as softened the targets. The pilots flew 12-hour days in shifts of 2.5 to 3 hours. One would return to base, refuel, reload ammunition, and change with the other pilot. It was a hard campaign for the pilots as well as for us in the ground."[33] The plan for this major military campaign is portrayed in Figure 3.

Mercenary and ANC forces were advancing rapidly. A unit from Bob Denard's 6 Commando, headed by Captain Le Bailly, with the help of a portion of the Cuban exile 58th Company, advanced on and took Lisala on September 15, 1964. Lisala was Unilever's company town and the Simbas were holding a number of European hostages. Juan (El Negro)

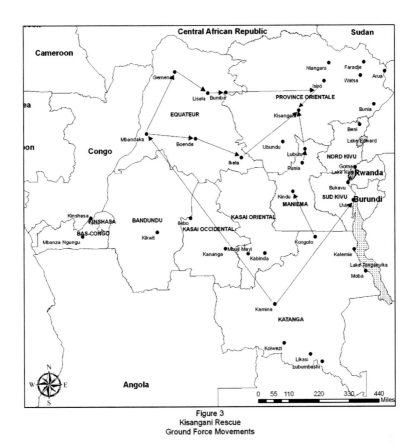

Figure 3
Kisangani Rescue
Ground Force Movements

Tamayo recalls: "While conducting house-to-house urban fighting in Lisala, [Cuban exile infantryman] Ricardo Morales found documents indicating that Che Guevara had attended a meeting at that location."[34] There is no record of Che Guevara having visited Congo prior to April 1965. If indeed Guevara attended a meeting in Lisala prior to September 1964, it had to have been as a side trip during one of his many African trips as Ambassador of the Revolution. The Simbas retreated to nearby Bumba, also on the north shore of the Congo River. Bumba was taken by Hoare's Company 51 and the Cuban exile 58th Company, on October 24, 1964.

A significant cache of Chinese weapons and equipment was captured in Lisala. On September 10, 1964, after ferocious battles, Hoare's forces under Major Siegfried Müller finally took Mbandaka, and moved on to take Boende, but had to retreat under heavy fire. Belgian Major Pierre

Lemercier and two ANC columns from Lima II reinforced Müller, and the combined force took Boende on October 24 and Ikela on November 6. Müller, an Iron Cross decorated former German soldier from the Wehrmacht, carefully obliterated anything that got in his way.[35] On October 28, 1964 the rebels announced that all Americans and Belgians in Kisangani had been placed under arrest.

Company 53 of Hoare's 5 Commando joined the ANC Lima I, under Colonel Mulamba, and commenced a mop-up operation in the Great Lakes area south of Bukavu, including the cities of Uvira, Lubero, and Butembo. The Congolese portion of the Great Lakes area is in the northeast area and it includes Lakes Edward, Kivu, and Tanganyika. After fierce fighting in the taking of Bukavu, Company 53 and the ANC Lima I, as planned, moved north to liberate Goma, Beni, and Mambasa, where they waited for orders to march to Kisangani. At Vandewalle's request, after taking Bukavu, Lima I was asked to cut mop-up operations short and join the Stan Column, which was debating whether to attack or bypass Kindu, a river port of around 50,000 people. The rebels were holding more than 100 Europeans at Kindu and had threatened to slaughter all of them if the troops got any closer to Kindu.

The joint American/Belgian military command agonized as to whether to capture Kindu before the Kisangani rescue. They feared that an attack on Kindu might put the lives of the Kisangani hostages at risk. Kindu had strong Simba support, and General Olenga was reportedly defending that city. The decision to take Kindu was made by Makasi pilot Gustavo Ponzoa.

Ponzoa recalls the situation: "I was flying a B-26K on a reconnaissance mission, with Fausto Valdéz as co-pilot. As we approached what appeared to be the town square we saw that the rebels had taken all male hostages to the square, stripped them to their underwear and prepared to execute them. There was no time to ask for a decision, we strafed the would-be executioners and radioed for the invading forces to move."[36]

The battle started on November 1, 1964. Kindu was the headquarters of the rebel forces for Maniema, and Nord- and Sud-Kivu Provinces. General Olenga had retreated to this stronghold following his resounding defeat at Bukavu. After a fierce five-day battle, the ANC Lima I, Hoare's Companies 55, 56, and 57, along with Belgium's Fifth Mechanized Brigade under Colonel Vandewalle, took Kindu with the help of the recently arrived Company 51 under Captain Ian Gordon and 58th Company of Cuban exiles under Rip Robertson. Air support by the Makasi Cuban exile air force made this operation possible. The takeover of Kindu prevented the massacre of more than 100 foreigners. Olenga was nowhere to be found, as he had fled to Kisangani.

The Simba rebels neither knew how to use the anti-aircraft weapons taken from the ANC nor employed defensive or camouflage techniques. Thus, any air strikes by the Cuban exile Makasi pilots were devastating. The Simba units were strafed with 50-caliber machine guns and 70mm wing-mounted rockets. The rebels, believing they were immune to enemy bullets, failed to disperse even when under relentless air attack. After each air strike, mercenary columns consisting of a few jeeps and trucks armed with machine guns would massacre the demoralized rebels. "The psychological impact of the airplanes was at least as important as their physical threat. The mercenaries and [Cuban exile piloted] planes quickly overwhelmed the militarily inexperienced and poorly equipped Simbas."[37] The mercenaries killed anything that moved. In the town of Kindu alone, the mercenaries killed more than three thousand rebels. The mercenaries were followed by Mobutu's reconstituted ANC, who were even more brutal than the mercenaries.

The western portion of Orientale Province was no longer under control of Simba rebels. As the forces of Vandewalle and Hoare advanced, as predicted, Simbas retreated to Kisangani, the Simba capital. The fear for the lives of the European hostages increased. A large battle was brewing. Colonels Vandewalle and Hoare prepared the revised strategy for the assault on Kisangani based on the location of their troops on or about November 10, 1964. After Vandewalle and Hoare interviewed the rescued hostages from Kindu, it became clear that the rebel threat to kill Kisangani Europeans was real.

Hoare's 5 Commando started to move in the direction of Kisangani. By this time, Gbenye's followers, under the command of General Olenga, held about 1,300 European (mostly Belgian) and American hostages, as well as 325 Pakistani and Indian citizens. Approximately 60 Americans were included, headed by U.S. Consul Michael Hoyt, along with U.S. consular officers and 4 of the CIA's own agents.[38]

Since the Kisangani rescue operation, America and Western Europe have learned much about hostage-taking as a mechanism of foreign policy and a method of generating funds for terrorist organizations. There are still many unanswered questions regarding the wisdom of Belgian and American diplomats continuing to negotiate with the terrorists until the last minute, to the detriment of military plans.

Most of the hostages were being held at the Victoria Hotel in the center of Kisangani, and the Simbas threatened to kill all hostages if Tshombé's forces came any closer to the city center. On November 16, the rebels announced that Dr. Paul Carlson, a well-known American medical missionary, would be executed as a spy. On this same date, political and military leaders of the U.S. and Belgium agreed on the logistics of a standby military rescue plan. On November 21, the rebels threatened to eat their prisoners.

The situation was similar at Isiro (then known as Paulis) a town some 360 kilometers northeast of Kisangani, where around 400 European hostages were being held. The hostages at Isiro had been brutalized by the Simbas. An American missionary had been tortured and beaten to death. There were also European hostages being held by Simbas at Bunia and Watsa, but the details were sketchy as communication with these cities had been cut off.

The Congolese, Belgian, and American governments had started negotiations with the Simbas on August 6, 1964, the day after the fall of Kisangani. These negotiations had dragged on for more than 100 days, including almost daily contacts between Christophe Gbenye and Gastón Soumialot with Belgian Chancellor Paul-Henri Spaak, in addition to the previously mentioned mediations of Kenya's President Jomo Kenyatta, representing the OAU. After all attempts to negotiate with the Simbas failed, the whole world waited while Washington and Brussels debated how to structure a rescue operation. In the meantime, Vandewalle and Hoare were instructed to wait for orders from Brussels, Washington, and Kinshasa.

Notes

1.   Benemelis, Juan F., Castro, *Subversión y Terrorismo en Africa*, Editorial San Martin, Madrid, 1988, p. 128.
2.   Weissman, *op. cit.*, p. 212.
3.   Quoted by Hellström, Leif, *The Instant Air Force: The Creation of the CIA's Air Unit in Congo, 1962*, Advanced History Course, Autumn Term 2005, University of Stockholm.
4.   García, René, Congo: Operación Valle del Kwilo. *Punto de Mira*, July 1989, p. 18.
5.   Fernández, Segisberto, Conversations with the author, Miami, October 19, 2007.
6.   Ros, Enrique, *Cubanos Combatientes: Peleando en Distintos Frentes*, Ediciones Universal, Miami, 1998, p. 87.
7.   "Congo Police Mutiny Put Down by Mobutu," *The Washington Post*, May 4, 1963, p. A8.
8.   Hoare, Mike, *The Road to Kalamata*, Lexington Books, Toronto, 1989, p. 19.
9.   García, *op. cit.*, p. 18.
10.   *Ibid*, p. 19.
11.   Fernández, *op. cit.*

12. Devlin, Larry, Conversations with the author, February 15 and 21, 2008.
13. *The New York Times*, April 26, 1964, Quoted by Victor Marchetti and John D. Marks, Jonathan Cape editors, London, 1974, p. 117.
14. "Whose War in the Congo?" *The New York Times*, June 18, 1964, p. 34.
15. Hoyt, Michael P. E., *Captive in the Congo: A Consul's Return to the Heart of Darkness*, Naval Institute Press, Annapolis, Maryland, 2000, p. xvi.
16. Guevara, Ernesto "Che," *The African Dream*, New York, Grove Press, 2000, pp. 14-15.
17. Annan's Congo burden: Déjà vu, *The Washington Times*, August 17, 2004.
18. Metrowich, F. R., *Africa and Communism*, Scanned and converted to PDF by Shangani, May 2005, p. 88.
19. Fernández, Segisberto, Conversations with the author, Miami, October 19, 2007.
20. *Ibid.*
21. Blanco, *op. cit.*
22. Odom, Major Thomas P., *Dragon Operations: Hostage Rescues in the Congo 1964-1965*, Combined Arms Research Library, Fort Leavenworth, Kansas, 1988, p. 42.
23. Carol, Oscar, Conversations with the author, Miami, July 26, 2006, plus additional communication on May 30, 2007.
24. Quoted by Blum, William, Killing Hope, *http://www.thirdworldtraveler.com/Blum/Congo_KHhtml*, downloaded September 17, 2004.
25. Fernández, Conrado, Conversations with the author, Miami, October 21, 2007.
26. Calas, Alicio, Conversations with the author, Miami, October 21, 2007.
27. Hernández, José, Conversations with the author, Miami, October 21, 2007.
28. Calas, *op. cit.*
29. Hernández, *op. cit.*
30. Calas, *op. cit.*
31. Price, James R. and Paul Jureidini, *Witchcraft, Sorcery, Magic, and Other Psychological Phenomena and Their Implications on Military and Paramilitary Operations in the Congo*, Special Operations Research Office, August 8, 1964.
32. Weissman, *op. cit.*, p. 240.
33. Fernández, Segisberto, *op. cit.*
34. Tamayo, Juan, Conversations with the author, Miami, July 30, 2006.
35. Schramme, Jean, Le Bataillon Léopard—*Souvenirs d'un Africain Blanc*, Laffont, Paris, c1969.
36. Ponzoa, *op. cit.*
37. Weissman, *op. cit.*, p. 240.
38. Quoted by Ros, *op. cit.*, p. 101, from the November 24, 1964 *New York Times*.

7

Rescue Operations

Both the command structure as well as the military plan for the Kisangani rescue were extremely complex and had to be adapted frequently to the constantly changing constraints the politicians imposed on the military planners. The two key politicians were, on the U.S. side Ambassador W. Averell Harriman, a man trusted by President Johnson, and on the Belgian side, Foreign Minister Paul-Henri Spaak. The politicians required the internationalization of the conflict, as well as a degree of secrecy, in an attempt to disguise the direct participation of U.S. and Belgian military. Additionally, they required the participation of Congo's military. Foreign Minister Spaak wanted Belgian and U.S. troops to leave shortly after the rescue and to minimize Simba casualties. Harriman was in closer agreement with the military in that the rescue troops should take Kisangani in order to break the back of the insurrection.

This international operation could not be carried out without the blessing of the Congo government. Belgium and the U.S. feared that Tshombé would view the Western strategy as a form of neo-colonialism and refuse to authorize the rescue operation. Tshombé, Mobutu, and Kasavubu were kept appraised of the multiple iterations to the rescue operation.

In addition to the joint U.S.-Belgium rescue plan, a separate American plan had been devised specifically to rescue U.S. Consul Michael Hoyt, David Grinwis (CIA officer under the cover of Vice-Consul), James Stauffer, Ernest Haule, and Donald Parkes who had been instructed by American Ambassador McMurtrie Godley to stay in Kisangani so that they could keep the American flag flying. This rescue plan, appropriately called *Operation Flagpole*, consisted of a diversionary attack on an area of Kisangani far from the American consulate with Cuban exile piloted T-28s, followed by assault and rescue with an H-21 helicopter and Rip Robertson's force of eighteen special operations Cuban exiles at the U.S. Consulate grounds. The operation was cancelled at the last minute due to the presence of a temporary Simba camp in the area of the U.S. Consulate.[1]

Larry Devlin recalls Operation Flagpole but believes that the origin of the name is different from the one provided by Odom or Hoyt. According to Devlin, "the helicopter was supposed to land by the flagpole on the Stanleyville [Kisangani] American consulate grounds, but no one could remember if the flagpole was in front or on which side of the building. After so much discussion on the location of the flagpole, we decided to code name the operation Flagpole."[2]

When the final joint Belgian/American rescue plan was accepted by the politicians, the command structure was made clear. En route to Kisangani, operational control of the Belgian paratroopers Dragon Force would be in the hands of the American airlift commander, USAF Colonel Burgess Gradwell. Gradwell was well-acquainted with Congo, as he had flown Irish troops during the UNOC operation in Katanga. Once the USAF planes arrived at the drop zone, operational control would pass to Belgian Colonel Charles Laurent, who was also well-acquainted with Congo. The Kisangani rescue operation was code named *Dragon Rouge*, which is French for Red Dragon. In addition to the Kisangani rescue, three additional rescue operations were planned: *Dragon Noir* (Black Dragon) at Isiro; *Dragon Blanc* (White Dragon) at Bunia; and *Dragon Vert* (Green Dragon) at Watsa.

The planned Dragon Force did not include enough Belgian paratroopers to hold a continuous perimeter around the airport while conducting the rescue operation in the center of Kisangani. Therefore the paratroopers had to rely on Vandewalle's ground forces arriving on schedule in order for the operation to be successful. Timing was critical as Vandewalle's troops could be slowed down by the enemy on their approach to the city. Vandewalle was convinced that Kisangani should be taken from the ground rather than the combined air-ground operation.

Regarding the ground troop movements, Colonel Vandewalle had operational control of all military operations against the Simba rebels. U.S. Army Lieutenant Colonel Donald V. Rattan and other American advisors representing COMISH accompanied Vandewalle's ground troops on the way to Kisangani.[3] Vandewalle, Rattan, and Hoare had decided to concentrate the bulk of their forces in the river city of Kindu (approximately 400 kilometers due south of Kisangani), recently liberated by their troops after a lengthy and ferocious battle. Further complicating troop movements, Kindu and Kisangani are on opposite sides of the Lualaba River, which becomes the Congo River when it starts flowing in a westerly direction after Kisangani.

While Vandewalle, Rattan, and Hoare waited for their orders for the Kisangani rescue, several operations were being conducted out of Kindu, one of which provided the first evidence that there were Cuban soldiers in the area. The operation in question was an armed reconnaissance flight on approximately November 10, 1964, conducted by pilot Ignacio Rojas, with Reginaldo Blanco as copilot. They were instructed to fly from Kindu to Bukavu in an effort to spot rebel transportation or other activity.

Reginaldo Blanco recalls the operation. "Our aircrafts were equipped with special FM radios which had a maximum range of about 2 miles [3.2 kilometers]. In this manner, we could communicate with the ground or between aircrafts, but the enemy could not easily listen to our transmissions. When we were near the town of Shabunda, we received a message in French from a Belgian unit which was pinned down below. Since Rojas spoke French, he translated to me 'To the airplane above us, please help us.' The situation was as follows, the Belgians were across the river from the rebels, there was a bridge, and the rebels were shooting at the Belgians with mortars and heavy machine guns. We made a circle, flew over the Belgians, and when we were over the bridge ready to fire, in our FM transmitter, in Cuban-accented Spanish, a voice said: 'no, no, you are mistaken.' We were not aware of any Cuban exile ground troops in the area, but startled, we made another circle. The Belgians identified their unit and asked us to please eliminate the enemy position. Again, we prepared to shoot, and the same voice said: 'no, no you are mistaken.' This time we shot 12 rockets in their direction, and the Cuban-accented voice said in Spanish: 'Mercenaries, sons of bitches.' We replied: 'Asshole, stick up your head, and we'll take it off.' There is no doubt these were Cuban soldiers, we believe stationed in Rwanda, who were making an incursion into Congo territory."[4]

The CIA was informed of the encounter immediately upon the return of the Makasi aircraft. No information as to the CIA's or other Western intelligence services' reaction has been found.

With the territory surrounding Kisangani mostly under control, the revised plan to conduct the final ground attack on Kisangani called for three columns, with the air support provided by Makasi, from their newly liberated base at Kindu. It is estimated that the total number of men for the three columns was 3,300. Column 1, known as the Stan Column, was the main force. Included in this detachment were: Hoare's Companies 51, 55, 56, and 57, Belgium's Fifth Mechanized Brigade under Colonel Vandewalle, the ANC Lima I, and Rip Robertson's experienced 58th Company, "which consisted of eighteen Cuban exiles armed with sixty-eight different weapons."[5] This column, which contained more than 200 vehicles, would move north from Kindu to Punia and Lubutu, then on to Wanie-Rukulu before entering Kisangani. Column 2 was composed of Company 54 and the ANC Lima II, which would come from the west through Ikela and Opala and on to Kisangani. The third column would result from the merger of Companies 52 and 53 coming from the northeast, starting in Kondolole and Mambasa respectively before joining forces to approach Kisangani.[6]

Mike Hoare, in his book *Congo Mercenary* chronicles the march north to Kisangani with the support of Lima I column from the ANC. He describes the Cuban exile ground force as follows: "I stopped to talk to a truck-load of [anti-Castro] Cubans who had just joined me. I called them 58th Company and they were proud of the title. They were as tough a bunch of men as I ever had the honour to command. Their leader was a remarkable man and the most dedicated soldier I have ever known. I wished them luck. They would need it; I had given them the job of finding [U.S. Consul Michael] Hoyt and his compatriots the following morning."[7] Hoare speaks of Rip Robertson when he refers to the Cuban exiles' leader. However, the job of rescuing American diplomats had been given to the 58th Company by COMISH and not by Hoare.

While American and Belgian military personnel worked out final procedures to drop the Belgian paratroopers, Ghana, Kenya, Belgium, the U.S., and other governments were trying to set up a last-minute negotiating session with the Simba leadership. The ground forces, under the command of Colonels Vandewalle, Rattan, and Hoare, were also gearing up for a final assault on Kisangani, still expecting to be the ones rescuing the hostages.

On or around November 14, 1964, American and Belgian military strategists had completed the details of what would be a multinational parachute rescue operation. The fighting unit was the Belgian paratroopers Dragon Force being flown by the U.S. Air Force, refueling at two other countries, going to a different continent several thousand kilometers away, with plans to rescue approximately 1,600 hostages of more than 10 different nationalities being held by a country, which did not exist. Additionally, the whole operation was to be conducted in the utmost of secrecy.

A timetable of the key events of the Kisangani rescue operation is presented at the end of this book.

Sometime around mid-November 1964, twelve C-130s transports and the crews of the Tactical Air Command from Pope Air Force Base in North Carolina were assigned to Evreux-Fauville Air Base in France. The crews were told to get some rest, as they would need to be at peak performance. On the morning of November 17, 1964, each pilot was handed a Manila envelope and told not to open it until his airplane had reached an altitude of 2,000 feet and there were no mechanical problems. After opening the envelopes, they learned that their destination was Kleine-Brogel, a Belgian military airfield located 60 kilometers north-east of Brussels. Upon arrival, the C-130s were promptly loaded with a total of 545 Belgian paratroopers, 8 jeeps, and 12 motorized tricycles. The pilots were handed another Manila envelope and told to take off.

This time they were advised to head for Morón de la Frontera Air Base in southern Spain. At Morón, after refueling, the navigators were given maps and instructions as to their next destination. This was Ascension Island in the south Atlantic, where they arrived on November 18, 1964, approximately 18 hours after leaving France. Ascension Island is a British possession and thus a third country had to be involved in this secret operation. Permission to use this British facility was secured from the newly-elected Labor party and Prime Minister Harold Wilson.

On November 15, 1964 the U.S. Joint Chiefs of Staff had issued a warning order for the Kisangani rescue. The following day, the U.S. Joint Chiefs of Staff and the Belgian Supreme Armed Forces Command ordered the U.S./Belgium Dragon Force rescue operation. Since this operation was to be carried out in Congolese territory, the authorization of the government of Congo was required before proceeding.

A concerted agreement by Washington and Brussels politicians under significant international pressure was not an easy task. A decision to give a last shot at a negotiated settlement was made. On November 18, 1964, the U.S. State Department contacted Gbenye and proposed to negotiate the release of U.S. hostages. Gbenye replied that he would only negotiate if the ground forces retreated. Belgian Chancellor Paul-Henri Spaak also tried to negotiate with Gbenye on November 20, 1964 without success.

Kasavubu, Tshombé and Mobutu authorized the rescue operation on November 21, 1964.

The entire force was flown from Ascension Island to the Kamina airfield, more or less in the center of Katanga Province on November 22, 1964. They were told to wait for instructions.

Red Dragon was activated on November 24, 1964 and the planes took off before daylight. Five C-130s became airborne from Kamina, each with 64 Belgian Red Berets in full combat gear. Behind them were the remaining seven C-130s and 225 Belgian paratroopers. The last aircraft had been converted into a hospital ship. Their instructions were to fly north at high altitude, then follow the Congo River at tree top altitude as they approached Kisangani. The operation had to be well-coordinated by American (COMISH) and Belgian military personnel and the CIA, as there were reportedly more than 200 Simbas guarding the Kisangani airport.

It was decided that the Belgian paratroopers would be dropped on the strip of grass alongside one of the runways at the Kisangani airport. USAF air reconnaissance disclosed the presence of two heavy weapons at said airport: a 20-mm anti-aircraft gun at or near the control tower and a 50-caliber machine gun mounted on an armored vehicle. These two heavy weapons were the objectives of the two Makasi B-26Ks, as given to them by Lieutenant Colonel Bouzin, the Belgian advisor to the Congolese air force.

As planned, at exactly 05:45 on November 24, 1964 two B-26Ks flown by Makasi Cuban exiles Castor Cereceda Coira, Tomás Afont Rodríguez, Francisco Alvarez, and Reginaldo Blanco made strafing passes over Sabena's Kisangani airport and disabled the two heavy weapons trained on the airport. They did not draw hostile fire. With the successful elimination of airport artillery, the USAF C-130s were hit only with light weapon fire, and no paratroopers were hit during the jump.

The C-130s approached Kisangani at an altitude of 500 feet, increasing their altitude to 700 feet when they were about one mile from the drop zone. The Belgian paratroopers selected a low altitude T-4 parachute in order to minimize the time the paratrooper was a potential target for Simbas on the ground. A total of 320 Belgian paratroopers and bundles of equipment were dropped, with only 3 casualties reported, all from men that hit the ground too hard. One paratrooper was killed afterwards by fire from the trees nearby while clearing the air strip to allow the C-130s to land. Within one minute of the initial drop, the 320 paratroopers had landed, and the airport was reported secured by Colonel Laurent about 45 minutes after the first group of paratroopers jumped. The Belgian rescue team immediately departed for the center of Kisangani, while the remaining C-130s landed, dropped equipment, and flew to Kinshasa for refueling.

The Makasi Cuban exiles returned to Kindu for refueling, and upon their return to Kisangani, the locations of Simba strongholds were provided to them by Belgian Colonel Laurent. After hitting these targets, the Makasi crews were instructed to land in Kisangani and provide logistical assistance, as the rescued hostages and the wounded would be processed through the Kisangani airport.

Concurrently with the Belgian-American air rescue operation, the Stan Column (Companies 51, 55, 56, and 57, Robertson's 58th Company of Cuban exiles, the ANC Lima I, and Vandewalle's Fifth Mechanized Brigade) was on its way into Kisangani. Air support was provided by B-26Ks flown by Cuban exiles Makasi. The ground force was a league of nations, for in addition to Congolese troops from the ANC there were Belgian, British, Cuban exile, French, German, Italian, Rhodesian, and South African fighters. These ground troops arrived in the Kisangani area around 10:00 on November 24, 1964 after encountering severe resistance by Simba rebels. According to Odom[8] the Stan column arrived in Kisangani around 11:00.

Cuban exile infantryman José Hernández describes their arrival in Kisangani: "We entered Stanleyville from the north. We had to cross the [Congo] river to gain access to the city. When you count logistics and medical personnel, we were a force of about 600. We had a number of ambushes along the way which slowed us down. We [the Cuban exile troops] were riding in three heavily armed jeeps. We crossed the river in a flat-bottom barge which we requisitioned from a guy that kept telling us something in a language we didn't understand. I think he was saying it was too much weight. Anyhow, we got to the other side, and as soon as we got going we fell into an ambush. The first jeep was hit by a grenade and machine gun fire. We all hit the ground. Alberto Pérez [Dr. Kildare] had a bullet wound in the stomach, Rip had been grazed by a bullet on the forehead, and Conrado [Fernández] was hit by a 50-caliber shell right on his side firearm. He had a perfect bruise with the picture of his pistol. Conrado was also hit by shrapnel on his leg, shoulder and neck. We took Alberto and Conrado to the hospital truck, and Rip kept on going."[9]

Later in the day, while securing the city, both Andrés Romero and Ricardo Morales were hit. These were not life-threatening wounds.

The battle plan for Operation *Dragon Rouge* is depicted in Figure 4. Upon landing, the paratroopers were to attack and control objectives 1, 2, and 3 in order to secure the airfield. Objective 3, The Sabena Guest House, was a rebel headquarters and the paratroopers expected to obtain information on the whereabouts of the hostages after securing this objective. Afterwards, one group would march into Kisangani via Avenue Monseigneur Grison and Avenue General de Gaulle. Other groups would secure objectives 4, 5, and 6 (accesses to the city) in order to block rebel reinforcements from entering Kisangani. It was expected that Simbas would retreat to Camp Ketele (objective 7), east of Kisangani, and this would become the next objective after all accesses to the city were blocked. As the Belgian paratroopers landed (around 06:00) on November 24, 1964, they were charged by a band of Simba fighters who had been hiding in the nearby bush. Unlike the ANC soldiers, there was no panic among the Belgian paratroopers. They annihilated the rebels with automatic weapon fire. The Belgian rescue team, under the able leadership of Colonel Charles Laurent, rushed to the Victoria Hotel in an attempt to arrive before the rebels followed through with their threat of killing the hostages. As Laurent's men approached the point marked with an "X" on Figure 4, they were attacked by a Simba group with machine gun and other light weapon fire. They were able to quickly counter attack and the Simbas dispersed. As one of the Belgian jeeps rounded a corner near the Victoria Hotel, at about 07:40, they saw the Simbas firing into the assembled hostages. The Belgian paratroopers opened fire on the Simbas. The Simbas lost their courage and ran. Their leader Gbenye had left the city even before the paratroopers had landed. His car had been ambushed by the Belgian paratroopers near the Sabena Guest House, and Gbenye was not in it.

In the meantime, air reconnaissance had spotted several enemy columns approaching Kisangani to reinforce the Simba defenders of the city. Makasi pilots were called in and the location of enemy troops was given to Cuban exile pilots on standby at the recently liberated airports of Punia and Lisala. Makasi did their job well and the survivors of the would-be reinforcement troops ran from Kisangani. While the paratroopers attempted to save as many hostages as possible, Vandewalle's ground troops joined in securing Kisangani: Lima I entered the city and blocked key crossroads; Belgian regular troops and Lima II occupied the Ketele Military Camp, which was secured after a brief but ferocious fight; and the 51st Commando controlled the Tshopo Bridge, an important access to Kisangani.

Each of the escape routes out of Kisangani had been sealed. General Olenga's car was found, but he, following the example of his leader Gbenye, had also already left town.

A number of versions of the events that occurred during the hours prior to the massacre of the hostages in the neighborhood of the Victoria Hotel are available, including those by Mike Hoare,[10] Major Thomas P. Odom,[11] the U.S. Army Airborne Operations website,[12] and U.S. Consul Michael Hoyt.[13] These versions, though strikingly similar, do contain some differences. The version provided by Dr. Joaquín Sanz Gadea, a Spanish surgeon working for the UN in Kisangani, is the best documented one. Dr. Sanz Gadea was conferred the Príncipe de Asturias (Spain's equivalent

Figure 4
Operation Dragon Rouge Battle Plan

KISANGANI/STANLEYVILLE

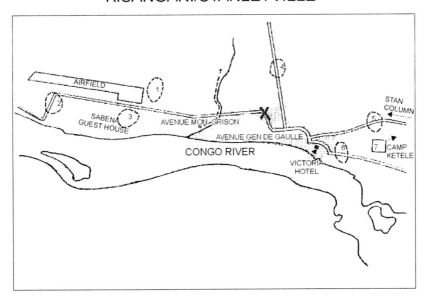

of the Nobel) prize for his humanitarian work in Congo, and has been nominated for the Nobel Peace prize a number of times.

Dr. Sanz Gadea, along with other Europeans, was evacuated from Kisangani on August 3, 1964, some 36 hours before the city fell to the Simbas. He was flown back to Kisangani to tend to the wounded hostages shortly after the airport was secured on November 24, 1964. His version of events, derived from conversations with the numerous hostages he treated, many of whom were his friends and neighbors, follows.

General Olenga had fled for the safety of Tanzania as soon as the invasion appeared imminent, leaving Colonel Opepe in charge of the hostages, with the specific instructions to kill them as soon as the invaders arrived. Colonel Opepe, in an attempt to hedge his bets, had decided to deliver the hostages to the airport and turn them over to the Belgians unharmed in order to avoid an invasion of their new nation. He told some hostages that he would save them in exchange for their putting in a good word about him with the invaders. In essence: I save you and then you save me. Colonel Opepe ordered his Simba troops to go to the Victoria Hotel and other places where hostages were being held and to instruct them to come out. Many of the hostages saved themselves by refusing to do so, instead hiding in closets, bathrooms, or under beds. Those hostages that did come out were assembled in rows three abreast, and Colonel Opepe and his Simbas started marching them to the airport. About this time, a truck full of Simbas under the command of Major Bubu, who was a deaf-mute (the Swahili word for deaf-mute is Bubu), announced in sign language that the invasion had already started, as he had seen U.S. Air Force transport planes land, and that Belgian paratroopers were heading to Kisangani. Reportedly, Colonel Opepe tried to communicate with Major Bubu and inform him that he was delivering the hostages to the airport. Major Bubu knew what his orders were, and to make sure there was no misunderstanding, he emptied the magazine of his automatic weapon on the helpless hostages. The Simba warriors, high on hemp and dazed after drinking alcohol all night, followed Bubu's example and opened fire on the hostages, women and children first. It was at this time that the Belgian paratroopers arrived at the scene and witnessed the Simbas killing hostages. Thirty-nine hostages were killed, or died later from their wounds, before the arrival of the Belgian paratroopers. There were two American casualties: Dr. Paul Carlson of California and Phyllis Rine of Mount Vernon, Ohio, both missionaries. Colonel Opepe was also killed. More than forty civilians were wounded.[14]

Hoyt, Grinwis, and the other U.S. officials saved themselves by running and hiding between buildings as soon as the Simbas commenced firing.

The hostages most badly injured were driven to the airport. The ones capable of walking were instructed to do so. When the wounded arrived at the airport and saw that the engines of one of the C-130s were running, the frightened Europeans ran to the airplane and tried to rush aboard. The crew was able to convince them to go to the hospital plane, where doctors waited to tend to their wounds.

As soon as the wounded were moved to the hospital plane, the C-130 took off for the safety of Kinshasa. All available aircraft continued shuttling as many as 120 former hostages at a time from Kisangani to Kinshasa. Nearly every plane landing or departing was hit by Simba light weapon fire. The airlift continued for two days, and approximately 1,600 hostages were rescued. The last Simba attack against the airfield was in the afternoon of November 24. Approximately 150 Simbas with the customary witch doctor support attacked. The Belgian paratroopers took no prisoners.

Four Makasi Cuban exile pilots were on the Kisangani airport grounds, assisting with hostage evacuation. Reginaldo Blanco recalls that the rescued hostages hugged them and kissed their hands.[15]

After taking the Ketele Military Camp, Lima II and the regular Belgian army ground troops soon joined the Belgian paratroopers and Robertson's 58th Company in securing Kisangani. Mop-up operations were conducted by Belgian ground forces, Mobutu's ANC, Hoare's 5 Commando mercenaries, and the Cuban exile Makasi air force (now operating out of the Kisangani airport).

While debriefing the rescued American hostages, Rip Robertson and former U.S. Consul to Kisangani John Clingerman learned from Al Larson, an American missionary, that about 25 missionaries were still being held by Simbas at the nearby Kilometer 8 mission. Larson tried to get the Belgians from the Fifth Mechanized Brigade to rescue the missionaries, but the Belgians claimed that they were short on transportation equipment. Clingerman, Robertson, and the Cuban exiles accepted the challenge, and with Larson as a guide, headed to the mission. "Larson was impressed by the swarthy band who took the time to explain they were 'Not Castro Cubans.' They saved 24 missionaries, but for one of them, a Canadian man, they were minutes too late."[16]

Juan (El Negro) Tamayo vividly recalls the rescue of the missionaries: "There were some regular Belgian soldiers with us. These were not paratroopers. The paratroopers were really courageous and excellent soldiers. As we reached the outskirts of Kisangani, the enemy engaged us with light weapons and we replied with 50-caliber machine gun fire. The enemy scattered. I looked around and the Belgian soldiers were all gone. There were a few Simbas guarding the mission, but we took care of them in short order. The missionaries had been tied up with barbed wire. There were also two wounded blonde children, I believe they were Belgian, a girl 1 or 2 years old and her older brother, of about 10 or 11. I will never forget the expression on that poor girl's face. She was terrified of the machine gun fire and her eyes seemed to be bulging out. The heated shell casings were falling on her, and I covered her with my shirt. Her brother was very brave and helped us reload our weapons."[17]

Segisberto Fernández relates his experience with the Kisangani rescue and his interaction with U.S. military: "I was at the Léopoldville [Kinshasa] airport assisting with the logistics of the rescue. At one point prior to the operation, I counted 32 U.S. transport planes unloading at the airport, and 12 more circling the area, waiting to land and unload. I went to Stanleyville [Kisangani] with the first C-130 which departed from Léopoldville after the landing of the paratroopers. We had to finish clearing the runways since the Simbas had left wrecked cars and all sort of debris scattered around the airport. Almost immediately, Makasi started using the Stanleyville airport for mop-up operations and to create a safe perimeter around the city. I have only praise for the U.S. military. In the four years I spent in Congo, every time we ordered fuel, ammunition and spare parts, it always arrived on time, the right parts, and in the right quantities. The CIA and the American embassy also took good care of us. We took anti-malaria medication daily, and had access to medical and dental care."[18]

On November 25, 1965 Dragon Force received instructions to undertake rescue operation Black Dragon at Isiro, 360 kilometers northeast of Kisangani. Troops and equipment for the operation were picked up at the Kisangani airport. The operation was initiated in the early morning hours of November 26, and it involved eight C-130s. The battle plan was not too different from the one at Kisangani. Makasi pilots strafed the airport and disabled the weapons intended to prevent the landing of aircraft. The Isiro airfield was secured within thirty minutes of the drop, but the troops were under heavy fire from small weapons. After eliminating resistance, the Belgians discovered quickly where the hostages were being held. While paratroopers secured the city, motorized patrols of ANC and Tshombé's mercenaries liberated 355 European hostages. This operation came too late to save 22 hostages who had been killed as soon as the parachutes could be seen over the city.

The balance of the combined Kisangani and Isiro rescues was astonishing: 63 hostages killed, 43 wounded and over 1,955 rescued. It is estimated that some 300 more Europeans were killed in plantations and isolated missions in Orientale Province. Regarding the rescue troops, 3 Belgian soldiers were killed and 11 wounded. The Cuban exile forces had 5 casualties: Alberto Pérez was shot in the stomach and was in critical condition for several days, Conrado Fernández was hit by grenade shrapnel on the head and leg, Andrés Romero had a non-life-threatening bullet wound, as did Ricardo Morales and the CO, Rip Robertson was grazed by a bullet on the side of the head. All 5 survived. No exact numbers are available on Simba casualties, but it is estimated that as many as 10,000 Simba warriors were killed during operations Red Dragon, Black Dragon, and the mop-up operations that followed.

Two other rescue operations were scheduled, White Dragon at Bunia and Green Dragon at Watsa. President Lyndon Johnson and the Joint Chiefs of Staff were pushing for the completion of all four rescue operations. Because of the strong Third World reaction after *Dragon Rouge*, Belgium's Chancellor Paul-Henri Spaak had wanted all operations stopped. Belgium's Foreign Minister Theo Lefévre and *Chef de Cabinet* Viscount Davignon had managed to convinced Spaak to approve *Dragon Noir*, but Belgium made it clear to the U.S. administration that the rescue at Isiro would be the last operation to be undertaken with Belgium's support. On November 26, 1964 U.S. Ambassador to Congo G. McMurtrie Godley II cabled Washington requesting the implementation of the rescue operations at Bunia and Watsa. Secretary of State Dean Rusk replied with an unequivocal no.[19]

The three leaders, Christophe Gbenye, Nicholas Olenga, and Gaston Soumialot had "kept the best available automobiles, usually Mercedes, at their residences, guarded and loaded ready to flee. They had divided among themselves the gold they found at the Kilo-Moto mines."[20] Gbenye and Olenga stayed in Khartoum, Sudan for some time, while Soumialot went into exile in Cairo, Egypt. General Olenga became a business associate of Ugandan military strongman Idi Amin. With all three leaders Gbenye, Olenga, and Soumialot in exile, by default Laurent Kabila had emerged as the new leader of the leftist revolution.

Third World reaction to the rescue operation was brutal. Demonstrations were held in Moscow, Prague, Cairo, Nairobi, and other cities denouncing American imperialism. The mob in Cairo, not finding any nearby U.S. businesses to attack, burned the JFK Library to the ground. There had been 270,000 volumes in this library.

The Soviet Union appeared to have been resigned to the imminent rescue attempt, for "on November 22, 1964, the USSR declared that Congo is being transformed into a second Vietnam."[21] This comment had to please Castro enormously.

A few days after the rescue, the Soviet Union sent a formal protest to the U.S., Belgium, and Britain, stating that a flagrant act of armed intervention had been committed and demanded the immediate withdrawal of mercenaries from Congo. In Accra, Ghana President Nkrumah condemned the rescue action as a brazen act of aggression and added that colonialism was not dead.

Beijing indicated that they would take all pertinent measures to help the Congolese rebellion. Chairman Mao Zedong made a rare appearance at a rally protesting U.S. imperialism, attended by more than 700,000 Chinese.

The Soviet bloc, the PRC, and most so-called non-aligned nations of Africa and Asia conveniently forgot about the atrocities committed by the Simba warriors. They also ignored the fact that the rescue operation was conducted to save U.S. and Belgian citizens from certain torture and death.

In Che Guevara's recently published Congo diary *The African Dream*, Guevara states: "[The Kisangani rescue] ... was the spark that launched Cuba's direct involvement in the affairs of Congo, for Cuba and Algeria had already been working together on revolutionary projects [in Africa]."[22]

Due to Soviet and other international pressure, Belgian paratroopers went home immediately, even though the job was not finished. On November 27, the airlift force picked up the paratroopers at Kisangani and Isiro and carried them to the air base in Kinshasa, beginning the return flight, which was somewhat different to their incoming itinerary. On November 29, the task force arrived in Ascension, and returned to Brussels the following day by way of Las Palmas (Grand Canary Island) and Torrejón Air Force Base (east of Madrid). Colonel Vandewalle also returned to Belgium, and the weight of putting down the rebellion rested on the shoulders of Hoare's 5 Commando, COMISH and the Cuban exile forces. The Belgian Paracommandos were given a hero's parade upon their arrival in Brussels on December 1, 1964.

Vandewalle, Rattan, and Hoare had planned their advance into Kisangani strategically targeting rebel strongholds, rather than taking the most direct path to Kisangani. Hoare knew where the Simbas were strong, and as the various companies advanced, they eliminated these rebel strongholds. By the time the Belgian paratroopers landed in Kisangani, most of the key cities in Equateur Province had been liberated. Surviving Simbas had moved in the direction of the Central African Republic border. Likewise, in Maniema and in Sud- and Nord-Kivu Provinces, the key cities had been freed of rebels, and the survivors had moved into Burundi, Rwanda, and Uganda. The situation in Orientale Province was different. Orientale was the traditional Simba stronghold. Many Simbas remained there, mostly in scattered groups in the northeast, near the border with Sudan. But Hoare now knew exactly where the rebels were, and he was able to design new operations accordingly.

The Cuban exiles fighting for democracy in Congo, when able to take a few hours away from war duties, also assisted with charitable operations. Dr. Sanz Gadea, in addition to running the UN hospital, also directed the operation of an orphanage. In his book *Un Médico en el Congo*, Dr. Sanz Gadea states that he could count on the generosity of Cuban exiles in the various money-raising activities of the orphanage. The Cuban exiles were always first in line to buy tickets for raffles or other benefits.

At the request of the Cuban exiles, WIGMO (the CIA-owned shell company responsible for the Cuban exiles) gave a party for war orphans: "Cuban exiles, Americans, Spanish, Swedish, Norwegians and Dutch took the children to a picnic, ate and sang songs."[23]

Dr. Sanz Gadea articulates that he was moved by the generosity of Cuban exiles. He once approached a pilot and asked him why they were so empathetic to war orphans. The answer was: "Doctor, we are, by obligation, the cause of so many orphans, but war is war."[24]

The two follow-up operations planned and executed by Mike Hoare after the Kisangani rescue were named *White Giant* and *Violettes Imperiales*. White Giant's purpose was to rid the north east portion of Orientale Province of rebel elements. Of particular concern was a large area along the borders with Sudan and Uganda, where weapons and ammunition were being moved at an estimated rate of "not less than thirty tons per day."[25]

Operation White Giant commenced in mid-December 1964. The area to be rid of rebel elements stretched through the cities of Bunia, Arua (then known as Aru), Aba, and Faradje. It was at Aba that the weapons were entering Congo from the Sudanese city of Yei. The first objective of this operation was to liberate the strategically important city of Bunia, which is at an altitude of 1,350 meters above sea level. Bunia is about 60 kilometers from the west shore of Lake Albert, which partially demarks the border between Uganda and Congo.

Bunia was liberated at the end of 1964, and during this battle Makasi pilot Fausto Gómez was shot down and killed. The airports at Bunia and Isiro would become two important bases for the Cuban exile air force to prevent rebel elements from returning to Congo from Sudan and Uganda.[26]

Shortly after the liberation of Bunia, an unlikely rescue operation was carried out by Juan Perón, a Makasi pilot operating out of this city.[27] Richard Holm, a CIA operative, wanted to scout the Congo-Sudan border, from where it was suspected that Simba rebels were being supplied. The two T-28s assigned to Bunia took Holm on his reconnaissance mission on February 17, 1965. One T-28 was piloted by Juan García Tuñón, while Holm rode in the other T-28 with Juan Perón at the controls. On the way back from their mission, they ran into severe weather. While attempting to go around the disturbance, they became lost, and with low fuel, they had no choice but to crash land. The remaining fuel ignited upon landing, burning Holm severely on the arms, chest and face. Perón was unharmed. García Tuñón was never found, but unconfirmed reports from missionaries in the area indicate that he had saved the last bullet for himself.

Perón continues: "I decided that the only chance for survival was to find some anti-Simba natives willing to help. Fortunately, I found a small group of Azande tribesmen, whose chief, Faustino, spoke English. Faustino told me that we were nearly 300 kilometers away from Isiro. We left Holm under the care of Azande women and set out in the direction of Isiro with Faustino and two other men. We traveled on bicycles, canoes and on foot. Seven days later, on the afternoon of February 24, 1965, we found some Belgian soldiers willing to help. The following morning, after traveling some 30 kilometers to Isiro, we met some CIA officers who had been desperately searching for us. The CIA arranged for a Belgian helicopter to find the Azande village, I flew as co-pilot of a T-28, as us Cuban exile pilots did not trust the Belgian helicopters, which we referred to as 'flying bananas.'"[28]

The Belgian helicopter crashed upon landing. There were no casualties, but the helicopter was seriously damaged. Perón and his Makasi pilot flew back to Isiro to ask for more help. The Belgians provided a second helicopter for the rescue. Holm was flown to Kinshasa, and then on to the U.S. for medical care. Holm survived, and years later would occupy the important post of CIA Station Chief in Paris.

Back to operation White Giant, Tshombé and Mobutu had provided a battalion (around 1,000 men) of well-trained Katangan soldiers to reinforce 5 Commando. This new force commanded by Hoare marched by land on March 15, 1965, to attack the rebel stronghold of Nioka, while a naval force composed of several large fishing boats under Lieutenant Roy Larsen (a Swedish mercenary) moved to strike Mahagi and Port Mahagi on the northern end of Lake Albert. Both operations were successful.

According to Benemelis, the flow of weapons through Sudan and Uganda was protected by a Cuban battalion (presumably from the troops left over from the Algeria-Morocco border dispute) operating from inside Sudan. "... The protection of the triangle Bunia-Watsa-Dramba was under the command of a black Cuban whose *nom de guerre* was 'Gombe.'"[29]

The forces of Hoare and Larsen again fought together in early May 1965 for the attacks on Arua, Aba, and Faradje. After taking Aba, Hoare went several kilometers inside Sudanese territory and destroyed the rebel's sanctuary, inflicting significant casualties on the enemy. Sudan did not protest, as they were probably happy to be rid of the foreign combatants.

On May 11, 1965, Hoare's forces destroyed the bridge on the road from Aba to Sudan, thus closing the Congo-Sudan border to truck traffic. In order to complete the pacification of the eastern portion of Orientale Province, it was still necessary to take the cities of Dungu and Watsa, thus sealing the access routes along the Uganda-Congo border. Watsa was particularly significant as it is the site of an important gold mine that was financing the purchase of weapons and supplies for the Simba rebels.

With the help of Cuban exile pilot Luis Fernández Ardois-Anduz, and his flight log, which he has preserved for more than forty years, the campaign can be reconstructed as follows.[30] The city of Dungu was taken around May 24, 1965 with the assistance of the Cuban exile Makasi, and the stage was set for the battle for Watsa, which was defended by some 1,200 rebels. Hoare called on Makasi and in response four T-28s and two B-26Ks softened the targets for a successful infantry attack on May 29, 1965.

On May 30, 1965, Hoare flew to Kinshasa to meet with Tshombé and Mobutu. After the initial pleasantries, Mobutu indicated that he was gratified with the military progress to date, but that he was concerned that the rebels were receiving aid through Burundi and from Tanzania across Lake Tanganyika.[31] Tshombé (apparently more concerned with his political future than with the military campaign) stated that he was pleased with the magnitude of his victory in the recent parliamentary elections.[32] The good news of his parliamentary victory was, at the end of the day, bad news for Tshombé as he had become too popular inside Congo and at the same time too unpopular with the remaining African nations.

Mobutu indicated that there were rumors that the rebels in the Great Lakes area had foreign advisors and that the CIA suspected that they were Cubans. Hoare's intention had been to tender his resignation during this meeting, but "the knowledge that a successful campaign to crush communist infiltration in the Congo would change the course of history"[33] changed his mind, and he accepted the new challenge. Hoare stated that he had to complete his job in Orientale Province, but that he would immediately start to hire replacements for his 5 Commando, as most of his men were finishing their six-month contracts.

The second operation was code-named *Violettes Imperiales* and its objective was to pacify the northern portion of Orientale Province and close its border with the leftist friendly government of the Central African Republic. Hoare, with help from Denard's 6 Commando took the cities of Niangara (then known as Niangana), Bili, Bondo, and Buta. This operation was completed in mid-June 1965.

It was during the assault of Niangara by 5 Commando troops under Major Ian Gordon that the possible Cuban military training, and perhaps participation, was detected for the second time. Gordon's soldiers fell into a carefully planned and better consummated ambush, while his armored vehicles were stuck in a trap. Simba rebels had not previously shown themselves to be capable of executing plans with such accuracy. Gordon and his men suspected that Cubans, known to be stationed in Sudan, had crossed into Congo to give a hand to the Simbas. These could have been the same Cuban troops that had gone to Sudan after the Algeria-Morocco border dispute. For reasons yet to be explained, these troops never joined the Guevara Congo operation. After suffering many casualties, Gordon had to retreat and later return with reinforcements. The CIA was promptly informed of the possible presence of Cuban soldiers in Congo.

Niangara is approximately 700 kilometers due north of Shabunda, the location of a similar incident that had been reported by Makasi's Ignacio Rojas and Reginaldo Blanco about six months earlier. It would not be until late June 1965 that material evidence of a Cuban presence in Congo would be obtained.

In his book published in 1979, Colonel Vandewalle describes the rescue episode in Congo and points out the practical difficulties in carrying out America's indirect wars. He states that the Americans tried not to transport the mercenaries in the U.S.-piloted C-130s; they were generally transported by Belgian-piloted C-27s. However war material as well as ANC troops being led by the mercenaries did travel by C-130s. Initially, the U.S. military attaché Colonel Knut Raudstein tried to avoid fighting alongside the mercenaries. On the other hand, several American military personnel were prominent in Vandewalle's headquarters and from the start fought alongside the Belgians and mercenaries. Vandewalle specifically mentions U.S. Army Colonel Donald Rattan and U.S. Army Sergeant Sam Wiesel. Later in the campaign, Colonel Raudstein did join in the fighting.[34]

The elapsed time from the taking of the hostages to the rescue operation was 111 days. The hope for a negotiated settlement delayed the rescue, as did the constant disagreement as to whether more hostages could be saved by air, by land, or a combination of the two. Vandewalle, Hoare, and Rattan had argued with U.S. and Belgian military planners to allow them to go into the city ahead of the Belgian paratroopers. Their argument was that the Simbas were likely to start executing hostages as soon as the parachutes were seen. Regardless, they were instructed to wait at a safe distance from Kisangani. As the synchronization of the arrival of the paratroopers and the mercenary-led columns was a near impossibility, the air rescue was chosen.

After interviewing more than one hundred participants of the rescue operation on both sides of the Atlantic, Weissman concludes: "It is quite possible—but not certain—that the parachute attack caused more white casualties than would have occurred had the mercenary columns continued their advance unaided."[35]

The same question regarding air versus land rescue was posed to Larry Devlin. His reply: "I could be wrong, but I believe that the paratrooper rescue was the right choice. If ground forces would have continued their advance on Stanleyville, rebel scouts would have known the exact location of the troops at all times. The rebels may have executed all the hostages in the case of a land rescue."[36]

Sometime in early June 1965, Jean Schramme and his 10 Commando were entrusted with peace keeping in Equateur and Bandundu Provinces. This was handled from Schramme's HQ in Yumbi, where the main concern was to stop infiltration of new troops across the Congo River from Congo (Brazzaville). It was well-known at the time that a large contingent of Cuban troops was present in Congo (Brazzaville).

A few weeks later, around mid- to late-June 1965, Bob Denard's 6 Commando was given the responsibility for safeguarding Orientale Province and the important borders with Sudan and Uganda. This he managed from his HQ at Kisangani, with the help of additional ANC troops at Isiro. With Orientale, Bandundu, and Equateur Provinces in a relative state of tranquility, Hoare and the Cuban exile forces were instructed by Mobutu to move to the Fizi-Baraka area to face a new enemy. Even though the information was unconfirmed, it was thought that regular Cuban troops (perhaps under the command of Che Guevara) had been operating with impunity in the Great Lakes area since late April 1965.

The area along the Great Lakes would remain insecure for the next two and a half years. Massengo and Kabila continued guerrilla warfare along the west shore of Lake Tanganyika. In spite of Soumialot's exile, his troops continued fighting in Sud-Kivu, particularly along the Fizi-Uvira axis. Mulele stayed in the Bandundu Province jungle and for some time conducted guerrilla warfare. The leftist Simba rebellion had been dealt a pernicious blow, but the Soviet Union, China, and particularly Castro's Cuba would not accept that the revolution had been defeated. Castro had assembled resources to breathe new life into the moribund Congolese revolution.

Notes

1. Odom, Major Thomas P., *Dragon Operations: Hostage Rescues in the Congo, 1964-1965*, Combined Arms Research Library, U.S. Army Command & General Staff, Fort Leavenworth, Kansas, 1988, p. 17.
2. Devlin, Larry, Conversations with the author, February 15 and 21, 2008.
3. Hoyt, Michael P. E., *Captive in the Congo: A Consul's Return to the Heart of Darkness*, Naval Institute Press, Annapolis, Maryland, 2000, p. 228.
4. Blanco, Reginaldo, Conversations with the author, Madrid, October 29, 2005.
5. Odom, *op. cit.*, p. 50.
6. Benemelis, Juan F., Castro, *Subversión y Terrorismo en Africa*, Editorial San Martín, Madrid, 1988, p. 144.
7. Hoare, Mike, *Congo Mercenary*, Lexington Books, London, 1967, p. 118.
8. Odom, *op. cit.*
9. Hernández, José, Conversations with the author, Miami, October 21, 2007.
10. Hoare, *op. cit.*, pp. 121-126.
11. Odom, *op. cit.*, pp. 55-64.
12. *The Congolese Rescue Operation* (November 1964), Airborne Operations [2-3.7 AC.F] – TAB E, *www.army.mil/cmh-pg/documents/abnops/tabe.htm*, downloaded October 20, 2004.
13. Hoyt, *op. cit.*, pp. 212-220.
14. Sanz Gadea, Joaquín, *Un Médico en el Congo*, Ediciones Temas de Hoy, Madrid, 1998, pp. 213-220.
15. Blanco, Reginaldo, Conversations with the author, Madrid, October 29, 2005.
16. Quoted by Odom, Major Thomas P., *op. cit.*, p. 69.
17. Tamayo, Juan, Conversations with the author, Miami, July 30, 2006.
18. Fernández, Segisberto, Conversations with the author, Miami, October 19, 2007.
19. Odom, *op. cit.*, pp. 121-150.
20. Hoyt, *op. cit.*, p. 177.
21. Benemelis, *op. cit.*, p. 146.
22. Guevara, Ernesto, *The African Dream*, Grove Press, New York, 2000, p. xx.
23. Sanz Gadea, *op. cit.*, p. 265.
24. *Ibid*, p. 263.
25. Hoare, *op. cit.*, p. 176.
26. Ros, *op. cit.*, p. 110.
27. Perón, Juan, Conversations with the author, Miami, August 23, 2005.
28. *Ibid*.
29. Benemelis, *op. cit.*, p. 177.
30. Fernández Ardois-Anduz, Luis, Conversations with the author, Miami, August 23, 2005.
31. Hoare, *op. cit.*, pp. 236-238.
32. *Ibid*, p. 237.
33. *Ibid*, p. 241.
34. Vandewalle, Colonel Frédéric, *L'Ommegang: Odysée et Reconquête de Stanleyville*, Brussels, Le Livre Africain, 1970, pp. 207-220.
35. Weissman, *op. cit.*, p. 253.
36. Devlin, *op. cit.*

Part III

Cubans versus Cubans in Congo

8

Castro Prepares to Invade Congo

Juan Benemelis, an early key strategist for Castro, states that even before the assassination of President Kennedy the Cuban General Directorate of Intelligence (DGI) had developed plans for intervention in Congo, and for extending Cuba's radius of influence in Latin America. The implementation of these plans was to be handled directly by Raúl Castro and Che Guevara.[1]

As the plans developed over time, it is likely that the key players changed. Evidence indicates that the KGB was in charge of executing Castro's plans in Latin America and that Spanish/Russian General Líster was pulling the strings through communist parties in the target countries. Further, there is no documentation that Raúl has ever been involved in an international military operation.

By late 1963, Guevara did not appear to be any longer in Castro's inner circle. If this assertion is correct, it would be unlikely that Guevara would be trusted to implement the exportation of Cuba's revolution to Africa. For the Congo operation, Guevara was clearly relegated to the position of commanding officer of approximately 200 soldiers, and in this capacity he had many bosses.

The Cuban armed forces had certainly seen action during the Bay of Pigs invasion in April 1961. Afterwards and even though no clear and present danger showed on Cuba's radar screens, the Cuban armed forces continued in the highest state of alert. This level of alert proved justified during the Cuban Missile Crisis in October 1962, but no action by Cuba's military was required at that time.

Following this crisis, Castro became more audacious in his support of African and Latin American revolutions, perhaps because of the "hands off Cuba" clause included in the agreement between Kennedy and Khrushchev.[2] Castro's support was primarily in the form of weapons and training, with no direct participation by Cuban soldiers. The only exception was the intervention in the Algeria-Morocco border dispute in the fall of 1963.

One year later, in the fall of 1964 still no direct major military action by the Cubans was anticipated. It is difficult, if not impossible, to maintain an army in the highest state of alert when no obvious need for its services is on the horizon. Consider a professional boxer who continues to train for a fight that never materializes. Eventually he will become frustrated, stop training and move on to other pursuits. In the specific case of the Cuban military, Castro possibly feared that his army might engage in the toppling of his own government.

In order to lessen the possibility of a military uprising, Castro split the Cuban army into three independent commands: Western, with headquarters in Havana; Central, with headquarters in Matanzas; and Eastern, headquartered in Santiago de Cuba.

He also declared the Isle of Pines (now known as the Isle of Youth) to be an autonomous military region. The idea behind compartmentalization of the armed forces was to minimize the probability of a *coup d'etat*, but in the event any one command would decide to topple the government, Castro was banking on the fact that the other two commands would fight against the rebellious one.

Castro went one step further in order to improve the odds: he decided to generate some action for his army. To minimize logistical and language problems, his logical preference would have been to enter into existing armed struggles in Latin America; however, in 1964, Brazil, Bolivia, Chile, and Uruguay broke diplomatic relations with Cuba. In 1964 revolutionary movements in Colombia, Peru, and Venezuela were essentially inactive. At the time, the only remaining possibilities for finding action for Castro's army were Guatemala and the Dominican Republic.

Castro continued to hope for Latin America while finalizing plans for a much more likely action in Congo. In early 1965, Cuba was expelled from the Organization of American States (OAS) for organizing a coup against Rómulo Betancourt, the democratically elected President of Venezuela.[3] Latin America was rapidly becoming a less likely theater for Cuban military operations. To provide action for his army, Castro was betting on the Dominican Republic revolt, which was supported by Cuba, both logistically and with advisors, such as Roberto Santiesteban, a high-ranking member of the DGI.[4]

The U.S. did not want a second communist regime near its shores, and therefore decided to invade and occupy the Dominican Republic in April 1965, at the request and with the blessing of the OAS. Evidence was presented by the U.S. to the OAS, which proved conclusively that civil war in the Dominican Republic was orchestrated from Cuba. The required 2/3 favorable votes were obtained, in accordance with OAS by-laws, to allow the U.S. to invade the Dominican Republic. President Johnson agreed to place the U.S. Marines under the symbolic command of an Inter-American Peace Force, to comply with terms of the Rio Treaty.

This preemptive action by the U.S. further entangled Castro's plans to intervene in Latin America. Castro directed a large portion of his well-oiled military machine to Oriente Province, eastern Cuba, under the command of Raúl Castro, to send a message to the U.S. that Cuba was prepared to defend the revolution of the Dominican Republic. A few days later, Castro chose not to challenge the U.S. militarily, ordering his troops back to their respective posts. At the end of the day, the well-trained boxer had not managed to schedule a fight.

Aside from the training of the Cuban armed forces and the idealism of helping revolutionary movements in other countries, did Castro's Cuba have a specific strategy? Professor Gleijeses[5] of Johns Hopkins University, in his 2002 book *Conflicting Missions*, provides an answer. After conducting numerous interviews with high-ranking officers in Cuba's military and obtaining permission to review Cuban secret documents, chosen by Cuban authorities, Dr. Gleijeses reached the conclusion that Cuba's strategy was self-defense.

Castro had tried to reach some level of pacific coexistence with Washington during the early 1960s, but his efforts had been rebuked. He became convinced that sooner or later Cuba would be attacked by the U.S., and similarly to American football strategy, where the best defense is a good offense, Castro decided to counter-attack. Not directly, but by creating other Vietnams. Castro believed that if the U.S. were to fight wars in several far-apart fronts, Cuba would become a nearby nuisance to the U.S., but would not be attacked.

Self-defense was certainly a motivating factor, but was it an initial strategy? After analyzing Cuba's later action in Angola, Mozambique, and Namibia, it appears likely that Castro wished to stamp his historical footprint in Central Africa as well as to inflict damage on the U.S.

Perhaps Castro developed his many Vietnams strategy to defeat the U.S. while watching a bull fight during his exile in Mexico City. Since it would be unlikely that in a fair fight the matador can defeat a healthy bull, the deck is stacked against the bull. The picadors jab the bull with a lance to weaken its neck and shoulder muscles. The banderilleros thrust darts into the bull's neck or shoulders, further weakening the animal.

After significant blood loss, a skilled matador can kill the bull with an accurate thrust of his sword through the bull's neck. Thus, the many Vietnams strategy was possibly intended to weaken the U.S. until Castro, or another matador, could deliver the final mortal blow.

It did not take long for Castro to complete his African strategy after he found a way to lend legitimacy to his brainchild. The U.S. had invaded the Dominican Republic with the blessing of the Organization of American States (OAS). Similarly, Castro would attack Tshombé with the approbation of the Organization of African Unity (OAU), which, along with most Congolese opposition leaders, had pronounced Tshombé the common enemy. In spite of its geographic absurdity, Cuba won full membership in the OAU by manipulating ethnic data on the percentage of black and mulatto Cubans. Castro must have also been convinced that Cuba's direct involvement in Africa would be better tolerated by the U.S. than similar actions in Latin America.

The question as to why Castro chose Che Guevara to command the Congo war is much more difficult to answer. Since Che Guevara will be a continuous player in the affairs of Africa and Congo, a brief biography follows.

*   *   *

Ernesto Guevara de la Serna was born on June 14, 1928, in Rosario, Argentina to an upper middle class family. He suffered from a serious asthmatic condition, which prompted his family to move to the drier climate of Alta Gracia, Córdoba.

He was mostly schooled at home, and his asthmatic condition exempted him from military service. In 1948, he entered the University of Buenos Aires and chose medicine. He received his medical degree in 1953, specializing in epidemiology. In Guevara's own account of the Congo campaign *The African Dream*, Guevara makes light of his chosen medical specialty: "... an epidemiologist—which, if this illustrious branch of the Aesculapian tree will forgive me for saying so, gave me the right to know nothing about medicine."[6]

Guevara's hatred for the U.S. apparently commenced in Guatemala, where he had chosen to live and practice medicine as this country was ruled by the radical socialist Jacobo Arbenz. Guevara witnessed the CIA engineer a coup in which Arbenz was replaced by the U.S.-selected Colonel Carlos Castillo Armas.

In September 1954 he moved to Mexico City where he found work at the general hospital. While working in Mexico, he met many Latin American radicals, including Fidel Castro who was planning the 1956 invasion of Cuba. It was in Mexico where he was given the nickname of *Che* for his habit of ending his phrases with that term, which is a familiar interjection, common in Argentina.

He joined Castro's expedition to provide medical services, but he devoured everything ever written about guerrilla tactics. His theoretical knowledge of unconventional warfare soon earned him the rank of *Comandante*. Upon Castro's triumph, Che was appointed to the job of Military Governor of *La Cabaña* Fortress. One of his duties, as such, was to supervise the trials of Batista's collaborators and their subsequent execution. Guevara sent hundreds of men to death. He forced each of his officers to take turns at executions to insure an adequate share of the blame. He was good at doing Castro's dirty work.

His second job has not been examined in detail in his many biographies. Guevara was head of the Industrial Department of the National Institute of the Agrarian Reform (INRA), and in this capacity he was able to carry out the land-confiscation work Castro was not comfortable personally doing at that time. He first arranged for the confiscation of land owned by foreigners, then of land owned by wealthy Cubans, with the final result being that the state owned all property in Cuba. This was an assignment that Fidel Castro could not have handled himself while he was claiming to be: humanist and not communist.

His third job was president of the Cuban Central Bank. At this time, the Cuban people considered him tied for number 2 with Raúl Castro, Fidel's brother, in the Cuban hierarchy. Then, Guevara started talking in public about doing away with money altogether and Castro kicked him upstairs to his fourth job, the important post of Minister of Industries. Guevara immediately showed immense hostility towards the few remaining U.S. interests in the Cuban economy. On the positive side, he worked hard and tried to set a good example, but failing to develop a cohesive strategy, the sugar sector was taken away from Che's ministry. His job instantly became meaningless, since sugar accounted for 90 percent of Cuba's industry. During the Cuban missile crisis, Che is thought to have advocated nuclear confrontation, even if it meant the obliteration of the Cuban population.

It was about mid-1964 when Guevara, having miserably failed in his last two assignments, was appointed to his fifth job, Ambassador of the Revolution. He then delivered his fateful anti-Soviet Algiers speech at the XI Economic Seminar of Afro-Asian Solidarity. Castro's options became limited: he could arrange to have Guevara killed, or he could find and/or create some military conflict, and send Guevara there, where he would die as a hero.

* * *

Critics of the Cuban revolution have speculated that Castro wished to remove Che Guevara from Cuba and from speaking in public. Castro and Guevara's ideological differences were insurmountable and Guevara was becoming too well-known internationally. Dariel (Benigno) Alarcón Ramírez, chief of Guevara's bodyguards and Guevara's close friend, also questions what could have happened between Guevara and Fidel, for their excellent relationship appeared to have soured after Guevara became Minister of Industries in 1962. According to Benigno, when Guevara left Cuba for Congo he was in a desperate mood, "... as if looking for another [country] in which to seek refuge."[7]

Contrary to this theory, evidence indicates that Castro was very protective of Guevara. Castro assigned three full-time men to safeguard Guevara in Congo in spite of Guevara's objections. Castro was also very careful to conceal Che's identity, although this could be dismissed as a measure of self-preservation, for Che's presence would identify Cuba as the aggressor in Congo. In order to further understand the differences between Fidel Castro and Che Guevara, the differences between Soviet and Chinese communism must be elucidated.

There were ideological differences between the U.S. and its fellow Western democracies. These differences are dwarfed when the differences in ideology, at that time, between the Soviet Union and The People's Republic of China are examined. Similarly, the ideological differences between Fidel Castro and Che Guevara were astronomical.

As Khrushchev was preaching peaceful coexistence with the Western powers and Castro was agreeing with Khrushchev, Che Guevara was openly talking about "fight without quarter against world imperialism."[8] While Castro was making speeches about Chairman Mao Tse-Dung being a fascist, Che was incorporating Mao's ideology into his speeches and, similarly to Mao, calling for People's War.

It is likely that Castro, perhaps as early as 1962, instructed Guevara to tone down his anti-Soviet rhetoric, but apparently he chose not to do so. To illustrate this point, Guevara was publicly verbally attacked in January 1965 by Carlos Rafael Rodríguez, perhaps the most analytical Cuban Marxist at the time. In a speech during INRA's (National Institute of the Agrarian Reform) yearly meeting, Rodríguez referred to Guevara as a "LaSallian Socialist."[9] He was comparing Guevara with Ferdinand LaSalle, a man who had been severely criticized by Karl Marx. Had Guevara been in Castro's good graces, Rodríguez would have never dared make this accusation. Since Rodríguez was not in Castro's inner circle,

Guevara's ideological differences with Castro must have been common knowledge among government officials in Cuba.

Castro's Cuba was economically dependent on the Soviet Union, and he was thus very careful to ensure that Cuban officials did not antagonize the Soviet Union, at least not in public. Castro had mastered the art of two-timing the USSR and the PRC, as both were courting new socialist countries, and he expected his high level officials to do the same. Unfortunately Che Guevara was not playing by the same rule book.

The Soviet Union believed that Africa was not ready for a proletarian revolution leading to communism. Their rationale was that to create a people's army, it was necessary to have exploited workers. And Africa was still years away from the full industrialization, which would give rise to the emergence of the proletariat. It would be then that armed revolution would be possible. The Chinese theoreticians believed that the agro-nomadic African tribes could be transformed into armies of revolution. The data that the Chinese missed were that the African tribes were neither hungry nor dissatisfied with their rulers. Most of them did not know who ruled them, and moreover they did not care. History has shown that the Chinese theoreticians were wrong. This does not necessarily imply that the Soviets were right.

A secret congress of Latin American communist parties, at the request of the Soviet Union, took place in Havana in November 1964. During this congress, Castro openly disagreed with Mao's theories. Castro's denunciation of Chinese policies did not come free of charge to the Soviet Union, as Castro obtained the support of the USSR to export his revolution to Colombia, Guatemala, Haiti, Honduras, Paraguay, and Venezuela.[10]

In October 1964, Khrushchev was replaced by the Cold Warrior Brezhnev whose ideas about exporting revolution were closer to Chinese theoreticians and thus to Guevara's. It is possible that Castro convinced and/or instructed Guevara that Latin America in general, and Argentina in particular, could wait, but that it was time to take action in Africa. It is also possible that Brezhnev had convinced Castro that the time was right to support Africa's revolutionary movements. A more likely scenario is that Guevara had antagonized key factions of the Soviet hierarchy and Castro was requested to keep Guevara out of the public eye. This last scenario could partly explain the unlikely choice of Guevara to lead the Congo action.

Ever since the day in 1961 when Castro announced that he was a Marxist-Leninist, historians have theorized that Castro was a Soviet puppet and that the Kremlin considered Castro and the Cuban armed forces as mercenaries to be used where and how Moscow saw fit. One example that supports the theory that Cuba's action in Congo was not Castro's initiative but rather an order from the Kremlin can be found in documents, which were recently declassified by the Kremlin. Sourcing these documents, American researcher Anne Appelbaum states in *The London University History Review*[11] that Moscow had instructed Castro to provide new divisions of black troops for African service. Che Guevara mentions many times in his posthumously published book *The African Dream: The Diaries of the Revolutionary War in the Congo*[12] that he cannot understand why only black soldiers were picked for the Congo action. This may only prove that at that time Che Guevara was not in Castro's inner circle, as details of Castro's agreements with the Kremlin were not provided to Guevara.

In the mid-1980s, some historians started to believe that Castro's involvement in Africa had been of his own initiative and that the Soviet Union was embarrassed into supporting him. Recent evidence tends to confirm Castro's independence when it came to effecting changes in the Third World. Anatoly Dobrynin, a high-ranking Soviet officer during the 1960s is quoted by Henry Kissinger as having said "the Cubans sent their troops [to Congo] of their own initiative and without consulting us."[13]

Why did Castro decide to export the Cuban revolution? Castro's actions showed his intent to prove to the world that he was important, the Missile Crisis notwithstanding. In his quest to be recognized as leader of the non-aligned world, Castro needed to spread communism and help countries held down by imperialistic colonialism. Additionally, Castro wanted to provide action for his armed forces, thus justifying having them on high alert status, and hence minimizing the possibility of a coup. Given Cuba's dismal economic situation, Castro coveted the financial and military aid provided by the USSR and the PRC to countries supporting liberation movements. Castro would also lessen the Cuban labor problems by having thousands of young men fighting abroad rather than applying for non-existing jobs in Cuba.

Why did Castro select Congo to be his first takeover target?

Congo was an immensely wealthy country in the process of fighting a cruel colonial legacy with little or no local leadership. Castro further theorized that he could secure the support of key African leaders by playing the card of avenging the assassination of Lumumba by the forces of imperialism. This would make Congo's neighboring states more receptive to Castro's rhetoric. On the logistics side, and going back to Figure

2, it is possible that Castro believed that once Congo was under Cuban and/or Soviet control, he could create a communist belt, extending from the Indian Ocean, to the Atlantic Ocean. From there, communism could be exported to southern Africa. On the self-preservation side, Castro believed that his activities in Africa would anger the U.S. significantly less than similar activities in Latin America. During interrogation, on the day of his execution, Guevara was asked why they had chosen Bolivia and his answer was: "I considered Venezuela, Central America and the Dominican Republic, but experience had shown that when Cuba tried to foment unrest so close to the U.S., the Yankees reacted strongly and the revolutionary activities failed."[14]

Considering that Castro wanted to maintain the export of his revolution secret, Congo was an ideal location. Not only was Congo far away from the U.S., but he would have the ability to deny being the culprit, by utilizing black Cuban soldiers of Congolese ancestry and physiognomy. Castro would not admit Cuba's involvement in Congo until 1995. If his operation was to be kept secret (long before the days of DNA testing) these Bantu-looking soldiers, with no identification documents or other incriminating evidence could not easily be connected to Cuba.

The first documented entry of slaves brought directly to Cuba from Africa was in 1521. Afterwards, there was a steadily increasing number of African slaves landing alive in Cuba, until 1886, when slavery was abolished in Cuba by the then ruling Spanish crown.

Professor Rafael López Valdéz, ethnologist from the Cuban Academy of Science, has provided an estimate of the time of arrival of the total of the approximately 1.3 million slaves brought to Cuba from Africa until the abolition of slavery.[15]

Number of African slaves

Years	Landing Alive in Cuba
1521-1762	120,500
1763-1789	15,500
1790-1820	249,000
1821-1870s	915,000
Total	1,300,000

The geographic distribution by ethnic group (African countries, as we know them today, did not exist then) of the 1.3 million African slaves arriving in Cuba provides an interesting statistic.

Total number of African slaves

Ethnic Group	Landing in Cuba during Slavery
Bantu	400,000
Yoruba	275,000
Ibo/Ibidio/Ijaw	240,000
Ewe/Fon	200,000
Other	185,000
Total	1,300,000

The Bantu (Congo) people lived in the Congo River basin, an area occupied today by Congo (Brazzaville), Congo, and northern Angola. Numerically, the Bantu were the largest group of African slaves introduced in Cuba. So dominant was the influence of the Bantu people that they formed a religion known as Palo Monte which survives in Cuba to this day. Also, in the field of music, Bantu rhythm is one of the basic elements of Afro-Cuban compositions. The basic cadence of some of the best known Afro-Cuban dances, the Conga and the Rumba, are based on Bantu rhythms.[16]

The second most important group, the Yoruba were mainly from southwestern Nigeria and since their voyage started in the port city of Calabar, they were known as Calabarí. There is a popular saying in Cuba to challenge the purity of the blood lines: *de San Antonio a Maisí, el que no tiene de Congo, tiene de Calabarí*. The westernmost point in Cuba is called Cape of San Antonio, while the easternmost point is called Maisí Point. Thus, the expression is translated as: "From San Antonio to Maisí, the ones that do not have some Congo ancestry, have [a bit of] Calabarí blood."

This hypothesis is supported by Benigno, who in addition to being Guevara's chief bodyguard and close friend, fought alongside Guevara in the Cuban mountains and later in Congo and Bolivia: "... because for Congo, in Cuba a [careful] selection of black combatants was made, [selecting] the ones that looked more like Congolese. Che was an active participant in the [final] selection process."[17] The initial selection of Cuban soldiers for Congo duty was likely made by high-ranking Cuban officers, possibly aided by anthropologists. Guevara was traveling in Africa at the time and could not have participated in this initial selection process. It is likely that Guevara and *Comandante* Victor Dreke had the final say on these recruits.

The final argument for the selection of Congo was that Castro expected to win, as Castro was convinced that he would. Jorge Risquet, one of

Castro's highest regarded military men, blames faulty intelligence for Cuba's failure in Congo: "In reality, Cuba possessed information which was fragmented and particularly exaggerated regarding the cohesion of the Lumumbist struggle."[18]

Why did Castro appoint Che Guevara to lead the Congo operation? And perhaps even more importantly, why did Guevara accept? Because of his asthmatic condition, and the heat and humidity of central Africa, Guevara was the worst possible candidate. Besides, he was white, and it would be quite difficult to camouflage him as a Congolese.

Castro chose Guevara for a combination of the following reasons. By sending Guevara to Congo, Castro was effectively silencing him. This was done to appease the USSR after Guevara's anti-Soviet speech of February 26, 1965 in Algeria, and possibly to punish him for going against Castro's party line. Guevara had also developed a warm rapport with key African and other Third World leaders who would be more willing to help Guevara than they would Castro himself. Thus, Castro needed to reassert himself as the man to deal with in Cuba. Che's growing popularity among the Cuban people as well as within the Cuban Army was likely perceived threatening to Castro.

These issues were discussed with Manuel Villafaña Martínez, who headed air operations during the Bay of Pigs invasion, and knew Guevara in Mexico before Che left to fight in Cuba, as well as later in Cuba, during the first year of the Castro government. Villafaña's answer follows: "Che had two ambitions, one was to be the supreme chief of the Cuban revolution, but he knew that was impossible because Castro could not be replaced, and Che was not Cuban. His second [ambition] was to *liberate* Argentina. There, he could be the supreme chief of the revolution. My guess is that Fidel promised to send him to Argentina once the mission in Congo was completed."[19] Jorge Risquet largely agrees: "What Che really wanted was [to start revolutions in] South America. He wanted to free Argentina."[20]

Guevara accepted because he was running out of choices in Cuba, and he had no other place to go without Castro's patronage. The carrot of later starting a revolution in Argentina possibly played a part in Guevara's acceptance of the Congo mission.

By late 1964, Castro had certainly formulated and tested his Africa strategy. Choosing Guevara to head any African military operation was likely far from Castro's mind at that time. Castro had contacted *Comandante* Victor Dreke in late December 1964, appointed him Chief of Military Operations, and told him to start selecting combatants: "all must be black and experienced soldiers"[21] for a mission to be later defined. The

Cuban operation in Congo was to be conducted in the utmost of secrecy. The soldiers were not told where they were going, and were instructed to tell their families that they were going to study in the Soviet Union. Training for the Cuban soldiers was conducted at the relatively flat area of Lomas de Candelaria, Pinar del Rio Province.

Castro selected approximately one third of the soldiers from each of the three regional military commands. This was probably done to underscore the separation of the three units but at the same time to show that the three commands were equal in importance.

It was roughly at this time that Castro instructed Guevara, in his role as Ambassador of the Revolution, to strengthen existing relationships with African leaders, as well as build new ones in the continent. It was in December 1964 when Che Guevara started collecting frequent flyer miles. Guevara spoke at a UN meeting on December 17, 1964, and from New York, at Castro's request he flew to Algeria, where on December 18, 1964 he met with President Ahmed Ben Bella.

On December 26, Guevara traveled to Mali where he met with President Modibo Keita. On January 2, 1965, he was in Brazzaville meeting with President Alphonse Massemba-Debat and Prime Minister Pascal Lissouba. After this meeting, both officials publicly stated: "... we are prepared to support liberation movements."[22] Also in Brazzaville, Guevara met with Agostinho Neto, leader of the revolution in Angola. During his visit to Congo (Brazzaville), Guevara established an Operational and Logistics Center in Dolissié (across the river from Congo) for the training of MNC fighters. This center was manned by Cubans who had stayed behind after the Algeria-Morocco conflict, and newly-recruited Haitians.[23] The presence of left-leaning troops from French-speaking Haiti working with Cubans in central Africa can be easily understood, as French is the lingua franca of Central Africa.

On January 8, Che met with leftist Guinea President Sékou Touré. Always looking to recruit African leaders, Guevara and Touré traveled to the border with Senegal, where they met with Senegalese President Senghor a Labe. On January 14, Che was in Ghana and back in Algeria on January 30. On February 2, 1965, Guevara arrived in the People's Republic of China where he met with Chairman Mao and Chou-En Lai. On February 11, 1965, he flew to Dar Es-Salaam, Tanzania's capital, where he met with key Lumumbist revolutionaries. In his diary, Che states that he did not like Gbenye or Soumialot, but he did like Kabila.[24]

It was during the Dar Es-Salaam meetings that Che separately offered both weapons and 30 instructors to Kabila and Soumialot, the latter having flown from his exile in Cairo to attend this meeting. Both accepted, but Soumialot insisted on black instructors. According to Soumialot, a number of his soldiers thought they were fighting against white supremacy, and they would be confused by white instructors. The number of instructors was later increased to 130 because the training was to be provided at a number of different locations. When Che clarified that the proposed training was to take place in Congo, Soumialot accepted, but Kabila balked at the concept. After prolonged and complex negotiations, Kabila finally accepted that the Cuban instructors would come to Congo. These instructors would be the Cuban soldiers that would arrive in Congo two months later. Kabila, Gbenye, and Soumialot would be astonished and concerned when they would later learn that Guevara would be the commanding officer. In their opinion, Guevara was too well-known, and his presence in Congo, if it should become public, would create an international scandal.[25] Guevara was probably equally as surprised when he learned, shortly after his arrival back in Havana from Algeria, that he himself would be leading the Congo operation.

Guevara continued accumulating frequent flyer points. On February 19, 1965, again following Castro's orders he was in Cairo and on February 24, he landed in Algeria for the third time during this trip. On February 26, 1965, Che Guevara made a presentation to the XI Economic Seminar on Afro-Asian Solidarity in Algiers. In this presentation, he blasted the Soviet Bloc on a number of issues, and publicly disclosed information that should have remained confidential.

It is known that on March 14, 1965, Guevara landed back in Havana for the first time since his infamous speech in Algeria. Castro met him at the airport. A few days later, Pablo Rivalta was appointed Cuban Ambassador to Tanzania, and one of his listed functions was "to coordinate the national liberation movements in Africa."[26] Rivalta was to report directly to Fidel Castro. Obviously Guevara was no longer involved in strategic political decisions; otherwise, Rivalta would have reported to Guevara. This was a strong early message from Castro to Guevara that he was no longer Ambassador of the Revolution, i.e., he had been demoted to his initial rank of a revolutionary.

With only a few key Cuban officials knowing that Guevara was about to commence Castro's secret war in Congo, a journalistic frenzy about Guevara's disappearance from public view took place in mid- to late-March 1965. The last confirmed sighting of Guevara was in Havana on March 21, 1965. Initial speculation was that because of his anti-Soviet pronouncements in Algeria during the XI Economic Seminar on Afro-

Asian Solidarity, Castro had instructed him to stay out of public view. As further time passed, tabloids started publishing derisory articles on the whereabouts of Guevara. During May 1965, many people claimed to have seen him in Chile, Brazil, Argentina, Peru, Mexico, and other countries. There were even reports that he was suffering from dementia and had been committed to a mental institution in Mexico City, as well as contradictory reports that he was dead and buried in the basement of a factory in Las Vegas, Nevada.[27]

During an international press gathering in Havana on April 20, 1965, Fidel Castro was asked where Guevara had gone after his well-publicized African speaking tour. Castro's answer: "All I can tell you about *Comandante* Guevara is that he will always be where he can be the most useful to the [Cuban] revolution. I think that his tour of Africa was very productive."[28]

The Cuban guerrillas were flown to Africa by airlines from inside the Iron Curtain in small groups of 10 to 15 men, by different itineraries, but their common destination was Dar Es-Salaam, the capital of Tanzania. The first group, with a total of 14 men including Guevara, arrived on April 19, 1965. They all had Cuban passports with assumed names. They gave themselves code names which corresponded to Swahili numbers. Victor Dreke was *Moja*, which is number 1 in Swahili, Martínez Tamayo was *M'bili*, number 2, and Che chose *Tatu*, number 3. Many think that at this time, Guevara was under the impression that he was still number 3 in Cuba, after Fidel and Raúl, and that is why he chose the code-name *Tatu*.

Since the Swahili numbering system becomes quite complicated as the numbers become larger, the groups of Cubans, which arrived later, were given African-sounding random code names. A somewhat complete list of the names of the Cuban combatants who fought in Congo is provided in Appendix III.

Meanwhile, in Congo, Mike Hoare was asked by Tshombé and Mobutu to meet at Kinshasa. This meeting took place on May 30, 1965, and both officials expressed their concern about renewed rebel activity in the Great Lakes area. The rebels had retaken Bukavu and were in firm control of Fizi and Baraka. The rebels controlled a strip of land about fifty kilometers wide, extending from north of Kalemie to south of Uvira, although both cities of Kalemie and Uvira were still under the control of the Congolese government. The areas immediately adjacent to two ANC garrisons within this area were also under government control. Mobutu asked Hoare to move his campaign to the Great Lakes area, where he would be in full charge of military operations. Hoare agreed, but first he still had some work to do in Orientale Province (Operations White Giant and *Violettes Imperiales*), and then, he would take a vacation.

Schramme's 10 Commando had taken control of the situation in Bandundu and Equateur Provinces, while Denard's 6 Commando was finalizing the pacification of Orientale Province. Hoare called on his Congolese friend General Bobozo in Lumumbashi to arrange for the crash training of the new troops. Hoare arranged with his CIA friends to have some aircraft and Cuban exile pilots from Makasi moved to the Kalemie area. He was also promised the support of a Cuban exile naval force that would be patrolling Lake Tanganyika shortly. With all these assurances, Hoare took a well-deserved brief holiday in Durban, South Africa. The stage was set for one of the most bizarre conflicts in recent history: Cubans fighting Cubans in Congo.

Notes

1. Benemelis, Juan F., *Las Guerras Secretas de Fidel Castro*, Fundación Elena Mederos, Miami, 2002, p. 96.
2. Carbonell, Nestor T., *And the Russians Stayed*, Morrow, New York, 1989, p. 237.
3. *Ibid*, p. 263.
4. Benemelis, *op. cit.*, Las Guerras Secretas de Fidel Castro, Chapter 7.
5. Gleijeses, Dr. Piero, *Conflicting Missions: Havana, Washington and Africa, 1959-1976*, University of North Carolina Press, Chapel Hill, 2002.
6. Guevara, *op. cit.*, p. 18.
7. Alarcón Ramírez, Dariel (aka Benigno), *Memorias de un Soldado Cubano: Vida y Muerte de la Revolución*, Tusquets Editores, Barcelona, 1996, pp. 103-108.
8. Closing phrase of Guevara's Algeria speech, quoted in Chapter Nine.
9. Quoted by Ros, Enrique, *Cubanos Combatientes: Peleando en Distintos Frentes*, Ediciones Universal, Miami, 1998, p. 195.
10. Quoted by Benemelis, *Castro, Subversión y Terrorismo en Africa*, Editorial San Martín, Madrid, 1988, p. 71.
11. Quoted in *http://www.sigloxxi.org/implacable.htm*, downloaded September 9, 2004.
12. Guevara, *op. cit.*
13. Kissinger, Henry, *Years of Renewal*, New York, Simon and Schuster, 1999, p. 816.
14. Rodríguez, Félix I. and John Weisman, *Shadow Warrior*, Simon and Schuster, New York, 1989, p. 166.
15. From a lecture given ca. 1992 by Cuban Professor Rafael López Valdéz, entitled Ethnic Influences in Cuba Resulting from the History of African Slave Trade to Cuba, *www.batadrums.com/background/ethnic.htm* downloaded April 2, 2005.
16. Ortiz, Fernando, *Africanía de la Música Folklórica de Cuba*, Editora Universitaria, La Habana, 1965.
17. Alarcón Ramírez, Dariel (aka Benigno), *Memorias de un Soldado Cubano: Vida y Muerte de la Revolución*, Tusquets Editores, Barcelona, 1966, p. 98.
18. Risquet Valdés, Jorge, *El Segundo Frente del Che en el Congo: Historia del Batallón Patricio Lumumba*, Casa Editorial Abril, La Habana, 2000, p. 224.
19. Villafaña Martínez, Manuel, Conversations with the author, Miami, February 25, 2005.
20. Risquet, *op. cit.*, p. 32.
21. Taibo II, Paco Ignacio, Froilán Escobar and Félix Guerra, *El Año que Estuvimos en Ninguna Parte*, Editorial Txalaparta, Pamplona, Spain, 1995, p. 23.
22. Risquet, *op. cit.*, p. 37.
23. Benemelis, Castro, *Subversión y Terrorismo en Africa*, p. 178.
24. Guevara, *op. cit.*, pp. 5-7.
25. Taibo, *op. cit.*, p. 52.
26. *Ibid*, p. 19.
27. Taibo, *op. cit.*, pp. 58 and 78.
28. Granma, *op. cit.*, October 22, 1967.

9

Guevara's Algeria Speech

Guevara traveled to New York around December 7, 1964 to address the General Assembly of the United Nations while transitioning from his post as Minister of Industries to his new capacity as Ambassador of the Revolution. Shortly after Guevara's departure, Castro began making arrangements to assemble Cuban troops to revive the fading Congo rebellion. These preparations were being made under the utmost of secrecy, and only a handful of Castro's closest associates were aware of his African plans.

Guevara's December 11, 1964 UN address is clear, well-documented and flows logically. His later good-bye letter to Fidel and the Cuban people is similarly orderly and intelligible. Both of these are closer in style to the numerous speeches delivered by Fidel, thus raising questions about the authorship of these two documents. In contrast, Guevara's mode of expression, whether he was writing or speaking in public, was rambling and disorganized, disjointed and often incomprehensible.

In his address to the UN, Guevara touched on many topics ranging from Puerto Rico's freedom to nuclear disarmament. Guevara is uncharacteristically supportive of Soviet policies. Regarding the Kisangani rescue, he stated: "That is why the government of Cuba supports the just stance of the Soviet Union in refusing to pay expenses for this crime."[1]

Excerpts from Guevara's UN address, translated into English, are provided by British historian Richard Gott in his introduction to Guevara's posthumously published *The African Dream*. In reference to the Kisangani rescue operation, which Guevara calls: "the tragic case of the Congo," he denounces "this unacceptable intervention," and likens the rescue operation to the assassination of Patrice Lumumba. Guevara proceeds to point his finger at the perpetrators: "Belgian paratroopers, transported by United States aircraft, which took off from British bases." He finishes his diatribe with the disclosure: "Free men throughout the world must prepare to avenge the Congo crime."[2] It seems unusual that while Castro is secretly preparing to send troops to Congo, he has provided Guevara with a speech that dwells on Congo unnecessarily.

After New York, Guevara embarked on a lengthy African tour, which included Algeria, Mali, Congo (Brazzaville), Guinea-Bissau, Ghana, Dahomey, and then back to Algeria. From there he traveled on February 2, 1965 to the People's Republic of China and had meetings with Chairman Mao and Chou En-Lai. It is surprising that Castro would have authorized this trip, since the PRC and the USSR were in a difficult moment of the Sino-Soviet split, and Cuba was supporting the USSR. Che departed the PRC on February 11, 1965 and traveled to Tanzania, where he met with Kabila and Soumialot. On February 19, 1965 he traveled to Egypt for meetings with Nasser and then on to Algeria for the third time to deliver his fateful address to the XI Economic Seminar of Afro-Asian Solidarity. Guevara's speech was given on February 26, 1965. From Algiers, Guevara returned to Egypt. Guevara arrived back in Cuba on March 14, 1965, after more than a three-month absence.

Due to the intensity of his travel schedule, it is unlikely that Guevara had much time to prepare his speech in advance. Guevara also had a reputation as a procrastinator and it is entirely possible that he finished writing his speech the night before its delivery. It is unlikely that Castro had an opportunity to review Guevara's Algiers speech, or that he influenced its writing. The style in Guevara's Algiers speech is his own and is easily recognizable as being radically different from the style of his UN address.

Guevara's English translation of his Algiers speech contains 56 paragraphs. Citations from the speech will be based on the paragraph number of the reference provided for this chapter.[3]

The timing of Guevara's inflammatory speech could not have been worse. Since the assassination of President Kennedy in November 1963, there had been attempts by Castro to improve relations with the U.S. Immediately after the November 1964 presidential elections, President Johnson, overwhelmed by the Vietnam conflict was himself attempting to reach an accommodation with Castro. The Johnson administration enforced U.S.'s neutrality and persecuted militant anti-Castro exiles. Evidence suggests that Castro had previously had several conversations with Guevara about toning down his rhetoric. Guevara incited the crowd with his pronouncement (in paragraph 6): "If the imperialist enemy, America or any other develops its attack against the underdeveloped peoples and the socialist countries, simple logic determines the necessity of an alliance between the underdeveloped peoples and the socialist countries." Having one of Castro's top men calling America the enemy and suggesting an anti-American alliance did not bode well for Castro's and President Johnson's pacific coexistence efforts.

Repeatedly throughout the otherwise rambling speech, Guevara attacks the Soviet Union (the first occurrence in paragraph 10): "The development of countries now starting out on the road to liberation should be paid for by the socialist countries." In the book *El Año que Estuvimos en Ninguna Parte*[4] the three authors interviewed a number of people who were involved with Guevara at the time of the Congo operation. Those interviewed agreed that Guevara believed that communist revolutions should be bankrolled by the USSR and the PRC, no strings attached. He was critical of the USSR because they sold weapons for a profit while Guevara thought they should be provided for free. The USSR and the PRC were having economic problems of their own at the time. Surely, they did not need Guevara announcing to the Third World that any and all liberation movements would be bankrolled by the USSR and the PRC, to the detriment of the health and welfare of their own citizens.

Che continued with additional criticisms of the Soviet Union (in paragraph 11): "There should not be any more talk about developing mutually beneficial trade based on prices rigged against underdeveloped countries by the law of value and the inequitable relations of international trade brought about by the law." Guevara, in his former job of Minister of Industries, had negotiated long-term agreements for the sale of sugar with the Soviets and Chinese. The Chinese had agreed to terms more favorable to Cuba than would have been permitted by World Trade Organization (WTO) guidelines. The Soviets, on the other hand, would not agree to pay more than WTO guidelines. This paragraph is a direct attack on the Soviets for not agreeing to go beyond then existing WTO guidelines.

Perhaps the most virulent anti-Soviet attack was given by Guevara (in paragraphs 12 and 13) when he berates the USSR for its trade and economic policies in exchanging goods with underdeveloped nations and accuses the Soviet Union of being an accomplice of imperialistic exploitation: "How can one apply the term 'mutual benefit' to the selling at world-market prices of raw materials costing limitless sweat and suffering in the underdeveloped countries and the buying of machinery produced in today's big, automated factories? If we establish that kind of relation between the two groups of nations, we must agree that the socialist countries are, in a way, accomplices of imperialist exploitation. It can be argued that the amount of exchange with underdeveloped countries is an insignificant part of the foreign trade of the socialist countries. This is a great truth, but it does not eliminate the immoral character of the exchange." This final sentence alone probably justified Castro in forcing Guevara to write his good-bye letter and placing him in charge of the dangerous Congo operation.

Paragraph 22 looks harmless on the surface. Guevara appears to be making a suggestion to the Soviet Union as to rules for investing in developing nations. "The states, in whose territories the new invest-ments are to be made, will have all the inherent rights of sovereign property over them without any payment or credit due, but they would be obligated to supply agreed-upon quantities of products to the inves-tor countries for a certain number of years at fixed prices." However, two critical errors are made by Guevara in this paragraph. One is that he is doing strategic thinking for Cuba, a job that Castro has reserved for himself. The second is that he is telling the USSR how to conduct its foreign policy.

Halfway through his presentation, Che temporarily halted his criticism of the USSR to proffer specific economic recommendations during what was an *Economic* Solidarity seminar (in paragraph 27): "If ... the under-developed [countries] could acquire all the technology of the advanced countries unhampered by the present system of patents, which prevents the spread of the inventions of different countries, we would progress a great deal in our common task." When Guevara had been President of the Cuban Central Bank, he had attempted, unsuccessfully, to do away with money. In his position as Minister of Industries he had never proposed eliminating the patent system within Cuba. Yet, in this international gathering, he is proposing that the attendees do so in their respective countries. It is difficult to judge the impact that Guevara's suggestions had on Castro, a man holding a doctorate of law degree.

Guevara once again departed from the central theme of the seminar and embarked on discussions about Congo and political matters. The mentions of Congo both in this speech as well as in his UN speech prob-ably alerted Western intelligence services as to Cuba's intense interest in Congo. Paragraphs 32 and 33 contain references to Congo. "... One is the brutal aggression we have seen in Congo ... Neo-colonialism has shown its claws in the Congo."

Paragraphs 34 through 38, though nearly ungraspable, contain a most unusual suggestion. Guevara proposes that the USSR and the PRC should include all socialist countries in some sort of a master economic plan. Under this plan, each nation would be told what they can and cannot pro-duce and what they can and cannot grow. At the time, neither the USSR nor the PRC were able to control their own economies. How could they be expected to control the economies of the Third World?

The USSR probably balked at the economic concept that Che next proposed, that free weapons should be handed to any set of socialist revolutionaries (whether or not legitimate) wanting to start a revolution in any country (paragraphs 40 and 41): "Our attitude toward liberation by armed struggle against an oppressor political power should be in accordance with the rules of proletarian internationalism.... Arms cannot be regarded as merchandise in our world. They should be delivered to the peoples asking for them for use against the common enemy without any charge at all, and in quantities determined by the need and their availability. That is the spirit in which the USSR and the People's Republic of China have offered us their military aid. We are socialists, we constitute a guarantee of the proper utilization of those arms; but we are not the only ones. And all of us should receive the same treatment." Surely, Castro was taken to task by the USSR on Guevara's pronouncements. The PRC had already been offering free weapons to any and all liberation movements, and never asked for payment.

Guevara's paragraph 42 illustrates his pro-Chinese sentiments as well as his open dislike of Soviet policies. Che said: "To the ominous attacks by American imperialism against Vietnam and Congo, the answer should be the supplying of all the defense equipment they [the rebels] need, and to offer them our full solidarity without any conditions whatsoever." This is a particularly strong criticism of the USSR. One of the chief reasons for the Sino-Soviet split was the degree of support the PRC was demanding the USSR give to Vietnam. The USSR had refused, and Guevara was castigating the Soviets in front of a major world body.

As evidenced by this speech, it must have been difficult for Guevara to stay on track on any subject. In the closing remarks of his presentation, he again tackled political issues in paragraphs 52 and 54. "For example, our peoples suffer the painful pressure of foreign bases established on their territories, or they have to carry the heavy burdens of foreign debts of incredible size. This is the time to throw off the yoke, to force renegotiation of oppressive foreign debts, and to force the imperialists to give up their bases for aggression on our territories." These are clear references to the Guantánamo U.S. Navy Base in eastern Cuba.

Guevara closed his speech, thanking his host. "And there are few settings from which to declare this as symbolic as Algiers, one of the most heroic capitals of freedom. And the magnificent Algerian people, steeled as few others in suffering for freedom, and firmly led by its party headed by our dear comrade Ahmed Ben Bella, serves as an inspiration to us in this fight without quarter against world imperialism."

Less than four months later, on June 19, 1965, Ahmed Ben Bella would be overthrown by Colonel Houari Boumedienne. This coup d'etat would occur a few days before a conference where Che Guevara would have been the guest of honor. Boumedienne expelled all Cubans from Algeria.

The fallout from this speech by Guevara signaled a major change in the leadership of the Cuban Revolution. It did not take Castro long to start evaluating the original *Comandantes* of the armed struggle against Batista. As Castro feared those that were the closest to him, the evaluation of the *Comandantes* became even more inexorable. Only the ones with complete obedience to Fidel Castro, able to support the USSR and without any vestige of pro-Chinese sentiments would survive.

There is no doubt that Castro received angry messages from the Kremlin, and it is clear that Castro had to discipline Guevara. Two important questions remain unanswered: Was Guevara aware of Castro's secret preparations to send Cuban troops to Congo? Did Guevara volunteer for Congo, or was this a punishment imposed by Castro?

The selection and recruiting of troops for Congo service commenced after Guevara had departed for New York in early December 1964. Fidel Castro had selected Victor Dreke, a black man with Congolese physiognomy to head the Congo operation.[5] It is unlikely that Castro planned to have two commanding officers for a troop of 200 men.

Intuitively, the answer to the first question is that Guevara was probably aware that some sort of military action was being planned, but did not foresee that he would head this operation. Recently, evidence has surfaced that suggests that Guevara was planning to take an active part in the Congo military operation and that he discussed this possibility with President Nasser of Egypt.

Richard Gott, in the introduction to Guevara's 1999 *The African Dream* book, describes an account of this conversation, ostensibly provided by Mohammed Heikal, a respected Egyptian journalist who was also Nasser's son-in-law. Gott provides an extensive bibliography at the end of this introduction, but there is no reference on Heikal's account. Nasser was allegedly astonished at Guevara's disclosure and warned him not to become: "another Tarzan, a white man among black men, leading them and protecting them."[6]

In a 2005 book, Martin Meredith, a well-known expert on Africa quotes the same conversation between Guevara and President Nasser.[7] No reference to Heikal, Gott, or anyone else is given.

The conversation between Guevara and Nasser may never have taken place. If indeed the conversation took place, Guevara may have gone to Congo of his own choosing. If however the conversation was fabricated, Congo was likely Guevara's punishment.

Regardless, Guevara had no other place to go. He certainly could not return to his native Argentina. He was about to give up his Cuban citizenship and would soon have no valid passport from any country. Possibly the only country that would have taken him would have been the People's Republic of China. But what could he have done there? He spoke no Chinese; hence, even practicing medicine would have been difficult.

Notes

1. Che's complete speech on the 19th General Assembly of the UN. Taken from *http:// www.companeroche.com/index.php?id=97*, downloaded February 3, 2008.

2. Guevara, Ernesto, *The African Dream: The Diaries of the Revolutionary War in the Congo*, Grove Press, New York, 1999, in the Introduction by Richard Gott, pp. xii-xiii.

3. A complete text of Guevara's speech in Algiers can be obtained from: *http://www. chehasta.narod.ru/eaasia.htm*, downloaded May 5, 2005.

4. Taibo II, Paco Ignacio, Froilán Escobar and Félix Guerra, *El Año que Estuvimos en Ninguna Parte*, Editorial Txalaparta, Pamplona, Spain, 1955, p.17.

5. *Ibid*, pp. 22-26.

6. Guevara, *op. cit.*, p. xxiii.

7. Meredith, Martin, *The Fate of Africa: From the Hopes of Freedom to the Heart of Despair*, Public Affairs Publishers, New York, 2005, p. 149.

10

Castro's Congo Intervention Fails

It is April 23, 1965, late at night, and fourteen combatants are crossing Lake Tanganyika from Kigoma in Tanzania to Kibamba in Congo. Thirteen men are black and one is white. There is nothing too unusual about this group. From a distance, an observer would have guessed they were local volunteers on their way to joining the languishing second independence revolution in Congo.[1] A serious blow had been dealt to the subversion in November 1964, when Belgian paratroopers were flown by the U.S. Air Force from Europe to Kisangani to rescue the nearly 2,000 hostages taken by the leftist rebels in that city as well as in Isiro. If the observer could have come closer, he would have been quite surprised to hear the fourteen men conversing in Spanish with a distinct Cuban accent. The observer would have been further astonished to recognize the white combatant as Argentinian-born *Comandante* Ernesto Che Guevara, Cuba's expendable high-profile man. The thirteen black men are handpicked experienced Cuban fighters. Over the next weeks these men will be joined by over 180 additional Cuban combatants, mostly black, and they will fight against various forces loyal to the Congo government.

Che and his 13 men were the first resident Cuban combatants to cross into Congo to initiate Castro's intervention in this central African country. They made the approximately 70 kilometer crossing of Lake Tanganyika under the cover of night. It is almost a certainty that most Cuban combatants called the Congolese port town of Kibamba, *kimbamba*, which in Cuban colloquial language roughly means *in the middle of nowhere*. They arrived on April 24, 1965.

At the time of Che's crossing, there were only two militarily active rebel areas left in Congo. One was the Kwilu River area, where Pierre Mulele and his rebel troops were operating from the cover of the dense jungle. The other was the Great Lakes area, where Kabila was the political leader. Castro chose the latter because of its proximity to the supporting country of Tanzania and the apparent ability to move supplies and person-

139

nel across Lake Tanganyika. The Kwilu River area was not logistically friendly for the Cuban intervention.

Che was fortunate that Mulele was fighting in the Kwilu River area, away from the Great Lakes. First of all, Mulele's outside help, mainly from the PRC, came from either Congo (Brazzaville), via river traffic, or overland from Angola. This meant that the rebel forces in the Great Lakes area did not have to share with Mulele the supplies coming from Tanzania, across Lake Tanganyika. Additionally, since the Kwilu River area is close to Kinshasa, the ANC had stationed a large number of troops near the capital city with the mission to fight Mulele. The Cuban exile Makasi air force bases in Kinshasa and Kikwit were given the priority to strike Mulele. Thus Kabila's Great Lakes front soldiers moved within their territory practically without opposition.

The theater of operations for the Cubans was the geographic area known as Fizi-Baraka, which stretches from Uvira in the north to Kalemie in the south, an approximate distance of 300 kilometers. To the east is the west shore of Lake Tanganyika, and available information indicates that the Cubans were seldom active more than 80 kilometers away from the lake. Therefore, all Cuban operations occurred within an area of some 25,000 square kilometers, or about 1 percent of the area of Congo. Figure 5 portrays the Cubans' operations theater. The terrain is ideal for guerrilla warfare, for the west shore of Lake Tanganyika is rocky, difficult for landing troops, and the Mitumba Mountain Range ascends straight from the lakeshore, shooting up to mountains of 2,000- to 3,000-meter altitude.

Che Guevara chose for the location of his HQ a site on top of a 3,000-meter high elevation called by the locals Luluaburg Mountain. He called this his high camp. This choice of location meant a 9-kilometer walk always climbing from Kibamba on the west shore of Lake Tanganyika. The four-plus hour walk took its toll on the Cubans, for their training had been on flat land and now they were spending all day in alpine exercises. There was also a low camp located at the foot of Luluaburg Mountain, in the direction of the village of Nganja.

The Cubans encountered a multitude of problems immediately upon their arrival in Congo. There were logistical problems as they were being supplied from Cuba, the PRC and the USSR, mostly through Tanzania, although Uganda and Sudan were alternate routes. The weapons from the USSR were frequently missing parts and/or the wrong caliber ammunition was provided. Cuban soldiers preferred Chinese weapons, which were replicas of U.S. ones with 1 millimeter added to the diameter of

Figure 5
Operations Theater
Che Guevara and Cuban Forces

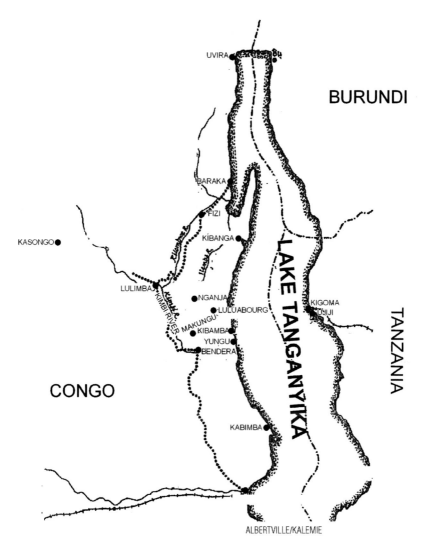

the bore. If the rebels captured enemy ammunition, it could be used, but not vice-versa.

Another significant problem that Che encountered was the quality of the local leadership. In his diary, Che states that during meetings with Congolese revolutionary leaders, a picture of Gbenye emerged: "… a man more suited to lead a gang of thieves than a revolutionary movement."[2] Guevara's opinion of Soumialot was not much better, as he considered him to be politically immature even though he was an older man. Guevara complained that Soumialot talked continuously and in vague phrases, as if trying to impress his audience. Guevara's perception was that Soumialot and Gbenye were not men capable of leading a country. Fortunately for Guevara, his high-level Congolese contact was neither of the two aforementioned leaders. It was Laurent Kabila, who impressed Guevara because of his youth and dynamic personality. Che did not consider Kabila to be perfect, but when compared with the alternate leaders (Gbenye and Soumialot), Kabila came out on top.

Other than supplies and local leadership, the Cubans also had the problem that their fighting partners were both Congolese and Rwandans, and these two nationalities did not get along. Ceaseless bickering over ownership of weapons, work to be done, and bland (no hot peppers are used) Cuban cooking created constant altercations. As the Congolese and Rwandans were both Simba fighters, they each relied heavily on their own variety of *dawa* or incantation. The witch doctors from the Kwilu River area and Orientale Province performed magic that supposedly turned enemy bullets into water (Mai Mulele). The *dawa* prepared by the mugangas from the Great Lakes was based on a liquid concoction, made from the juice of various mysterious plants, which they claimed made the warriors immune to enemy bullets. The *dawa* was poured over the warrior before battle, and a mystical drawing was made on the warrior's forehead with carbon. However, conditions were attached to the success of the *dawa*, for it would only work, provided they did not steal, touch a woman, look back, or feel fear. In order for the *dawa* to be effective, all four requirements had to be met.[3] The witch doctors probably had some good legal advice, for they could always claim that the warrior died because he felt fear. Since the Congolese *dawa* was different from the Rwandan one, the treatment would only be effective when applied by a witch doctor with the correct nationality. Even if under attack, these warriors would not fight until their own form of *dawa* was performed by their own witch doctor.

The Cuban ranks rapidly grew to some 115 to 120 men.[4] The original mission of the 130 Cubans to be provided for the Congo revolution was to train guerrilla fighters. Guevara was under the impression that he and the Cuban troops would be working with Congolese and Rwandan soldiers with some level of military experience, as the fighting in that area had been going on for approximately 4 years. To his surprise, these men were new recruits, had seen little or no military action, and thus did not even have the most rudimentary knowledge of warfare. In keeping with the warfare methods of their ancestors, they thought the bullets were meant to scare, rather than kill, the enemy. Their idea of doing battle was to quickly shoot all 30 bullets of their semi-automatic weapons into the air and run.

Bored with the routine of training green recruits, Che suggested that in addition to training, they should start planning military operations. The Cubans' Congolese contact was Leonard Mitoudidi, a French-speaking university graduate who was the on-site chief of military operations. The revolutionary leader, Kabila, stayed safely in Tanzania drinking scotch. The overall military chief, Idelphonse Massengo, usually stayed away from any fighting and came by only to visit with the Cubans, but never for more than a day or two.

Victor Dreke Cruz (*Moja*) was usually introduced to the rebels as the commanding officer of the Cuban unit. Perhaps this was done because Guevara was a white man, an unwelcome reminder of colonial days. It was not necessary for the Rwandans and Congolese to know Spanish in order to quickly determine that the real boss was Guevara.

On May 23, 1965, Che and Mitoudidi agreed to send out teams to scout the following four targets: Kabimba; Bendera; Baraka, Fizi, and Lulimba; and finally Uvira.

Incomplete and contradictory reports from the reconnaissance patrols slowly trickled in. The ANC fort at Lulimba was far away and had thousands of men. The Congolese team sent to Fizi could not agree on the number of men and weapons at this fort. They did agree that there were white officers at the camp, and that there was a helicopter pad and a small landing strip. At Kabimba as well as at Bendera, there were significant men and weapons, but no training or organization. The trip to Uvira never took place.

A significant event occurred on June 7, 1965. Mitoudidi, the best contact the Cubans had, drowned while crossing Lake Tanganyika. Guevara wrote in his diary for the month of May 1965: "Until Mitoudidi's arrival all of [our] time was wasted."[5] It appears that the wind was blowing hard that June morning and a large wave made two or three soldiers fall into the water. In general terms, Lake Tanganyika is moderately calm at night, but quite rough during the day. Mitoudidi, who was reputed to be a good swimmer, jumped in to save his men and never came back.

On June 9, 1965, Cubans and Congolese attacked an ANC supply boat in Lake Tanganyika and captured weapons. Several ANC soldiers were killed and one French mercenary was captured and delivered to Congolese Simba fighters operating in the Kibamba area. Guevara was horrified when he later learned that the Frenchman had been buried standing up with only his head above ground, and allowed to starve to death.

At approximately the same time as the attack on the ANC supply boat, Mike Hoare was in Lumumbashi, southern Katanga Province, talking to General Louis Bobozo and arranging for the crash training of new 5 Commando troops, as well as their subsequent transportation to Kalemie upon completion of training. The first newly-trained recruits arrived in Kalemie in late June 1965, and until Hoare's arrival in that city around September 1, they were used as escorts or scouts by the ANC.

Hoare's new 5 Commando troops did not commence their military campaign in the Fizi-Baraka area until sometime shortly after Hoare's arrival. Other than Makasi, it is evident that the Cubans had little or no meaningful opposition during their first four or five months in Congo.

The entire Fizi Baraka area was protected by two ANC battalions, one at Bendera and the other at Lulimba, but they seldom left the protective confine of their respective forts.[6] The number of men in a Congolese battalion is variable and to some extent depends on the rank of the commanding officer. Normally, a battalion would be commanded by a lieutenant-colonel and have a fighting strength of 600 men. During the day, the Cubans were harassed by the Cuban exile Makasi, flying out of Kalemie. Several aircrafts had been moved to Kalemie in September 1964 after the liberation of that city as a result of operation Watch Chain. Makasi did not have the benefit of professional ground scouts, and thus Cuban exile pilots had to rely mostly on their good senses to spot targets. According to Makasi pilot Jorge Navarro, the native ground scouts would construct an arrow with white rocks, indicating that from that point on, everyone was the enemy.[7]

The first documented action of Cuban exiles versus Cubans from Che Guevara's Congo group took place on June 19, 1965. Information had been obtained by the CIA from local tribesmen that foreign soldiers had a camp west of Yungu. Two B-26Ks and four T-28s from the Makasi unit at the Kalemie airport strafed the Cuban camp. Guevara had instructed his men not to shoot back, so that their exact position would not be disclosed to the enemy. But contrary to Che's orders, the Cubans shot back with 12.7 mm anti-aircraft machine guns. The planes did not return fire. Guevara was furious, but chose not to punish the soldiers who disobeyed his orders. It would be weeks later before the Cubans learned that they had been fired at by Cuban exiles. The Cuban exiles would learn about ten days later that they had strafed the Cuban camp. The original battle report from the Cuban viewpoint indicated that these were "Canberra aircraft flown by Belgian mercenaries."[8] There were no Canberra aircrafts at this time in Congo. Perhaps Cuban report writers relied on old battle descriptions from the days of the Katanga secession.

On June 24, 1965, thirty-nine new Cuban soldiers arrived, including three medical doctors. They reported that they were attacked by both air and water as they crossed Lake Tanganyika. The lake was patrolled by aircraft piloted by Cuban exiles during the day, but the SWIFT boats manned by Cuban exiles did not start patrolling until early September 1965, close to five months after the first Cubans arrived in Congo. If they were indeed attacked by water, it was not by Cuban exiles.

By late June 1965, with a total force of about 200 Cuban fighters, Guevara divided the Cubans into four units. Che and a large contingent were stationed at the high camp HQ at Luluaburg Mountain. The HQ was called *La Base*. Santiago Terry Rodríguez (*Aly*) was at Kibamba in charge of coordinating the logistics. Eduardo Torres (*Nane*) was with Congolese fighters in Makungo, and Víctor Dreke Cruz (*Moja*) with Rwandans fighters had his camp at the mountains near Bendera.

Other than a few well-executed ambushes, the only major offensive operation carried out under Cuban command was a large scale attack on the ANC barracks near the city of Bendera. The ANC barracks are located in a steep mountainous region where the water running down to the Kimbi River is utilized for electricity production. The hydroelectric plant is located along the river bank, and the town of Bendera is nearby. The ANC base to be attacked was around 40 kilometers (on foot, using mountain paths) south from Che's La Base, approximately 100 kilometers north of Kalemie, and about 25 kilometers west of the lakeside city of Yungu. The mountains west of Bendera were controlled by Victor Dreke (*Moja*) and his Cuban and Rwandan combatants. Within the ANC fortification, there was another building, which contained a military school.

A week or so prior to the Bendera action, Kabila and Massengo had appointed the Rwandan Mundandi to be on-site chief of military operations, in replacement of Mitoudidi. Guevara had to obtain Mundandi's approval for his military plan. This first and only major offensive military operation by the Cubans was personally planned by Guevara at La Base. After much deliberation, Mundandi reluctantly conceded to allow Cubans to command the main battle points. It was agreed that there would be three assault units, and that the commanding officers would be Victor Dreke Cruz (*Moja*), José-María Martínez Tamayo (*M'bili*), and Norberto

Pío Pichardo (*Inne*). Because of some local numerology superstition, the date for the attack was set for June 29, 1965.

The assault force consisted of approximately 200 combatants, 44 of which were Cubans, while the remaining 156 were Rwandans and Congolese rebels in an unknown proportion.

During this battle, a Cuban unit commanded by First Lieutenant Norberto Pío Pichardo (*Inne*), unable to reach its assigned target, attacked the military school, thinking that it would be an easy target. They were received with intense heavy weapon fire and *Inne* was killed instantly.

There were five Cubans killed in action. Due to the fierceness of the fighting and the haste of the retreat, the Cuban troops were only able to retrieve three of the bodies of their fallen comrades. One of the dead Cubans, contrary to instructions issued by Guevara, had with him his passport and a diary written in Spanish. Another dead Cuban was wearing underpants with a label which read *Hecho en Cuba* or Made in Cuba.[9]

According to Cuban military writers Gálvez and Taibo II, as well as Guevara's own diary, most of the Rwandans refused to fight, claiming they were sick. The few that did agree to participate in this action ran after the first shots were fired. Cuban publications also affirm that as soon as the planes piloted by Cuban exile Makasi arrived, the few remaining Congolese and Rwandans ran.[10] *El Año que Estuvimos en Ninguna Parte*, a chronicle of this battle from the Cuban viewpoint, written by three journalists, blames their defeat on the numeric superiority of the Tshombé forces. Using a somewhat similar reasoning system, the Congolese probably blame their defeat on a poorly-trained witch doctor with weak *dawa*.

There were two key elements to the defeat of the Cubans, Rwandans, and Congolese in the one-day Bendera action. The most significant one was that the ANC troops, in one of their rare outings, were conducting exercises in full gear away from the fort. As they returned, the rebels were caught in a cross-fire. "The ambushers ended up ambushed."[11] The other element was the support from the Makasi Cuban exile air force. Located at Kalemie, only a short distance to Bendera, they were able to arrive at the battle area in only a few minutes and engage the enemy. The Cubans had underestimated the enemy and overestimated the will to fight of Rwandan and Congolese soldiers, and this resulted in a costly and resounding defeat for the Cuban forces.

The diary of the dead Cuban was given to Cuban exile Makasi pilot Antonio (Tony) Soto Vázquez to read and translate[12] and he reported that the writer was definitely Cuban. Additionally, his passport showed that he had traveled to Tanzania from Havana, via Moscow. This tangible evidence offered the proof Western intelligence services had been missing. By late June 1965, the CIA had confirmed that Cubans were in Congo and that in all likelihood Che Guevara, who had gone off their radar screens back in mid-March 1965, was their commander. The Cuban exile Makasi was instructed to patrol Lake Tanganyika more intensely. Additional CIA resources were quickly mobilized to capture or kill Guevara.

The Johnson administration wanted the world to know that Cuba, with an active military presence in Congo, was interfering in the internal affairs of this independent African nation. However the U.S. did not want the world to know that the CIA and Cuban exiles were involved in the Congo struggle trying to tip the scale in favor of the West.

A small article entitled *Congo has Diary of Cuban Agent* appeared in the July 18, 1965 issue of *The Washington Post*. Said article, ostensibly released by the Congolese army, states that the diary was taken from a Cuban soldier killed in the failed attack on Bendera. The article goes on to say: "The diary, in Spanish, is said to describe how the owner and three other Cubans [soldiers] flew from Havana to Moscow and on to Dar-Es-Salaam and then crossed Tanzania to the Congo."[13]

The Cuban combatants had traveled from Havana to Dar Es-Salaam following different itineraries, making random stops along the way. There is no information available to indicate if Western intelligence services were aware of this troop transportation strategy. Whatever the Cubans did, it worked as intended. Once the troops arrived in Dar Es-Salaam, the arrangements to infiltrate the combatants into Congo were made by Pablo Rivalta, the Cuban Ambassador to Tanzania.

Larry Devlin was asked if the CIA was aware that there were Cuban soldiers in Congo before the diary of the dead Cuban soldier was read. Devlin's answer follows. "Yes the CIA was aware that there were Cuban soldiers in Congo several weeks before the [June 29, 1965] attack in Bendera. However, we were under the impression that there were only a handful of soldiers and we certainly did not know that Che Guevara was their commanding officer."[14]

There was a significant contingent of Cuban logistics personnel at Ujiji, Tanzania who assisted the Cuban combatants in crossing Lake Tanganyika. Ujiji was the location where Stanley had found Livingstone in 1871.

The defeat at Bendera was highly demoralizing for all rebels, but particularly for the Cubans. Many wanted to return to Cuba, including two of the three medical doctors. The soldiers wanting to return to Cuba asked for non-combat duties.

The ANC had career officers who had been schooled in discipline, training, and leadership under Belgian military officers. The ANC troops were generally well-trained militarily, although consciously or unconsciously most of them truly believed that the powers of the witch doctors could render the Simbas invincible. A turning point had been the battle for Bukavu on August 19, 1964 when ANC Colonel Mulamba, with the assistance of U.S. military officials, the CIA, and the Cuban exile Makasi, inflicted a crushing defeat on the Simba forces of Olenga. This victory was a significant morale booster for the ANC troops who saw that bullets did kill Simbas and witch doctors alike. At the same time the Simbas realized that they were vulnerable and started to have doubts about their leadership. Operation *Dragon Rouge*, the loss of Kisangani, and the fact that Gbenye, Soumialot, and Olenga ran away before bullets began flying provided the final message of defeat for the Simba rebels. The high level ANC officers were aware that they were fighting to prevent the installation of a communist regime in their country. The Simbas, in general terms, did not know who Marx and Lenin were, and moreover did not care.

New ambushes were set by the Cubans July 7 and 10, 1965. Although these were successful and provided a measure of much needed confidence, these ambushes further helped the CIA and Makasi pilots to pinpoint the Cubans' positions. There were other ambushes, but a very significant one was on the road from Kalemie to Bendera, on approximately July 22, 1965. In this carefully-planned and well-executed ambush, the rebels blew up an important bridge while several supply vehicles were crossing. The vehicles were then attacked and several of the newly arrived 5 Commando troops escorting the supply convoy were killed. The Cubans took the weapons and the Rwandans drank all the whiskey being transported, under the watchful eye of the Cubans who were not allowed to drink.[15]

By early August, the rebel factions were weakened by internal strife. Soumialot, the Defense Minister, fired Gbenye, who was the president. Kabila had communicated to Guevara that Soumialot did not have the authority to fire Gbenye. Massengo left for Kigoma to confer with Kabila.

In the middle of this political confusion, Guevara decided he wanted to be in the battlefront and on August 18, 1965 he joined Victor Dreke and his Rwandan fighters in the mountains near Bendera. After a few days, however, Guevara was convinced by his troops and bodyguards to return to La Base at Luluaburg Mountain.

The Cuban exile infantry group had returned to Miami during January/February 1965. Around August 1965, former Navy and Coast Guard

Cuban exiles were recruited and asked to crew two SWIFT boats, named *Monty* and *Gitana* to patrol Lake Tanganyika. According to Cuban exile Eulogio Reyes who served in SWIFT boat *Gitana*, their orders were to prevent rebel cadres from crossing the lake from Tanzania, prohibit transportation of weapons and supplies into Congo, attack rebel camps near the shore, and finally to rescue airmen from the lake.[16]

It did not take long for Guevara's Cubans to develop a great deal of fear and respect for the Cuban exile navy. This force of 16 men, operating out of Kalemie, was equipped with state of the art navigation and communication equipment. Considering that they were patrolling a stretch of lake covering an area with a length of 300 kilometers and an average width of 50 kilometers, this small but highly efficient navy made a meaningful contribution to the stability of Congo's government.

The original SWIFT boats were used as water taxis to serve the oil rigs in the Gulf of Mexico. These boats were manufactured by Sewart Seacraft of Berwick, Louisiana, and modified versions had already been used by the CIA for infiltrations against Castro's Cuba and were also being used by the U.S. Navy in Vietnam.

There were a total of sixteen Cuban exiles in this Congo navy: Ricardo Chávez, Serapio Cepero, Anael Alvarez, Roberto Cao, Jorge Arroyo, Justo (Papá) Salcedo, Félix Toledo, Remigio Arce, Generoso Bringas, Domingo Borges, Andrés Sánchez, Luis Fernández, Eulogio (Papo) Reyes, Pedro Ramírez and Gumersindo Hernández on lake patrol, plus Roberto Pichardo who was the radio/radar technician.

The SWIFT boats used for Lake Tanganyika were steel-hull, about 16 meters in length, had enough fuel for a 720-kilometer patrol, were designed for quiet operation and had a maximum speed of 25 knots. Armament consisted of three 50-caliber machine guns, one 30-caliber machine gun, and one 57-millimeter recoilless cannon, mounted on the rear deck. The parts required to fabricate the two SWIFT boats were flown to Kalemie in large crates.

Generoso Bringas recalls: "The SWIFT boats had been shipped disassembled in 3 sections plus the engines from Louisiana. Several Louisianans came along to assemble and test the boats. They were really nervous in the African jungle, and worked day and night at a frantic pace. It was not a matter of being dedicated workers or not, they just wanted to get the hell out of the African jungle as soon as possible."[17]

The Cuban exile Lake Tanganyika Patrol arrived in Kalemie in early September 1965, and they would soon join the battle against Guevara and the reluctant Congolese and Rwandan rebels. Eulogio Reyes "Papo" was one of the first navy Cuban exiles to arrive. "I came with the first group, because we were to help assemble the SWIFT boats. When the remaining 2 or 3 groups of men arrived, the boats were practically ready for testing. Commandant John Peters, from Mike Hoare's Fifth Commando took us out for the first time and showed us how to navigate in the treacherous waters of Lake Tanganyika. The rebels were so used to crossing the lake without opposition that during our first days of patrolling, we practically fought continuously. We were told that there were Cuban soldiers in the area, but when someone starts shooting at you, you don't ask to see their passport, you just shoot back. Scouting reports were rare. We occasionally obtained information from Makasi aircrafts flying out of Kalemie, but we mostly relied on radar for night navigation. We had good accommodations, were well fed and well treated and medical care was available. Near the end of our tour, I became ill. I got some sort of parasite which lodges in the liver, but I was hospitalized in Miami after our return and cured. I also remember the powerful storms in Lake Tanganyika. One day we saw this horrible black cloud heading in our direction. We did not know much about African animals, but we certainly knew what a tornado looked like. We went below deck and hoped for the best. It only lasted a few seconds, but when we came back out, the tornado had damaged the cabin, ripped out the cannon, the machine guns, and ammunition boxes. We were very lucky to have survived that tornado."[18]

Meanwhile, Hoare's contacts in Johannesburg and elsewhere were busy hiring mercenaries for action in the Great Lakes area. The recruits were primarily South Africans and Rhodesians. General Bobozo in Lumumbashi was training the recruits and arranging for their transportation to Kalemie. The newly constituted 5 Commando was ready for action by mid-August 1965. Likewise, the CIA had redoubled its efforts and had sent to Congo a team, which included several Cuban-American agents, with the mission of tracking down Che Guevara.

By mid-September, Hoare had a good idea of the location of the Cubans and other rebel camps and had developed his strategy. The operation was code-named *Banzi*, which was the pseudonym used by Mobutu during his short tenure as a journalist, and it was scheduled to commence on September 24, 1965. All arrangements were made by Hoare and his staff in complete secrecy.

Hoare described his plan of attack as follows. Lulimba would be attacked by land, starting from the ANC fort at Bendera. This was intended to be a diversionary attack prior to assaulting Baraka. Baraka, the rebel stronghold and a strategically important city, would be attacked by water by the Cuban exile navy, by air by the Cuban exile Makasi, and by land by himself and some 200 men. After capturing Baraka, the troops would then attack Fizi, followed by Lulimba, which would be attacked from both front and rear, thus encircling the enemy.[19]

By this time, the cities of Baraka, Fizi, and Lulimba had been in rebel hands for over a year, as in late June 1964 the rebels had gained control of the northwest shore of Lake Tanganyika. It was time for a change.

In order to execute his Baraka battle plan, Hoare secured the assistance of *Compagnie des Chemins de Fer du Congo Supérieur aux Grands Lacs Africaines* (CFL), the local railway and transportation organization. CFL would provide three ships capable of transporting an assault force of 200 men from Kalemie to Baraka. CFL would also convert a barge so it could carry 18 vehicles. Due to the abruptness of the coastline, Hoare selected a beach 8 kilometers north of Baraka as the landing spot.

Baraka is a beautiful city on the northwest shore of Lake Tanganyika. The city was defended by rebel Lieutenant Colonel Lambert and approximately 2,000 well-trained Congolese and Rwandan combatants. Predicting that an attack on Baraka was imminent, Lambert had asked Guevara for help to defend the city and Guevara obliged by sending Santiago Terry Rodríguez (*Aly*) and 35 Cuban soldiers. *Aly* was instructed by Guevara that he and the Cuban soldiers were to leave the city if it became clear the city would be lost to the enemy.

The Cuban exile Navy was given the job to weaken rebel forces at the beach selected by the 5 Commando for their landing. Félix Toledo described this battle. "Our job was to clear the beach prior to the landing of 5 Commando. Both *Monty* and *Gitana* participated in this ferocious battle. There were not too many places to land for an assault on Baraka, and we think that the enemy was expecting us. The enemy had installed a cannon, don't know what caliber, had several 50-caliber machine gun nests, and a couple of mortars. The rest of their fire power was light weapons which could not reach us. The battle started at sunrise. I distinctly remember there was a long warehouse parallel to the beach. We began making passes in front of the beach, shooting with all our weapons. Sometimes we reversed our direction to confuse the enemy. These were not Simbas. They were well trained military men, accurate in their shooting, and they wasted no ammunition. There was a mother ship anchored at a safe distance and we returned to her to replenish our ammunition. At one point, I noticed bullets hitting some 20 meters in front of our boat, and I thought the enemy had planes. Then I asked the machine gunner on the upper part of the stern to stop shooting for a moment and then start again. The bullets were coming from his machine gun. The grooves inside the barrel were completely worn and the barrel had apparently overheated. We rushed to the mother ship and obtained a new 50-caliber machine gun which we quickly mounted in place. When we finished our job at sundown, the entire peninsula was on fire, and the warehouse had been literally cut in half."[20]

The initial landing was under the command of John Peters and Hugh van Oppens, and took place at first light on September 24, 1965. The force departed from Kalemie, but Hoare was careful to leak a battle plan for a target in the opposite direction, just in case the rebels had spies in the area.

The diversionary attack on Lulimba was carried out by Lieutenant Alastair and around 100 men. Their orders were to keep the enemy busy for as long as possible. This diversionary attack did not go well, as Alastair's forces met strong resistance and had to withdraw. Hoare ordered these troops to join him in Baraka.

The battle for Baraka was directed by Hoare and Congolese General Bobozo. Even after the 12-hour pounding by the Cuban exile navy, the enemy had regrouped, fighting was fierce, and Hoare lost four men from the first landing. Hoare estimated that 2,000 defenders met them at the beach with heavy machine guns and 76-millimeter cannon fire. The battle lasted for five long days. On the second day, Hoare requested the support of Makasi from their base in Kalemie. Thirty minutes later, six T-28s began to strafe the enemy. Hoare describes the action: "... the [anti-Castro] Cubans put on a show of aerobatics to beat any flying display, their white wings flashing in the sunlight. An aggressive spirit now surged through the men and fighting patrols went out, intent on avenging the death of our four men."[21]

According to Hoare, the defense of Baraka, at least for the first four days, was led and organized by Cubans. "The enemy were [sic] very different from anything we had ever met before. [The Simbas] were obviously being led by trained officers. We intercepted wireless messages in Spanish ... it seemed clear that the defense of Baraka was being organized by the Cubans."[22] On the fifth day, however, the pattern changed and the rebels attacked Simba-style. This likely meant that the Cubans, following Guevara's orders, had left the city.

A quite different version of the battle for Baraka is offered by Cuban military historian William Gálvez, as he affirms: "When Hoare took Baraka on September 30, 1965 there was no resistance and there were no Cubans defending the city."[23]

On September 28, 1965, Victor Dreke (*Moja*) sent a report to Guevara in which he stated that there was an increase in enemy activity in the mountains near Bendera. Air attacks and patrols were on the rise. Martínez Tamayo (*M'bili*) reported on the following day that many of his men were sick. Martínez Tamayo, following Guevara's orders, had taken 14 men to the Lugoma area to set up ambushes. Guevara learned via a radio broadcast from Kinshasa that the offensive was being commanded by Mad Mike Hoare with 2,400 men and that the city of Baraka had fallen. Over the next few weeks, Baraka would change hands several times.

Based on the available Cuban publications, it appears that the Cuban officer who best understood Hoare's overall strategy was Victor Dreke. Sometime in late September, early October, when referring to enemy troop movements, Dreke stated: "We thought they [the enemy] were trying to close the lake ... then I realized they were pushing us into the lake to force us to get the hell out."[24]

Even though Guevara respected the beliefs of his Congolese and Rwandan fighters, he viewed the *mugangas* as a destabilizing influence on the troops. On one occasion, Che, wanting an additional able-body fighter, tried to convince a newly arrived *muganga* to accompany the troops to an ambush where the wait was expected to take several days. Che's argument was that the *dawa* could lose its effect over time. The obviously intelligent *muganga*, not wanting to be too close to where bullets would fly, retorted that he would do a time-release *dawa*, which would last for two weeks. Che, clearly outwitted by the young African, had to accept the *muganga's* logic.[25]

Hoare had seen evidence of the Cuban troops' genius as guerrilla fighters, and he knew that it would be difficult to defeat the Cubans at their game. Therefore, by staying on the offensive, he intended to force Guevara's troops to fight in a conventional style. Hoare and the Cuban exiles would prove that they were better conventional warriors than the Cubans.

The war campaign was not the only area creating problems for Guevara, for the political front was also in turmoil. Gaston Soumialot had visited Havana during the late August, early September 1965 time frame, and had made statements to Castro, which created concerns in the mind of the Cuban dictator, as they differed from Guevara's reports.

During his trip to Havana, Soumialot complained during a press conference that anti-Castro Cubans were fighting against his troops in Congo: "At Congo (Léopoldville), fighting against us in increasing numbers, there are Cuban counter-revolutionaries. There are pilots and others are in the infantry and other sectors of Tshombé's army."[26]

As a result, Castro sent a number of high level Cuban officials to corroborate Guevara's assertions. The first wave of auditors consisted of: Aldo Margolles, Óscar Fernández Mell (President of the Cuban Medical Society), Emilio Aragonés (member of the Central Committee of the Communist Party), Victor Shueg Colás (who later became a General in Castro's army), José Palacio (appointed by Castro to conduct and refresh political indoctrination of Cuban forces on Congo duty), and various physicians. At least this first group decided to stay and join in the fighting. The selection of some of the *noms de guerre* of these VIPs indicates that Cubans never lose their sense of humor. Fernández Mell, because of his perennial foul mood was named *Siki*, Swahili for Vinegar and Emilio Aragonés was named *Tembo*, Swahili for Elephant because he was tall and heavy set. The remaining new combatants were given random Swahili names.

Around October 1, 1965, a second group of inspectors arrived, headed by Dr. José Ramón Machado Ventura, Cuba's Health Minister.

After Guevara had arrived back in Cuba from his African speaking tour in mid-March 1965, and before his departure for Congo, Guevara had supposedly authored a letter exculpating Fidel Castro and the Cuban government from his actions in international revolutionary activities.[27] There are many theories on this letter, including one that says that Castro wrote it and Guevara never signed it.

In keeping with the secrecy of the Congo operation, Castro kept Guevara's letter in a secure place. In this letter, Guevara resigned all duties to the Cuban revolution, his army commission, and his Cuban citizenship. Just to make sure his letter was not misunderstood, he stated "Nothing legal ties me to Cuba," adding "Cuba is not responsible for my actions." This letter has never been seen by anyone but Castro, who still supposedly keeps it in a safe place.

In his revealing book,[28] Benigno claims that there was an agreement between Fidel Castro and Che Guevara that this letter would not be made public unless an international crisis created by Guevara's presence in Congo had to be alleviated, or Guevara was killed. Yet Castro read the letter to a large audience on October 3, 1965, while Guevara was alive and fighting in Congo and with no international crisis in view.

Volumes have been written, and volumes will continue to be written, about this letter. Some historians have attempted to read Guevara's mind, others claim that Guevara neither wrote nor signed this letter, while others have concluded that this letter represents a disclosure of Che's exile. An English translation of Guevara's letter to Castro follows.

Year of the Agriculture

Havana

Fidel:

At this time, I remember many things, when I met you at María Antonia's home, when you suggested that I come [to Cuba] and all the tension [associated with] the preparations.

One day they came by asking who should be notified in the event of my death and the reality of this possibility hit us all. Afterwards, we learned that this is true, that in a revolution, in the true sense of the word, one either triumphs or dies. Many comrades were lost on the way to victory.

Today, everything has a less dramatic tone because we are more mature, but history repeats itself. I feel that I have fulfilled my duty to the Cuban Revolution in its territory, and I [therefore] bid farewell to you, our comrades, and [the Cuban] people who are already [also] my people.

I am formally resigning my duties in the Directorate of the Party, my post as Minister, my rank of Comandante, and my Cuban citizenship. Nothing legal ties me to Cuba, only nexuses of the kind which cannot be broken [in the same manner] as appointments.

Making an inventory of my past life, I believe that I have worked with sufficient honesty and dedication to consolidate the revolutionary victory. My only mistake of any seriousness was not to have trusted you more from the first moments in [the mountains of] Sierra Maestra and not to have understood with sufficient clarity your leadership and revolutionary qualities. I have lived magnificent days and I have felt by your side the pride of belonging to our people in the shining and [also] sad days of the Caribbean Crisis.

Few times has a statesman shone more brightly than in those days. I am also proud to have followed you without vacillation, identified with your way of thinking and to see and appreciate the dangers and the principles.

Other nations of the world claim for my modest help. I can do what is denied [to you] for your responsibility in Cuba and the time has come for us to say good bye.

Let it be known that I do this with a mixture of happiness and grief: here I leave the purest of my hopes as a builder and the most dear of my loved ones and I leave a people that admitted me as a son; that lacerates a piece of my spirit. In the new battlefields I will carry the faith I learned from you, the revolutionary spirit of my people, and the knowledge that I am complying with the most sacred of duties: to fight against imperialism wherever it may be; this comforts and heals thoroughly any wound.

I say once again that I liberate Cuba from any responsibility, except the one resulting from its example. If my final hour arrives under different skies, my last thoughts will be for the [Cuban] people and in particular for you. I give you thanks for your teachings and your example, to which I will try to be faithful until the last consequence of my acts. I have always been a part of the foreign policy of our Revolution and I am continuing to be so. Anywhere I stop I will feel the responsibility of being a Cuban revolutionary, and I will act accordingly. I leave no material things to my children and wife and I am not sorry to say so: [in fact] I am proud that this is the case. I ask nothing for them since the State will give them enough to live and be educated.

I would have many things to say to you and to our people, but I believe that this is not necessary, for words cannot express what I would like [to say], and it is best not to scribble on too much paper.

Until victory always! Fatherland or death!

I embrace you with all revolutionary dedication,

Che

Guevara's reference to the Caribbean Crisis likely pertains to the Cuban Missile Crisis.

The Cuban Popular Socialist Party had been dissolved and replaced with the Cuban Communist Party, and its first meeting was on October 3, 1965. Reading Guevara's good-bye letter at that gathering may have been Castro's chosen way to justify to the Cuban people the reasons why the highly-regarded *Comandante* Guevara was not appointed to the Party Central Committee. Perhaps more important than the letter itself and the fact that it was read by Castro to such a large audience and ostensibly without consulting with Guevara, was what Castro said after reading the letter. Castro, in an attempt to explain Guevara's absence from the newly constituted Central Committee of the Cuban Communist Party said: "If we ask ourselves who is missing, there is no doubt about the fact they are indeed missing. It would be impossible to constitute a Central Committee of 100 revolutionary comrades without many comrades missing. The important fact is not the ones that are missing…; what is [really] important are the ones that are here, and what is represented by the ones that are here."[29]

Castro's message was clear: Guevara was no longer a part of the Cuban government. What prompted Castro to make Che's letter public at that moment is a very important yet unanswered question. Guevara was so embarrassed by the publication of his letter that he initially refused to return to Cuba after his defeat in Congo.

La Base had a short-wave radio transmitter, so it can be assumed that Guevara learned of Castro's betrayal of his trust shortly after the infamous letter was read. Considering the time difference between Havana and eastern Congo, perhaps Guevara knew on the morning of October 4, 1965.

On October 5, 1965, Che Guevara arranged a meeting of all unit commanders of Congolese, Rwandan, and Cuban rebel groups fighting in the Fizi-Baraka geographic area. The meeting took place at a hill between Fizi and Baraka. The consensus of the group was that they were running out of places from which to carry out ambushes. Due to the superiority of enemy forces, they were approaching the point of either having to run and hide or engage in conventional warfare. They decided to stay and fight. As a result of the October 5, 1965 meeting, Che wrote a letter to Castro that because of its importance has been translated into English and follows in full. There was no reply from Castro.

This letter[30] was written on approximately October 6, 1965 after Guevara's meeting with the rebel bosses on the previous day. Che's mood is desperate, and reading between the lines it appears that Guevara is considering disobeying Castro's orders and fighting the war his own way.

The reader must be impacted by the unusually harsh tone in a message addressed to Castro. The fact that the Congo campaign is not going well does not solely justify writing to the Commander-in-Chief in such terms.

Perhaps the bitter tone of this October 6, 1965 letter from Guevara to Castro can be explained as Guevara expressing his anger for Castro having made his letter public to the world on October 3, 1965. The truth may never be known.

Clarifications on points made by Guevara follow after the letter.

Guevara used the notation (...), and it has been deleted in the translation. Words or phrases in brackets have been added to improve the readability of the English translation. Parentheses originally provided by Guevara have been retained in the translation.

Dear Fidel:

I received your letter which provoked me to have contradictory feelings, since in the name of [the] international proletariat we commit errors which can be quite costly. Besides, I am personally preoccupied that either because of my lack of seriousness when writing, or perhaps because you do not totally understand, it could be thought that I am suffering from the terrible disease of pessimism without cause.

When your *Greek gift* (Aragonés) arrived, he told me that one of my letters had provoked the sensation [that I was] a condemned gladiator, and the [Health] Minister (Machadito) when communicating your optimistic message, confirmed the opinion that you have made. With the bearer you will be able to converse at length and [he] will give you his first hand experiences, for he traveled a good portion of the [battle] front; I am, therefore suppressing the anecdotes. I will only tell you that here, in accordance to the people familiar with the situation I have lost my reputation of objectivity. I have maintained optimism without foundation, when faced with the existing reality. I can [further] assure you that if it were not because of me, this beautiful dream would be totally disintegrated in the midst of a general catastrophe.

In my prior letters, I have asked you not to send too many people, but rather well-trained team players, and I also said that here we practically have no need for weapons, with the exception of some of a specialized nature. We have too many armed men and not enough soldiers. I also gave you a special warning not to hand out money, except with a medicine dropper, and after many petitions. None of my warnings have been taken into account and fantastic plans have been elaborated that put us in danger of international ridicule and could place me in a very difficult situation.

I will proceed to explain [to you]:

Soumialot and his buddies have sold you a large street car. It would be pointless to enumerate the great number of lies they told; it is better to explain the real situation with the enclosed map. There are two zones where it can be said that there is some sort of an organized revolution, this one where we are, and in a portion of Kasai Province, where Mulele is located and that is the great unknown. In the rest of the country, all there is are disconnected bands that survive in the jungle; they lost everything without a fight, as they lost Stanleyville without a fight. I know Kabila well enough so I can have no illusions [about him], but I cannot say the same about Soumialot, but I have some antecedents such as the string of lies they adorn themselves with, and the fact that he does not have the decency to come by these God damned lands. With regard to the necessity to select well the men and not to send to me [just] quantity, you assure me with the messenger that the ones here are good; I am sure that the majority are good, otherwise they would have quit long time ago. That is not the point, you do have to have a well-tempered spirit to put up with what happens here; it is not a matter of good men, what we need here are super-humans.

And then there are my 200 men; believe me that these people would be a hindrance at this moment, unless we definitely decide that we are going to fight on our own, in which case we would need a division and we would have to see with how many [divisions] the enemy will bring [into battle]. Perhaps my last statement is an exaggeration and we need a battalion to recover the territory we had when we arrived and to be a menace to Albertville, but the number is not important in this case, we cannot alone liberate a country which does not want to fight. We have to create this fighting spirit and search for the soldiers with Diogenes lantern and Job's patience, a task which becomes even more difficult as these [Congolese] people find additional idiots to do their work for them.

The subject of the boats is a different kettle of fish. It has been for a long time that I have been asking for two [marine] engine technicians to prevent the Kigoma landing from becoming a [boat] graveyard. Three brand-new Soviet boats arrived a bit more than a month ago and two are already useless, and the third, in which the messenger crossed, takes water from all sides. The three Italian boats will follow the same path as the prior ones, unless they have Cuban crews. For this subject and the one of the artillery we only need Tanzania's acquiescence, which will not be obtained so easily. These countries are not [like] Cuba that will play all [of its money] on one card, regardless of how large it may be.

What pains me the most is the matter of money, for I gave you repeated warnings. It is the utmost of my audacity as scatterbrain that after much crying I had committed to supply a new front, the most important one, with the proviso that I would direct the operations and that a special mixed unit would be formed under my direct command; for this, I calculated, with pain on my soul, $5,000 per month. Now I find out that a sum twenty times bigger is handed out to any passerby, with only one [of those payments] one could live well in any capital [city] of the world. To a miserable [battle] front, where the peasants suffer all imaginable misery, including the rapaciousness of its own defenders, not one cent of that money will arrive, neither to the poor devils who are trapped in Sudan.

With the 50 physicians in the liberated zone, Congo will count with the enviable position of one per 1,000 inhabitants. Better than this exaggeration, why not send a group of revolutionary doctors.

A few recommendations which I pray you will take into account in an objective manner: forget about all men in an executive position and all the ghost organizations, and arrange for ten well-trained team players, and it is not necessary that they all be black, and from Osmany's list choose whoever you want. Regarding weapons, [please send] the new bazooka, electric fuses, a little R4 [explosive] and nothing else for now. No mortars, for we have too many, forget the Burundi matter and treat with much tact the subject of the boats (do not forget that Tanzania is an independent country and we must play cleanly there, forgetting about the small indiscretion which I committed).

And I say good bye to you with an embrace.

Che

Guevara refers to Fidel's letter brought by Health Minister Machado, where Castro discussed Soumialot's request for fifty Cuban medical doctors for the Congolese battlefront.

Guevara speaks of Emilio Aragonés (Tembo) who had recently joined the ill-fated Congo adventure. It is common knowledge that Aragonés and Guevara argued bitterly in Congo. The expression *Greek gift* is more difficult to decipher, as there are at least two obvious explanations. One possibility is that Guevara considers Aragonés a Trojan horse, which was a present of the Greeks and finally allowed the destruction of Troy. The other alternative is that he refers to a strategy in chess called *Greek gift*, where one player sacrifices pieces of lesser value while setting up for the kill. In either event, the expression does not speak well of either Aragonés or Fidel Castro.

Guevara's letter was to be hand-delivered to Castro. The only person who left the camp during the following days and was traveling to Cuba was Machado, the Health Minister, but it cannot be stated with certainty that he was the messenger. It may be acceptable to refer to a child or teenager named Machado as Machadito, but when speaking of a Minister, it should be considered an insult.

Guevara's reference to a street car is an Argentine expression, probably equivalent to the Spanish expression "to sell a motorcycle," which is closely related to the American expression "to sell the Brooklyn Bridge." Che's opinion was that Soumialot was a frequent liar and exaggerator.

It is surprising that Guevara stated that Stanleyville (Kisangani) was lost without a fight. The rescue operation involved ferocious fighting. Thousands were killed. It can only be surmised that Guevara speaks of the leaders rather than the soldiers, as Gbenye, Soumialot, and Olenga had abandoned Kisangani when the rescue operation appeared imminent. Guevara's reputation was that of speaking the truth rather than distorting facts to make a point.

Guevara's reference to "these people" pertains to the 50 Cuban physicians Soumialot had requested for the various battle fronts in Congo; Guevara was obviously opposed to this idea.

Guevara specifically mentions the city of Albertville (Kalemie), indicating that he would need several divisions to become a threat to Hoare's HQ, which was located in this city.

In the Spanish original, instead of idiot, Guevara uses the Cuban term *comemierda*, which literally means "those who eat excrements," but in Cuban dialect it means unintelligent or stupid people.

Guevara speaks of *Comandante* Osmany Cienfuegos, a man trusted by Castro, who had visited Congo in May.

It appears that Guevara was frustrated about everything. The subject of the number of men assigned to him particularly bothered him, as Guevara knew that there were Cuban training and logistics units located in Sudan, Tanzania, and Uganda, which could have been ordered to Congo to reinforce the embattled Cuban contingent. There is little or no information available on the numbers of Cuban soldiers in Africa at that time. It can safely be estimated that there were at least 2,500 Cubans stationed within a one-day journey to the Tanzanian side of Lake Tanganyika. Guevara was well-aware that a column of approximately 200 Cubans under the command of Jorge Risquet was in Congo (Brazzaville). Had the Congo campaign been successful, this column was intended to replace Che's column. It is possible that as a result of his letter to Castro, Guevara was hoping to get Risquet's column to reinforce his. There is no logical explanation as to why Castro did not provide help to the embattled Guevara. Castro did not build his reputation as a winner by engaging in losing ventures.

Meanwhile 5 Commando, after securing the perimeter around Baraka, continued executing Hoare's strategy and commenced clearing the road to Fizi around October 5, 1965. Coincidentally, the meeting that Che and the rebel group leaders were having on that day was quite close to where Hoare's forces were at the time. Surprisingly, they did not meet.

With Baraka secured, Hoare's forces and the ANC troops moved south and took Tembili, after Makasi softened the target. They then continued, almost undisturbed, into Fizi, which was defended by some 400 Congolese rebels and approximately 10 Cuban combatants under the command of Oscar Fernández Mell (*Siki*). Fizi was taken on October 10, 1965.

After air reconnaissance, and based on ongoing reports of attacks on Makasi aircraft, Hoare correctly concluded that the main Cuban camp had to be in the mountains immediately west of the Yungu-Kibamba area. Hoare then arranged for the ANC battalion at Bendera to move in the direction of the lake and capture the port city of Yungu. Hoare predicted that all the Cuban soldiers would move either to Kibamba to protect their retreat into Tanzania or to Luluaburg Mountain to protect Guevara. Thus, the enemy would be trapped in an ever decreasing semi-circle with its center on Kibamba-Yungu, and its radius initially extending to the Cuban camp at Lulimba. Hoare further assumed that the Cubans might move into the mountains to continue their fight as guerrillas. In fact, Guevara did entertain this idea.

After losing Fizi, the surviving Cubans joined Guevara at La Base at Luluaburg Mountain. Hoare did not follow as he had become familiar with Guevara's ambush tactics. For some time, Guevara had felt safe at either his low or high Luluaburg Mountain fortress. He was aware that the high camp HQ was at a location, which could only be attacked by troops having to cross 3,000 meter mountains (if coming from the west), or by ground troops by way of Lake Tanganyika. But he knew that Hoare would now have the advantage of taking the initiative, as the rebels could only defend themselves.

Hoare left a small contingent of soldiers to defend Fizi and moved on and took Lubondja on October 12, 1965. Guevara was aware of Hoare's troop movements, for Victor Dreke recalls that Che said: "... now the enemy could merge their forces in Lulimba with those that landed in Baraka."[31]

The political front took center stage on October 13, 1965. General Bobozo flew into Fizi and informed Hoare's garrison that President Kasavubu had dismissed Prime Minister Tshombé. In his book *Congo Mercenary*, Hoare states: "The news ran like wildfire through the Commandos with much speculation as to our future."[32]

The Cubans were startled when they learned the political news on the radio, also on October 13, 1965. Kasavubu had terminated Tshombé's mandate and named Évariste Kimba as Prime Minister designate. Army Chief Mobutu issued a radio proclamation promising amnesty to all rebels that surrendered their weapons. He further asked the Congolese not to listen to the Chinese or Cubans, for as he explained, they were there only to steal the riches of Congo.[33] The ouster of Tshombé was a highly significant event, for the rebels had received the support of African nations for the specific purpose of replacing Tshombé. It is likely that at this point, Castro had already received messages from the Organization for African Unity stating that the Cuban troops had to be removed from Congo.

After the USSR became convinced that the military option in Congo was essentially defeated, they joined the cease-fire negotiations. One of the conditions imposed by the OAU was that all foreign troops must abandon Congo. A cease fire was far from Guevara's mind. He was not prepared to accept defeat for many reasons, one of which was that he had no place to go, as he had been officially removed from the Cuban hierarchy on October 3, 1965.

Che Guevara understood warfare tactics as well as the terrain in which they were operating. He knew that if fighting were to continue, they must retake and make secure some territory in the Fizi-Baraka geographic area from where they could continue to replenish provisions, weapons, and army personnel across Lake Tanganyika. Under the best conditions, they would continue to be in a difficult situation as the lake was under the close surveillance of the Cuban exile SWIFT boat patrols as well as Makasi aircrafts. Guevara regrouped his forces into three units. One unit, commanded by Victor Dreke (*Moja*), would stay with Guevara at the low camp near Kilonwe (around 6 kilometers from what Guevara considered the Cuban port of Kibamba). The second unit under Martínez Tamayo (*M'bili*) would dig foxholes and emplace machine guns at Kibamba. This second unit would prepare the getaway. The third unit, commanded by Santiago Terry (*Aly*), would try to retake Baraka and in general establish a presence in the northern lakeshore.

Even if it meant hiding for a while, or fighting a stronger foe, Guevara needed to buy time for some 3,000 Congolese rebels to complete their training by Cubans at the nearby Tanzanian lakeshore city of Ujiji. It was estimated that this group would not be ready to fight for a few months. There was another very good reason for continuing to fight: Fidel Castro's Central Africa strategy, which included taking over Katanga Province using the Fizi-Baraka geographic area as the launching zone. The plan would then have Katanga establishing a federated revolutionary state together with Tanzania, followed by Castro attacking Angola. Surprisingly, Guevara had decided to obey Castro's original intent even after the good-bye letter incident.

The political front took over on October 23, 1965, at the summit of African Heads of State in Accra, Ghana. President Nkrumah had great plans for the event, but the French-speaking countries decided to boycott the gathering, as they were not running the show. Then, Congolese President Kasavubu delivered a bombshell when he decided to blame all the ills of Congo on Tshombé, whom he had just removed from office. Kasavubu called for renewed diplomatic relations with the leftist government of Congo (Brazzaville) and an end to the white mercenaries brought in by Tshombé. Mobutu was furious, for the employment of mercenaries was a military decision, and he was the Commander in Chief of the Congolese military. Opening the river traffic, with left-leaning Brazzaville, would pave the way for communist infiltrators to enter Congo. Mobutu ordered Kasavubu to retract his statements, but instead Kasavubu asked Prime Minister-designate Kimba to do his dirty work. After a half hearted retraction by Kimba over Radio Kinshasa, Mobutu seemed ready to stage his second *coup d'etat*.

Now that Hoare knew the location of the Cuban camps, it was only a matter of time before he would attack. On October 24, 1965, exactly six months after Guevara's arrival in Congo, the Argentinian revolutionary came close to meeting his death. During the early afternoon, the Luluaburg Mountain lower base was attacked by Hoare's mercenaries and ANC troops from the Lulimba barracks, under the command of John Peters.

Victor Dreke (*Moja*) described the action: "It was one-thirty or two in the afternoon, I had gone to the toilet, and suddenly I hear a barrage of bullets in the direction where Che was reading a few minutes ago ... I see Che and *M'bili* shooting and backing away ... Che was shooting standing up and some fellow Cubans, trying to protect him, told him to lay down, he became angry and said: 'There is only one *Comandante* here!' ... The Congolese disappeared to the hut of the muganga to do the dawa ... Che gave the order to retreat, but a group of four Cubans did not hear and kept on fighting ... they saved us.... Che almost got killed that day."[34] On that day, the Cubans had one soldier, Orlando Puente Mayeta (*Bahasa*) killed. On the material side, they lost a significant amount of weapons and ammunition, and most importantly, their long-range radio transmitter.

Approximately 90 kilometers north of La Base, a large contingent of Congolese rebels, commanded by Santiago Terry Rodríguez (*Aly*), retook Baraka around October 30, 1965. They met little resistance, as Hoare and his troops had continued in the direction of Fizi, leaving only a small number of soldiers behind to protect the city. Baraka was again in rebel hands, now defended by about 2,000 Congolese rebel soldiers and some 45 Cubans. Hoare ordered an immediate counterattack, and his 5 Commando units were able to secure a perimeter around the city. Fighting was fierce, but Hoare's 5 Commando forces slowly took the city, one block at a time. In spite of the continued support provided by the Cuban exile Makasi pilots, the tenacious resistance offered by the Cubans made the battle difficult. It took three days of fierce fighting and the loss of hundreds of lives on both sides.

At the same time, some 80 kilometers south of Baraka, Cubans under the leadership of Oscar Fernández Mell (*Siki*) and Emilio Aragonés (*Tembo*) were defending the port of Yungu (by the lake front village of Kibamba) with tooth and nail, since it was through this port that they were receiving weapons and munitions. The Cuban exile manned SWIFT boats, utilizing their 57 mm recoilless cannons, destroyed the machine gun nests on the lake shore, thus allowing Hoare's ground forces to gain control of Yungu. Casualties were heavy on both sides. Cubans retreated to their original port of entry of Kibamba, from where they could either escape across the lake to Tanzania, or make a run for their mountain hideout and continue their fighting later.

By the end of October, Cuban combatants were demoralized and a large percentage wanted to quit. Medic Rafael Zerquera (*Kumi*) summarized the feelings of his fellow countrymen: "We want to fight elsewhere, perhaps Vietnam or Peru ... we are no cowards, but the majority of Congolese are not interested in the liberation of Congo."[35]

On November 1, 1965, a messenger from Pablo Rivalta, Cuban Ambassador to Tanzania, delivered a dispatch to Guevara that basically said that with Tshombé no longer in power, it was time to abandon the fight.

Guevara knew that he had lost the important territory, which was necessary to implement the following phases of Castro's Central Africa strategy; nevertheless, he wanted to continue fighting. On November 4, 1965, Che reported that the mercenaries were very active and assumed they were planning the final assault on his command HQ.

Guevara's men did not want to continue fighting. On November 9, 1965, Martínez Tamayo (*M'bili*), now in the Lubondja area, reported that most of the Cubans under his command wanted to return to Cuba. Lubondja is located around 20 kilometers west of the lakeshore, and about halfway from Kibamba to Fizi.

With the mountain area west of the Fort Bendera area now under ANC and mercenary control, all Rwandans under *Moja's* command had been forced to evacuate the area to the safety of La Base area. The Rwandans announced they wanted to quit. To further complicate matters, the rebel area of Nganja was being attacked daily, but the Cubans had to defend it, for they kept cattle there. Without Nganja, they could not eat, as this was their last source of food. The Cuban exile navy had significantly slowed down the flow of supplies via Lake Tanganyika.

The ANC was emboldened by their recent victories, as well as by the massive desertions of both Congolese and Rwandans on the rebel ranks. It did not take long for many of the deserters to provide information to the ANC and Hoare's troops, probably in an effort to save their skin. After this information was analyzed, government troops possessed detailed and accurate information on the location of rebel camps, number of men at each camp, and the weapons at their disposal. An entry in Guevara's diary summarizes the situation: "On Wednesday, November 10, 1965, planes were seen in the entire region.... The enemy was marching in the direction of all guerrilla fronts, guided by local farmers."[36]

There is enough information in various books published in Cuba to be able to reconstruct the location of Cuban forces on or around November 10, 1965. *M'bili* with twelve Cubans and an unknown number of Rwandans were on the road from Nganja to the lake. Ramón Armas (*Azima*) plus nine Cubans and sixteen Congolese were protecting the road from Nganja to La Base. *Moja* with around thirty Cubans and an unknown number of Rwandans were defending the lake from Kazima (north of Kibamba), while *Aly* with thirty-five Cubans were defending the lake north of Kabimba. Guevara (*Tatu*) plus the rest of the Cubans, Congolese, and Rwandans were based at the low camp.

Guevara, who boasted to have written the textbook on guerrilla warfare, surely knew that without the support of local farmers, waging unconventional warfare is impossible.

By mid-November the situation of the Cubans became untenable. They commenced destroying all documents and weapons that they would not be able to carry, and started to retreat in the direction of the lake. Che sent a message to Chinese Premier Chou En-Lai who, in his reply, suggested not to quit, but to try instead to join Mulele in the Kwilu River area. Guevara knew of no other way to take his men to join Mulele other than to walk there, and he estimated the distance to be more than 1,000 kilometers. Additionally, he did not know how to contact Mulele.

Guevara's situation provides an excellent example of the philosophical differences between the USSR and the PRC that caused the Sino-Soviet split. The USSR, seeing that the battle was lost, was prepared to abandon ship and negotiate. The PRC, on the other hand, wanted to continue fighting. Even though much of the information on the Congo war has now been declassified by Washington and Moscow, little is known about the PRC's involvement. It is suspected that in addition to weapons, significant advisory personnel were provided from their newly opened (1964) embassy in Bujumbura, Kingdom of Burundi. The Chinese had targeted five sub-Saharan countries, and have continued in their quest to install Communist governments in these countries.

Massengo, who was now traveling with the Cubans, convinced Guevara that they must stop fighting for the time being. A message by Guevara to his Tanzanian logistics officers asked for transportation across the lake stating: "Total men to evacuate less than 200, will be more difficult each day that passes."[37]

The Cubans, aware that retreat was imminent, on November 12, 1965 mined a lane on Lake Tanganyika in order to slow down the Cuban exile

SWIFT boats and facilitate their evacuation. Guevara and his men arrived at the lake on November 20, 1965, and decided to sail the next day at 02:10, the idea being that they would be beyond the lake's mid-point (and in Tanzanian territory) at daylight.

The evacuation of Guevara and the Cuban combatants was to be handled by Captain Roberto Sánchez Bartelemy (*Changa*), but also known alternatively as Lawton or The Admiral of the Lake. His job throughout the Congo operation had been to shuttle supplies across the lake, working with their logistics personnel in Tanzania. His new assignment was to provide the boats and attempt to get the men back to Tanzania safely.

The evacuation plan, according to Cuban sources, was based on three boats. The VIPs, Oscar Fernández Mell (*Siki*), Ernesto Che Guevara (*Tatu*), and Emilio Aragonés (*Tembo)* would be in Boat 1. Boat 2 would be under the command of *Aly*, while the skipper of Boat 3 would be *Moja*. If the group should come under attack, Boats 2 and 3 would face the enemy, thus allowing Boat 1 to continue for the safety of Tanzania.

Although Cuban publications always indicate that there were three boats, U.S. and Cuban exile versions claim that there were either four or five boats.

Guevara and the surviving Cubans started to cross Lake Tanganyika in heavily armed boats. The Cubans had installed 75 mm cannons on the stern of each boat and 50-caliber machine guns on the prow. As planned, they departed from a point 10 to 15 kilometers south of Kibamba, at 03:00 on November 21, 1965. Contrary to Cuban publications, evidence indicates that a naval battle between Cuban and the Cuban exile navy took place shortly after the departure of the Cuban troops.

The action that follows is described by Cuban exile navy veteran Félix Toledo. "We had been warned that a radio communication had been intercepted and there could be some action that night. Before we talk about the battle, I must explain two things. The day before, SWIFT boat *Gitana*, while in port, came under mortar attack. Our boats were diesel-powered, and as such required that the engines be warmed up for about 4 or 5 minutes. When you see mortar shells hitting near you, you don't think much about the safety of the engines. Therefore, the crew of *Gitana* sped away from the port, out of the reach of the shore mortars. The engines were damaged and it took several days to carry out the repairs. On that night, SWIFT boat *Monty* was alone. I must also explain that in Lake Tanganyika, perhaps because of the way trees and plants are dragged by the rivers before flowing into the lake, floating islands are formed which move quite fast with the lake's currents. On many occasions, we approached what we thought was a boat, only to find out it was a large clump of plants and branches. The way we checked this out was to idle our engines and watch the islands. If they were stationary, or moving slowly with the lake current, we did not worry. That particular night, there were five islands, and when we idled our engines, we saw that the islands were moving around one another. It was clearly the enemy and we decided to attack. Four boats came in our direction, while one moved out of the way. A shooting battle ensued. Our boats' fixed firing power was concentrated in the stern, two 50-caliber machine guns, plus the 57 millimeter recoilless cannon on the cabin. On the prow, we had another 50-caliber machine gun, and we had an additional 30-caliber machine gun which we moved around. I am very lucky to be alive. During battle, I normally took the 30-caliber machine gun to the prow and laid flat on the deck, at the feet of the 50-caliber gunner. At a certain moment during the battle, our skipper, Ricardo Chávez told me to get the 30-caliber machine gun and get to the stern as quickly as possible. I moved, and within seconds, the boat that had moved out of the way made a pass in front of our prow and a bullet hit the gunner, Justo Salcedo, in the foot, almost exactly where my head was seconds before. Salcedo was bleeding badly, and we could not stop the bleeding. We were afraid that without medical attention, he would have died. We did the prudent thing and returned to Albertville. We don't know who those people were, but they were experienced and well trained soldiers. I believe we sank one of their boats, perhaps two, but I have no way to know for sure."[38]

Cuban publications offer a radically different version of the lake crossing. According to Cuban publications, there were no enemy boats, nor were they challenged while crossing the lake. Cubans further claim that the CIA aviation escorted them to the Tanzanian shore and that they suffered no loss of lives in their exodus.[39]

The interviewed Makasi pilots confirm that they manned the only aircrafts in the region, and that they never patrolled at night. If they would have known that Guevara was in one of those boats, they would have gone out patrolling that night and opened up with any weapon available to them, continuing for as long as they had bullets. This sentiment was expressed by each Makasi pilot interviewed. Jorge Navarro, with his typical Cuban sense of humor added: "I have a bridge for a missing tooth. Had I run out of ammunition, I would have thrown my tooth to Guevara's boat."[40]

Another information discrepancy pertains to the number of casualties suffered by the Cubans. Guevara admitted that their total force was 200 men. Yet, according to a listing of the names of all of the Cuban combatants transported across the lake, there were only 123 men.[41] Cuban sources would later claim that only *six* men were lost in battle. This disparity in numbers is further discussed in Appendix III.

Upon arrival in Tanzania, Che, apparently following Castro's instructions, made a brief good-bye speech to the men and vanished. Castro had obviously planned the evacuation, for he had sent a man he trusted completely, at least at that time, General Arnaldo Ochoa to take over the troops, arrange for medical attention for the ill and wounded, and move everyone to Dar Es-Salaam for their repatriation to Cuba.

The Cuban surviving combatants were given some initial medical treatment for a few days in Kigoma. Then, they were taken to Dar Es-Salaam in three trucks and a jeep. After two or three days at the Tanzanian capital, they were flown to Moscow, where they were met by the Cuban military *attaché*. From Moscow they were flown to Havana by two Soviet aircraft to a cool reception by Fidel and Raúl Castro. Victor Dreke recalls: "We returned in defeat, and Fidel told us that we had fulfilled our duty and that we had done everything possible within what was available to us. At the end of the conversation Fidel criticized that we had fragmented the (Cuban) forces."[42]

History would repeat itself many times on this subject. Castro, the military strategist, would second guess his high ranking officers and embarrass them in public by telling them what *he* would have done under the same circumstances. Years later, General Ochoa, the commanding officer of the Cuban troops during the Angola War, would comment on several occasions that Castro was trying to run the Angola campaign from behind his desk in his office in Havana.

There were many reasons for the defeat of the Cubans in Congo. Perhaps the most significant one was poor timing. If the Cubans had arrived in Congo six months earlier, or at about the time the Simba forces had taken Kisangani, they might have been able to make a difference in the conflict. Also, had the well-disciplined Cuban soldiers been involved in the defense of Kisangani, perhaps the outcome of Operation *Dragon Rouge* would have been significantly altered. By the time the Cubans arrived, the Simba revolt, which had controlled more than one half of Congo's territory, had been reduced to isolated pockets of resistance, scattered through perhaps 15 percent of the territory of Congo. It would be a stretch to assume that 200 foreigners could rally a moribund revolution back to life.

A large percentage of the mercenaries had their employment contracts expire shortly after the Kisangani rescue. The three mercenary columns had barely commenced to reorganize about the time of Che Guevara's arrival. It had been previously difficult to recruit qualified mercenaries, but after the victory of *Dragon Rouge* at Kisangani, many soldiers of fortune in the world wanted to be a part of the Congo action. Although the new recruits were somewhat green, there was no shortage of manpower.

In the defeat of the Cubans, the size of their contingent also played a very significant role. There were only 200 Cubans at the peak of the action. Castro sent 3,200 soldiers to a simple border dispute between Algeria and Morocco. During a December 2, 2005 speech delivered by Fidel Castro to his armed forces to commemorate the 30th anniversary of his Angola war, he admitted that: "Cuban forces numbered 55,000 troops in Angola."[43] Prior to this speech by Castro, the number of Cuban troops in Angola was a carefully-guarded State secret, but historians had estimated the number to be around 30,000. The number of Cuban troops killed in Angola is still unknown. During the critical battle at Cuito Cuanavale, Angola there were 40,000 Cuban and 30,000 Angolan troops. Why did Guevara only get 200 men?

In addition to timing and troop strength, other reasons for failure must be mentioned. One was the initial false sense of security held by Guevara and the Cuban troops, as they were essentially unopposed for about four or five months. Another was the military genius of Mike Hoare, who organized a brilliant campaign in a few weeks. The vision of the CIA must not be underestimated. The U.S. administration was fully immersed in the Vietnam conflict and the Congo insurrection was left in the hands of the CIA and a few (COMISH) American military advisors. The CIA engaged the services of experienced Cuban exiles, who considered any battle against communism to be their battle. The CIA indeed did what had to be done, at a reasonable cost, and they were able to keep international reaction to a minimum.

When the Cubans realized they had to work with untrained soldiers, they scattered in four groups to provide a crash training course in military operations. Before they left Havana, it would have never occurred to the Cubans that the Congolese were not interested in their revolution, and that the Rwandan volunteers would often become ill before battle.

Guevara himself was likely another reason for the failure of Castro's intervention in Congo. Even though as an individual contributor he was honest, highly intelligent, and a very hard worker, as a *Comandante* he was disorganized, a poor military planner and an incompetent leader. He had not performed well in the previous three jobs Castro had given him in Cuba. Considering how many good military leaders there were in Cuba at that time, Che was without a doubt, one of the worst choices Castro could have made to command the Congo intervention forces.

Castro did such a good marketing job to promote Guevara as a super-hero of the revolution, that after his death, Che Guevara continues to inspire young people who think of him as an honest and pure champion of the oppressed.

The public reading of Guevara's good-bye letter by Castro also had an impact in the failure of the Cuban intervention in Congo. Che's renunciation of his Cuban citizenship had a negative impact on the morale of his troop. In the epilogue of his Congo diary, Guevara states: "... my farewell letter to Fidel played a role in my relations with the men in the final days ... just as they did many years ago, when I was starting out in the Sierra—the comrades saw me as a foreigner in contact with Cubans. The letter ... caused a distance to develop between myself and the combatants."[44]

Guevara never expected to have to fight against the dedicated and experienced anti-Castro Cuban exiles. These men had also fought against communist-led rebels in the Dominican Republic, Nicaragua, El Salvador, Venezuela, Bolivia, Vietnam, Laos, and many other places. But Congo was special. The Cuban exile Air Force, Makasi, of experienced pilots and aircraft maintenance owned the skies over Congo. After interviewing ground troops on their way to Kisangani a few days before the Kisangani rescue, *The New York Times* reported: "Most troops term the air cover as decisive in their success on the ground."[45] The 58th Company of infantry Cuban exiles under Rip Robertson performed courageously in their march to Kisangani and during the rescue operation. And the anti-Castro Cuban navy essentially stopped the flow of supplies to the rebels across the waters of Lake Tanganyika. In the future, military historians are likely to agree that this small but audacious group of men tipped the balance against international communism in Congo.

A total of 101 Cuban exiles served in Congo. The most important campaigns were from September 1964 (prior to the Kisangani rescue) through November 1965 (exit of Che Guevara and Cuban soldiers), and during this time, it is doubtful that there were ever more than 65 Cuban exiles fighting at any one time in Congo, probably 60 is a better estimate. The total number of Cuban exiles in patrol at Lake Tanganyika was 16, always in 2 boats, and generally patrolling at night. There were 18 men in the ground forces. When the Lake Tanganyika patrolmen arrived, the infantry had already departed. And Makasi pilots, even though they were literally scattered throughout Congo, at one time in as many as 13 air bases, seldom numbered more than 25 at any given time, ground maintenance and administrative personnel included. A total of 67 men served in the Cuban exile air force.

What became of the aircrafts the Cuban exile air force used? The U.S. government left them in Congo for the ANC to use. Regarding the SWIFT boats, Eulogio Reyes recalls: "I believe the boats were given to the ANC, and when we left, the 5 Commando mercenaries and the ANC were manning them. The boats were well maintained and all the spare parts were flown from the U.S."[46]

Félix Toledo relates a story which, even though not an integral part of the conflict, is worthy of repeating. "Some of us in the Cuban exile navy had befriended a Spanish missionary priest. He was the sole survivor of a congregation which ran a school and a hospital. One day we asked him why he was still there. His answer moved all of us to tears. He replied: 'I can't go. I'm the only one left and I must continue my work until I can meet with my friends.' The Simbas had killed the priests and nuns in the school and hospital. He had survived because he was visiting an out-of-town patient the day of the massacre."[47]

The following table represents the airports Makasi operated from, and the approximate date when operations began at the given airport. It was difficult to get agreement on the dates, but they are probably within a month of the actual time. These airports were available to Makasi, but that does not imply that there were men there at all times. Makasi personnel moved around Congo, depending on where their services were needed.

City	Approximate Date
Kinshasa	September 1962
Kikwit	October 1963
Kamina	November 1963
Kabinda	July 1964
Kamembe, Rwanda	August 1964
Kalemie	September 1964
Kongolo	October 1964
Endolo	October 1964
Punia	November 1964
Lisala	November 1964
Kindu	November 1964
Kisangani	November 1964
Isiro	December 1964
Bunia	January 1965

Guevara's diary of his Congo experience starts as follows, "This is the history of a failure."[48] The start of the failure was to apply a method that had worked in Cuba in a country 11,000 kilometers away. In one of his letters to Castro, Guevara asks for super humans, for he knew that the war could not be won with normal human beings. This was a revolution for the Congolese people, yet apparently only the Cubans and from time to time the Rwandans were taking the fighting seriously.

Perhaps the most insightful view was given by Víctor Dreke who stated: "The Congo revolution had been lost before our arrival, but it is always sad to be present at the time of the defeat of a revolution."[49]

Guevara was revered by the Cuban soldiers under his command at least until they found out Guevara had resigned his Cuban nationality. He could point his pistol at his soldiers and tell them to preserve their dignity and not to allow defeat to change their attitude. But he could not do that with Congolese rebel soldiers, even if he could have spoken their language. After six long months Che finally realized that the Congolese did not want a revolution. They were neither hungry nor unhappy. After all, when you are immune to enemy bullets, who needs a revolution?

Notes

1. Taibo II, Paco Ignacio, Froilán Escobar and Félix Guerra, *El Año Que Estuvimos en Ninguna Parte*, Editorial Txalaparta, Pamplona, Spain, 1995, pp. 43-47.
2. Guevara, Ernesto, *op. cit.*, p. 17.
3. Taibo II, *op. cit.*, p. 77.
4. Taibo II, *op. cit.*, p. 128.
5. Guevara, *op. cit.*, p. 25.
6. Hoare, Mike, *Congo Mercenary*, Robert Hale, London, 1967, p. 248.
7. Navarro, Jorge, Conversations with the author, New Orleans, August 5, 2006.
8. Gálvez, William, *El Sueño Africano de Che ¿Qué Sucedió en la Guerrilla Congolesa?*, Casa de las Américas, La Habana, 1997, p. 120.
9. Taibo II, *op. cit.*, p. 116.
10. *Ibid*, pp. 117-120, Gálvez, op. cit., pp. 105-111, Guevara, op. cit., pp. 38-50.
11. Ros, Enrique, *op. cit.*, p. 113.
12. *Ibid*, p. 114.
13. *The Washington Post*, "Congo has Diary of Cuban Agent," July 18, 1965, p. A1.
14. Devlin, Larry, Conversations with the author, February 15 and 21, 2008.
15. Taibo II, *op. cit.*, p. 132.
16. Reyes, Eulogio, Conversations with the author, Miami, October 19, 2007.
17. Bringas, Generoso, Conversations with the author, Miami, July 24, 2006.
18. Reyes, *op. cit.*
19. Hoare, *op. cit.*, pp. 253-277.
20. Toledo, Félix, Conversations with the author, Miami, October 20, 2007.
21. Hoare, *op. cit.*, p. 264.
22. *Ibid.*
23. Gálvez, *op. cit.*, pp. 200-201.
24. Taibo II, *op. cit.*, p. 178.

25. Guevara, *op. cit.*, p. 136.
26. Quoted by Ros, *op. cit.*, p. 102 from Revista Bohemia, September 17, 1965.
27. Quoted in Gálvez, William, *op. cit.*, pp. 207-208. Translated by the author.
28. Alarcón Ramírez, Dariel (aka Benigno), *Memorias de un Soldado Cubano: Vida y Muerte de la Revolución*, Tusquets Editores, Barcelona, 1996, pp. 337-340.
29. Quoted by Ros, Enrique, *op. cit.*, p. 149.
30. Taibo II, et al, *op. cit.*, pp. 183-185. Translated by the author.
31. Taibo II, *op. cit.*, p. 189.
32. Hoare, *op. cit.*, p. 267.
33. Guevara, *op. cit.*, p. 112.
34. Taibo II, *op. cit.*, pp. 194-196.
35. Gálvez, *op. cit.*, p. 266.
36. *Ibid*, p. 281.
37. Guevara, *op. cit.*, p. 215.
38. Toledo, Félix, Conversations with the author, Miami, October 20, 2007.
39. Taibo II, *op. cit.*, pp. 233-237.
40. Navarro, *op. cit.*
41. Gálvez, *op. cit.*, pp. 360-364.
42. Taibo II, op. cit., p. 242.
43. Quoted in Africa News *www.afrol.com,/articles/17553*, downloaded January 15, 2006.
44. Guevara, *op. cit.*, pp. 234-235.
45. *New York Times*, November 22, 1964, p. 4.
46. Reyes, Eulogio, Conversations with the author, Miami, October 19, 2007.
47. Toledo, *op. cit.*
48. Guevara, *op. cit.*, p. 1.
49. Taibo II, *op. cit.*, p. 242.

Part IV

Aftermath

11

Constitutional Deadlock

While Mobutu's ANC, Tshombé's mercenaries, and the Cuban-exile Makasi pilots, naval and ground forces were doing battle with Cubans, Simbas, and other rebels a different battle was being fought in Kinshasa. It was a political struggle for control of Congo.

Tshombé's prestige throughout Africa had been severely damaged by the Belgian-American rescue operation in Kisangani. Nationalistic African movements viewed this operation as a neo-colonial attack on Congolese patriots fighting for their second independence. In contrast, Tshombé's popularity within Congo was soaring. He controlled forty-nine of the fifty political parties, the exception being Kasavubu's ABAKO party. The coalition of Lumumbist revolutionaries was too busy fleeing from Tshombé's mercenaries to vote.

Taking advantage of his immense acclaim, Tshombé organized a new political party, *Confédération Nationale des Associations Congolaises* (CONACO). Riding on Tshombé's popularity, CONACO won a landslide victory in both chambers in a parliamentary election in March 1965, with a total of 122 out of 167 parliamentary seats.

The other Congolese leader, Kasavubu, was envious of Tshombé's popularity. In the eyes of the Congolese people, Tshombé was the perceived hero who had saved the country from Simba domination.

At the time of Congo independence, when Belgian jurists threw together the Congo constitution (they were given only 36 hours), they overlooked setting a time limit on the office of the president. Hence, Kasavubu believed that he was *President-for-Life*, and was therefore within his rights to remove the Prime Minister.

Kasavubu had purposefully avoided taking part in the continent-wide reprobation against Tshombé; however he had criticized Tshombé for the use of white mercenaries against the Simba rebels. Kasavubu did not want the other African leaders to perceive him as agreeing with Tshombé's policies, nor did he want to continue playing the limited role of a figure head president.

On October 13, 1965, Kasavubu arbitrarily declared the end of the transitional mandate of the Tshombé government, and named Évariste Kimba, a leading figure of the anti-Tshombé forces, as Prime Minister-designate. On November 14, the Tshombé-controlled Parliament blocked Kimba's investiture by a vote of 134 to 121.

Another candidate, Victor Nendaka sought to be invested Prime Minister, but Kasavubu blocked Nendaka and renominated Kimba, as Kasavubu thought he could easily manipulate Kimba. The ensuing government crisis lasted for ten days and paralyzed the Congo government. This constitutional deadlock paved the way for a second military takeover by Mobutu.

On November 24, 1965, fourteen members of the ANC high command met in Kinshasa with Mobutu in an emergency session. The next day, Mobutu ordered his troops to the streets, removed Kasavubu and Kimba and proclaimed himself President of Congo. Colonel Léonard Mulamba became Prime Minister of the Government of National Union. Parliament approved the new government by acclamation and announced that it could remain in office for a five-year term, considering the state of national emergency.

Mobutu seemed to be a suitable compromise leader for Congo. He was not identified with European colonial powers, and he had always been careful to blame Tshombé for the hiring of white mercenaries. Additionally, his support by the U.S. was low key enough as not to offend the USSR and the PRC.

At the end of the day, Mobutu had read the situation correctly. After his *coup d'etat*, Uganda became friendly towards Congo, as did Tanzania, halting the flow of weapons across Lake Tanganyika. Even Sudan stopped aiding Congolese rebels, for they had problems of their own in the southern part of the country.

12

Revolt of the Mercenaries

On October 13, 1965, Kasavubu had terminated Tshombé's presidential mandate. On November 24, 1965, Mobutu, with the full support of the CIA and the Congolese armed forces, took over the reins of Congo. This was only three days after Che Guevara and the Cuban soldiers had left Congo in defeat.

At the time of Mobutu's final *coup d'etat*, there were a few isolated Simbas fighting around the Great Lakes area. And then, there was Mulele continuing to fight in the Kwilu River area. The Cuban exile Makasi force and navy were still fighting the leftist rebels, but compared to previous months, the situation was calm.

Mobutu concentrated his efforts on destroying any remnants of prior opposition to his regime. On June 2, 1966, four key politicians, including former Prime Minister-designate Évariste Kimba, were charged with conspiring to assassinate Mobutu, and after a kangaroo court trial publicly hanged in the *Grand Place* in Kinshasa.[1]

Mobutu was concerned about Tshombé's popularity, as Tshombé was credited with having suffocated the Simba rebellion. Tshombé's decision to remain in Congo, even though he had been ousted by Kasavubu several months earlier, was further threatening. In early June 1966, Mobutu brought charges of treason against Tshombé, who promptly went back into exile in Spain.

In early 1967, Tshombé was tried in absentia and sentenced to death. Mobutu then turned his attention to the mercenaries, as their loyalty, if they understood the meaning of the word, rested with Tshombé, the man whom they had served for many years.

Mad Mike Hoare was considered to be the mercenary chief closest to Tshombé, and thus Hoare was the first to receive his termination letter from Mobutu. From the human resources viewpoint, this was a quite normal termination, for the mercenaries had been hired under standard six-month employment contracts. But the mercenaries were far from normal people. Strangely, Hoare accepted his dismissal and moved on to different pastures. Mobutu's intention was to slowly eliminate the three commando units, and he started by significantly reducing the size of 5 Commando. Once Hoare and his trusted South African mercenaries left Congo, they were replaced by a much smaller group of Italian and Spanish soldiers of fortune.

Commandos 6 and 10 were temporarily maintained under Denard and Schramme respectively. The mercenaries returned to their bases, concentrating their energy in parties and drinking their salaries. But Mobutu kept a watchful eye.

The mercenaries were very much aware of the power they possessed, as they were referred to by the Congolese as *"Les Affreux"* or "the feared ones."[2] They were further convinced that Congo was meant to stay in a permanent state of anarchy. The possibility of a strong central government in Congo would deprive them of all their perks as well as a handsome salary. The mercenaries had been a significant element of Congo's defense for the previous five years, and each Commando had been its own country, accountable to no one. They saw no reason for this situation to change. Since they did not have any towns to ransack, they drifted into the protection business, extorting money from miners and merchants.

Compared to previous years, life was quite boring for the mercenaries. Conspiracies continued. Denard was having secret meetings with Tshombé in Madrid, while Schramme was using the 10 Commando troops (which Schramme called his *Bataillon Léopard*) to build a complex military base in Yumbi, by the Congo River, on the border between Bandundu and Equateur Provinces, which he intended to use as his own quasi-feudal slave state.[3]

In 1960, at the time of the Katanga secession, Tshombé had organized his own army, which were called the Katangan *gendarmes*. These units had been placed in moth balls after Tshombé's defeat by UN troops during the Katanga secession, and had moved into Angola, for they were ethnic Luba and could blend with the local Angolan population. The Katangan *gendarmes* were reactivated by Tshombé in mid-1964 to put down the Simba rebellion. After Mobutu's *coup d'etat* in 1965, the Katangan *gendarmes* were precariously integrated into the ANC. Mobutu made sure that they were scattered to posts far away from Katanga, but somehow their individual units managed to stay together.

In July 1966, the Baka Regiment of the Katanga *Gendarmerie* stationed in Kisangani mutinied and seized the airport when they heard the rumor that their unit might be disbanded. This regiment, led by Colonel Ferdinand Tshipola, was one of the original units that had returned from Angola in 1964,[4] had stayed in Congo and had been relocated by Mobutu.

Sometime in July shortly after this mutiny, Makasi pilots Juan Perón and Jorge Navarro, while on a routine reconnaissance mission landed in the Kisangani airport. They were unaware that the Katangans had just taken over the airport. When the aircraft came to a stop, they were surrounded by Katangan *gendarmes* with automatic weapons. Perón, who spoke a little Swahili, asked if everything was okay, to which the highest ranking officer replied: "Everything is fine, for you are our friends."[5] Perón and Navarro were taken to the safety of the Victoria Hotel, where they remained for nearly a week. There was a CIA operative also staying at the Victoria Hotel waiting for the storm to pass, who told Perón and Navarro that this was an internal problem and that they were to sit there and relax until the situation was sorted out. They were apprehensive, for they could hear heavy automatic weapon fire, particularly at night, but eventually they were able to return to duty safely.

The mutinous Katangans resisted government offers to negotiate a settlement for more than two months. Mobutu sent Schramme to put down the revolt. Schramme was able to negotiate an end to this mutiny after promising the Katangan *gendarmes* amnesty and giving them a large cash bonus. During these negotiations, Schramme developed an even closer relationship with the mutineers.

Mobutu continued executing his plan to dissolve the mercenary units. First, he dismissed the remnants of 5 Commando. Then, concerned with Schramme's strong relationship with the Katangan *gendarmes* stationed in Kisangani, gave Denard orders to march against Schramme and disarm his unit. Instead, both mercenaries drank several bottles of Scotch, and after deciding that their respective positions with the Mobutu government were coming to an end, created an alliance to take over the country.

Denard's and Schramme's intention was to expand their position in Kisangani until they had full and complete control of the city. From there, they could more easily extend their domination into other cities in eastern Congo, finally moving into Katanga. In Lumumbashi they would wait for Tshombé who would fly in from Madrid, and together they would march into Congo's capital city of Kinshasa, thus completing their plan to take over Congo.

The mercenaries' battle plan was to use Schramme's Yumbi base to launch three simultaneous attacks on Kisangani, Kindu, and Bukavu. Kisangani is about 1,300 kilometers due east of Yumbi. Kindu is 440 kilometers south of Kisangani, while Bukavu is 520 kilometers southeast of Kisangani. After the three towns were taken, Denard's troops would maintain control of them, while Schramme's troops would march into the Tshombé stronghold of Katanga. Plans would be made there for the final takeover of the government of Congo. The chosen date for the three simultaneous assaults was July 5, 1967.

It is likely that the CIA was aware of the planned revolt of the mercenaries and as such Tshombé was being closely watched in Madrid. The U.S. had put their support behind Mobutu, and they felt compelled to protect his government.[6]

Tshombé's bodyguards in Spain had been hand-picked by Denard and Schramme. At the risk of using an oxymoron, both Denard and Schramme considered the Frenchman Bodenan to be a most trusted mercenary. The CIA and/or Mobutu offered Bodenan an increase in salary, and in June 1967 he proceeded to hijack Tshombé's flight from Ibiza to Mallorca. Tshombé had been taking a small holiday in the Balearic Islands. The hijacked plane was diverted to Algeria and Tshombé was delivered to the local authorities, who threw him in prison. With Tshombé incarcerated, the mercenaries had lost the political side of their conspiracy, but they still had their weapons and Congo's perception of their military supremacy.

On July 5, 1967, as scheduled, and not deterred by news of the hijacking of Tshombé's plane, Schramme and Denard executed their planned Revolt of the Mercenaries. Schramme, with 11 white mercenaries from 10 Commando, and some 100 Katangan *gendarmes*, attacked and gained control of Camp Ketele, an ANC base in Kisangani full of troops and their families. The ANC troops were accustomed to seeing mercenaries around their camps, and thought nothing of their presence. The slaughter was horrible. A portion of Denard's troops, under the command of mercenary Major Fougères, attacked other ANC installations in Kisangani at the same time as Schramme's attack on Camp Ketele. In response to both attacks, Mobutu's troops rounded up 30 former mercenaries who were not involved, and executed them. Other mercenaries able to do so, immediately joined Schramme.

Concurrently on July 5, 1967, a unit of Katangan *gendarmes* and some of Schramme's white mercenaries under Captain Raymond overran Bukavu. Denard's troops, led by mercenary Major Noddyn and Katanga *gendarme* Major Kanini, joined on the assault on Bukavu. The Congolese ANC unit defending Bukavu fled upon being attacked by the mercenary forces.

An additional group of attacking forces, led by Captain Michel, also from Schramme's 10 Commando, advanced on Kindu and overran the city without difficulty. Denard's troops under Major Pinaton assisted in the takeover of Kindu.

Mobutu wisely decided to counterattack at Kisangani first. Denard's and Schramme's forces were heavily pounded by CIA-trained ANC troops and strafed by the same CIA Cuban exile Makasi pilots who had previously guaranteed them success during the Simba and Cuban campaigns. Both Denard and Schramme were wounded. While Schramme's wounds were superficial, Denard had a bullet wound in the occipital region, and the right side of his body was temporarily paralyzed. The mercenaries seized a Makasi aircraft at gunpoint and kidnapped pilots as well as Dr. Sanz Gadea to tend to the wounded in route. "Makasi pilot [Francisco] Panchito Alvarez was one of the pilots who flew Denard, as well as other mercenaries and their families to Salisbury, Rhodesia [currently Zimbabwe] to seek medical treatment."[7] Dr. Sanz Gadea and Alvarez were freed by Rhodesian authorities and after their aircraft was released, they were allowed to return to Kisangani.

Schramme was attacked with T-28s and B-26Ks, while the CIA arranged for USAF C-130s to ferry ANC troops to the battle zones. Schramme's men also came under attack by Congolese paratroopers trained by Israel. The mercenaries fled through enemy lines and hid for several days in the dense jungle. Suddenly, on August 8, 1967, they reappeared at Lake Kivu, where they joined the mercenaries holding the city of Bukavu. Kisangani was once again under the control of Mobutu and the ANC.

Mobutu then decided that the liberation of Bukavu was the next priority. Schramme and his men were in a strenuous state of siege in Bukavu. Their only source of supplies was by parachute, organized by Schramme's friend Gerry Puren and carried out by the Rhodesian entity ATA (Air TransAfrica). From this rather weak negotiating position, Schramme made unusual demands. He demanded Mobutu's resignation and proposed an alternative government headed by a totally unknown Katangan.

Having almost miraculously healed from his wounds, Denard traveled from Zimbabwe to Angola, where he gathered his troops, as he planned to enter Congo by bicycle from the south. Denard's troops fell into an ambush as they crossed the border into Congo, and Mobutu's troops executed the captured soldiers. Denard, and those able to engage the ANC, made a fighting retreat back to Angola, and morale broke. This was the end of Denard's Invasion of the Bicycles.

After almost three months in this precarious state of siege, Schramme and his remaining troops crossed into Rwanda and surrendered their weapons on November 5, 1967. This was a contingent of 130 white mercenaries, 800 Katanga *gendarmes*, and their dependants (1,500 women and children). It is interesting to note that during the eleven weeks that Schramme and his men held on to Bukavu, they repeatedly defeated any ANC unit thrown against them. Schramme crossed into Rwanda only after Mobutu sent 15,000 fresh ANC troops to take Bukavu. It was the combination of the Israeli-trained paratroopers and the American airlift of ANC troops to Bukavu that convinced Schramme that he could not win.[8]

The mutiny was essentially over and the American (most of the Cuban exiles were, by now, naturalized American citizens) Makasi pilots were all back home before the end of 1967. The Cuban exiles of Lake Tanganyika's Navy had returned home in February/March 1966, except for Domingo Borges and Anael Alvarez who had returned to Miami in December 1965 suffering from a tropical disease. The Cuban exile infantrymen had returned to the U.S. in January 1965, except for the wounded who had returned home in February 1965.

There was no fanfare and no ceremony to pass the baton to the ANC. The Cuban Americans quietly returned to Miami, were given a medical check-up and sent on to their families.

The Cuban exiles were satisfied, and rightfully so, about what they accomplished in Congo. They had been stopped in their efforts to depose the communist dictatorship in their beloved Cuba, but they had been able to assist in stopping Castro in his African expansion plans. Mobutu may not have been a perfect leader, but he did not deliver Congo to international communism.

The Katangan *gendarmes* who crossed into Rwanda with Schramme were offered amnesty by Mobutu. Upon their return to Congo, they disappeared mysteriously, and there is no doubt in the minds of most historians that they were executed. Not many living people opposed to Mobutu's regime were left in Congo.

The stage had been set for Mobutu's long, bloody and oppressive regime.

Notes

1.   From *http://workmall.com/wfb2001/congo_democratic_republic_of_the/congo*, downloaded November 29, 2004.
2.   Marzo, Jorge Luis and Marc Roig, eds., Planeta Kurtz. *Cien Años de "El Corazón de las Tinieblas de Joseph Conrad,"* Random House Mondadori, Barcelona, 2002.

3. Jean Schramme, *Le Bataillon Léopard—Souvenirs d'un Africain Blanc*, Laffont, Paris, 1969.

4. Odom, Lieutenant Colonel Thomas P., US Army Combined Arms Research Library, *http://cgsc.leavenworth.army.mil/carl/resources/csi/odom2/odom2.asp*, downloaded January 5, 2005.

5. Navarro, Jorge, Conversations with the author, New Orleans, August 5, 2006.

6. Schramme, *op. cit.*, p. 121.

7. Perón, Juan, Conversations with the author, Miami, August 23, 2005.

8. Le Bailly, Jacques, *Une Poignée de Mercenaires*, Presses de la Cité, Paris, 1967.

13

Postscript

In Chapter Eleven it was described how Mobutu seized power in November 1965, taking advantage of a power struggle between President Kasavubu and Prime Minister Moïse Tshombé. It did not take long for Mobutu to realize he was a fish out of water in the field of politics. Therefore, he sought to reconcile with Kasavubu as a means of securing legitimacy for his regime while he learned the game of politics.

One did not say no to Mobutu. Kasavubu accepted Mobutu's offer and an honorary seat in the Senate. About two years later, Kasavubu retired to a farm in Mayombe, where he died on March 24, 1969. He was approximately fifty-nine.

Tshombé died of heart failure in his Algerian prison cell in 1969, at age fifty. Many people over the years have questioned the real cause of his death.

Pierre Mulele continued fighting in the jungles of the Kwilu River area, but in September 1968, he made the fatal error of accepting Mobutu's offer of amnesty. On October 2, 1968, Mulele was picked up by members of the ANC, ostensibly to take him to the football stadium where he was to be honored as a loyal friend of Lumumba. Instead, he was taken to a military camp where he was tortured and later dismembered with his body parts thrown into the crocodile infested Congo River. Mulele was forty-nine. Ten years later, in 1978, Mulele's mother was hanged by Mobutu's soldiers.

With Mulele out of the way in 1968, and the deaths of both Kasavubu and Tshombé in 1969, a partial eclipse of the first generation of Congolese politicians had occurred. Mobutu had paved the way for his long and cruel administration. And in 1969, Mobutu was still a young man of thirty-nine.

By this time, Mobutu had already established a presidential form of government and had proclaimed himself Chief Executive. The constitution was reestablished in 1970 when Mobutu became old enough to serve as president.

In 1971, Mobutu embarked on a campaign of anti-European cultural awareness. He changed the name of Congo and its river to Zaïre. Any city in Congo having a European-sounding name was renamed with a clearly African one. Congolese were required to drop their Christian names and replace them with African ones. In 1972, he set the example by changing his name to Mobutu Sese Seko Nkuku Wa Za Banga, which means "The all-powerful warrior, who because of his endurance and inflexible will to win, will go from conquest to conquest, leaving fire in his wake."[1]

Gaston Soumialot joined Laurent Kabila in Tanzania and continued the anti-government, anti-American Simba movement. Christophe Gbenye, apparently with the gold taken from the Kilo Moto mines, established a successful transportation company in Uganda. Nicholas Olenga continued in his smuggling business in partnership with Idi Amin in Uganda, and ended up imprisoned in Khartoum, Sudan. In 1971 Mobutu asked Olenga, having been released from prison in Sudan, and Gbenye to return from exile. They accepted and lived in Kinshasa under some form of house arrest. It is difficult to understand why Mobutu invited them back to Congo instead of having them killed. A possible explanation is that Gbenye and Olenga still had some popular support and the political climate had changed. Having them in Congo would make it easier for Mobutu's secret service to ensure that they did not try to organize a revolt. Perhaps there is an African proverb similar to the English one: "keep your friends close and your enemies even closer."

Olenga never adjusted to civilian life, was imprisoned in Kinshasa, and was later lost in Mobutu's prison system. He is believed to have died in the early 1980s. Gbenye, at age eighty-one continues his involvement in Congo politics as president of the MNC. Gaston Soumialot continued his revolutionary activities in Tanzania and the Fizi-Baraka area of Congo. It is believed that his own men killed him in the late 1960s.

There were three Cuban soldiers left behind when Che and his surviving troops retreated to Tanzania. The missing men were Roberto Hernández Calzada (who does not appear on the list of combatants given in Appendix III), Luis Calzada Hernández (no apparent relation to Roberto, only a coincidence), and one of the Semanat brothers (who had been missing for a few weeks prior to the exodus). General Ochoa asked for volunteers, and a rescue party was organized by PFC Martín Chibás González (*Ishirine*) about forty-five days after the Cuban evacuation. Both Roberto Hernández and Luis Calzada were found and repatriated to Cuba. Semanat was never found, but he is not listed as having been killed (or missing) in action. Chibás is now a General in the Cuban Army.

Ernesto Che Guevara stayed for a few months in Tanzania after his defeat in Congo. In early 1966, he traveled to Prague suitably disguised. Several personalities of the Cuban revolution traveled to Prague in an attempt to forcedly convince him to return to Cuba. The conditions under which he returned are unknown.

It is widely believed that General Líster and other Soviet strategists stationed in Cuba were violently opposed to having the defeated and anti-Soviet Guevara involved in revolutionary activities in Latin America. For reasons not yet clear, Castro overruled the Soviets, and allowed Guevara to travel to Bolivia.

In August 1966, Guevara traveled to La Paz with a counterfeit Uruguayan passport, no beard and no hair, and wearing glasses as a disguise. He promptly started guerrilla fighting in the Bolivian jungle. He was wounded in action at Quebrada del Yuro and taken prisoner by Bolivian Rangers to the town of La Higuera, where he was executed by firing squad on October 8, 1967. He was thirty-nine.

This book is about Castro's intervention in Congo and the performance of Cuban-Americans in the Congo conflict, but Guevara is such a central figure in this book that the readers would want to know the reasons for his demise. To prevent antagonizing the Soviet's Latin American network, Castro misinformed Mario Monje, the then head of the Bolivian communist party. According to Cuban-American researcher Enrique Ros,[2] Castro originally told Monje that Guevara was in Bolivia only in transit, that his destination was Argentina. When Guevara actually set up guerrilla operations in Bolivia, he became a bitter enemy of the only people who could have helped him survive. When Monje confronted Castro and asked him what sort of help should be given to Guevara, Castro reportedly replied: "not even an aspirin," meaning that he should not even help Guevara to get rid of a headache.[3]

Castro could have arranged to extricate Guevara from Bolivia, but he never attempted to do so. It is also possible that the Soviets engineered Guevara's capture (perhaps by having local farmers guide Bolivian rangers to Guevara's camp) to insure his defeat.

A number of the survivors of Guevara's Congo fiasco returned to Africa to fight in other wars, such as Guinea-Bissau, Ethiopia, Angola, and Congo (Brazzaville). A group of the soldiers closest to Guevara accompanied him to Bolivia. Only three Cubans survived in Bolivia, one of whom did not participate in Congo. The other two are: Harry Villegas (*Pombo*), and Dariel Alarcón Ramírez (*Benigno*). *Pombo* is now a General in the Cuban Army. *Benigno* was granted political asylum by France in

1996, where he resides today under constant police protection, as it is rumored that the Cuban government has offered a bounty for his head.

Survivors in Congo, later killed in Bolivia include: José María Martínez Tamayo (*M'bili*), Israel Reyes Zayas (*Azi*), Carlos Coello (*Tumaini*), and Dr. Octavio de la Concepción Pedraza (*Moro Goro*). It is possible that there were others, but the information available from Cuban sources is limited and highly censored.

A fable teller by the name of Aesop lived in Greece in the sixth century BC. He wrote a fable entitled *The Fox and the Grapes*. A hungry and thirsty fox saw a cluster of beautiful ripe grapes on a high vine. The fox tried every trick to get them, but all he managed was to wear himself out. Finally, to hide his disappointment, the fox said: "The grapes are sour and not ripe as I thought." After the resounding defeat of Guevara and the Cuban forces in Congo, Castro lost interest in Congo, at least militarily.

But all was not lost to the Cuban leader. Even though he could not take Congo militarily, Castro decided that Cuba could profit commercially from the riches of Central Africa.[4] Castro is believed to have instructed the identical twins (Colonel Antonio de la Guardia and Brigadier General Patricio de la Guardia), both of whom are better known as the *Cuban James Bond*, as well as Division General Arnaldo Ochoa to set up a network to smuggle diamonds, gold, and ivory. The sophisticated network was indeed set up, the key geographic points being Congo (Brazzaville), Tanzania, Angola, Congo, and finally Panama (for money laundering). Mobutu did not care who he did business with, as long as he could increase his personal fortune. The difficult mission was thus accomplished and Cuba obtained huge profits from this illicit trade for many years.

In the late 1980s, a Cuban military investigation uncovered (ostensibly without Castro's knowledge) that cocaine had been added to the product portfolio of this smuggling enterprise. Castro appeared on television and seemed to have been taken by surprise by the news, although it is unlikely that anything important happened in Cuba without Castro's knowledge and blessing. Ochoa was arrested in mid-June 1989 and two days later the de la Guardia twins and other lower-level officers were also arrested. There were a total of fourteen officers arrested.

Division General Arnaldo Ochoa, the man who took care of the Cuban troops defeated in Congo after Che Guevara vanished, subsequent to their crossing into Tanzania, was executed in Havana in 1989, having been convicted of drug trafficking. Ochoa had commanded Cuban military operations in Venezuela, Ethiopia, Angola, Yemen, and Nicaragua.

Coincidentally, Ochoa was a popular *Hero of the Cuban Republic*, the highest honor which can be accorded to a military man in Castro's Cuba. He was forty-nine. Colonel Antonio de la Guardia was also executed. He was fifty. Brigadier General Patricio de la Guardia is serving a thirty-year prison term.[5] The moral of this fable is clear: it is wonderful to make money for Cuba, just don't become too popular in the process.

More than fifty years after Fidel Castro's takeover of Cuba's government, Cuba is still ruled without democratic elections. Castro has transferred power to his younger (seventy-six years old) brother Raúl. In spite of the poor living conditions Cubans must endure, Castro has not abandoned his internationalist aspirations. What he failed to do with bullets and rockets in Africa during the 1960s and 1970s, now, at age eighty-one and in failing health, he is trying to do with the ballot box in Latin America. Oil-rich Venezuela and natural gas-rich Bolivia are already under his protective wing. Nicaragua has recently joined the organization, as has Ecuador. Close election results precluded the addition of Mexico as an ally to the newly revived forces of communism. A commitment made by President Kennedy to Premier Khrushchev in 1962 is still allowing Castro to attempt to rule nations in 2008.

Even after Congo's fiasco, Castro continued his involvement in Africa's political landscape. At one time in the 1970s and 1980s there were Cuban soldiers fighting in Ethiopia, Angola, Mozambique, and many other countries. The CIA continued utilizing Cuban exiles to collect intelligence in the area, but the U.S. did not fall for the many Vietnams trick.

Mad Mike Hoare left Congo in early 1966. In keeping with the axiom that "once a warrior, always a warrior," Hoare led an aborted coup to take over the government of the Seychelles Islands in 1981. Hoare received a ten-year prison term but was released after serving three years. He lives in France and is eighty-four.

Also not content to live a peaceful life, Bob Denard invaded the Comoros Islands in 1978 and took control of the government. French authorities sent a force to establish order in the region, and rather than fight his countrymen, Denard went into exile in South Africa. He voluntarily went to France to serve a five-year prison term for a failed coup in Benin in 1977. Instead, he received a five-year suspended sentence. He lives in Comoros and is seventy-six.

Black Jack Schramme returned to Belgium in 1968, and in 1969 escaped to Spain to avoid being tried in Belgium for the murder of a Belgian in Zaïre. In 1970, he moved to Portugal and in 1974 to Brazil. He was expelled from Brazil in 1976 and moved to Paraguay. His track was lost then, but he is thought to live in Bolivia. If he is still alive, he would be seventy-seven.

Rip Robertson contracted malaria during an operation in Central America in the mid-1950s. After Congo, William Rip Robertson went to Vietnam where he continued to employ counter-guerrilla tactics to fight international communism. Sometime in 1970, following a bout with malaria, this brave man died. When Rip Robertson's name is mentioned, many of the battle-hardened Cuban exiles become teary-eyed.

Mobutu ruled Congo until May 1997. The only positive comment on his administration is that he minimized tribal conflicts and encouraged a sense of nationhood. Otherwise, his government was marked by nepotism, violence, and corruption. Congo was hit by uncontrolled inflation and the country became poorer as Mobutu amassed an immense personal fortune estimated at $4 billion, mostly kept safely in Swiss banks. In order to describe Mobutu's form of government, a new word had to be coined: *kleptocracy*. Just as democracy is government by the people, kleptocracy is government by the thieves.

Laurent-Désiré Kabila copied the steps followed by Soumialot some thirty years earlier. He negotiated a deal with ethnic Tutsi and commenced waging war against the ANC in the eastern part of Congo with the objective of ousting Mobutu. On May 16, 1997, Tutsi rebels and other anti-Mobutu groups captured Kinshasa. The ailing Mobutu fled to Morocco where he died of prostate cancer in September 1997.

Laurent Kabila, the patient playboy, became the new President in 1997, after almost a forty-year struggle, and changed the country's name to Democratic Republic of Congo. He was shot by a bodyguard in mid-January 2001. After some days without news, his death was confirmed on January 18, 2001. He was sixty-two. During Laurent Kabila's presidency, ethnic strife resurfaced. The level of corruption was not too different from the one that existed during Mobutu's presidency. Congolese Tutsi occupied key positions. His government was weakened by a split between Luba-Katanga (ethnic group of Kabila's father) and Lunda (ethnic group of his mother). Kabila's assassination was originally blamed on soldiers from Kivu, but after the investigation was completed, Lunda figures were arrested.

His thirty-one-year-old son, Major General Joseph Kabila assumed the Presidency, and is still in power. Joseph Kabila is given mixed reviews among Congolese. While most political figures in Congo speak French and Kikongo, Joseph speaks English and Swahili, since he grew up mostly in Rwanda. Some question whether he is the son of Laurent.

There are also questions about his mother's nationality. Critics say that his mother is a Rwandan Tutsi. The official version is that his mother is a Bangubangu from Maniema.

Antoine Gizenga provides an excellent example that anything is possible in politics, as long as you survive long enough. He stayed in Congo until 1966, when an assassination attempt against him failed. He then lived in exile for more than twenty-five years, primarily in Mali, the Soviet Union, France, and Angola. He returned to Congo in 1992 to head PALU (Unified Lumumbist Party), which he had helped create in 1964. He was an important voice of the opposition against Mobutu, until Mobutu's ouster in 1997. He then opposed the rule of his former comrade in arms, Laurent Kabila. Gizenga continued his political activities, and in the July 2006 general election, PALU came in third place with about 13 percent of the vote. The other two candidates, Joseph Kabila and Jean-Pierre Bemba were virtually tied. In a masterful move, Gizenga signed a coalition agreement with AMP, Kabila's party, where Gizenga would back Kabila in exchange for the job of Prime Minister. Kabila won the October 2006 runoff election and appointed Gizenga as Prime Minister on December 30, 2006. At age eighty-three, Prime Minister Antoine Gizenga is a politician worthy of admiration. The Kabila-Gizenga administration has been recognized by many foreign governments.

The 2006 election in Congo was the first general election since the one that had been held immediately after independence in 1960. In the democratic context, Congo seems to be ahead of Cuba. Congo has had two general elections since 1959, while Cuba has had none.

Western Europe and the U.S. have found alternate supply sources of critical minerals and appear to be no longer interested in Central Africa, although several U.S. and European corporations are still operating in Congo. Joseph Kabila and Antoine Gizenga have an excellent relationship with the OAU and the African socialist countries, particularly Angola. Their relationship with China is good, but their association with Cuba is outstanding.

After returning to the U.S., the Cuban Americans who fought in Congo entered into diverse activities. Some continued to fight communism on different fronts, including Vietnam. Others started businesses or practiced varied professions. The majority of them stayed in the U.S. or Puerto Rico, although some live in Latin America and Europe. It was a great honor for me to meet and interview some of these brave men. I did find out that I have something in common with all of these men: we all hope to live long enough to see our native country free of communist rule.

I sincerely believe that the Cuban Americans who assisted in preventing international communism from taking over the riches of Congo should be recognized by the United States government for having helped the West at a critical moment of the Cold War. Not many people are aware of what these brave men did for liberty and democracy, and I trust that this book will be a first step in honoring these courageous patriots.

Notes

1.   From *http://encyclozine.com/Joseph_Mobutu*, downloaded October 28, 2004.
2.   Ros, Enrique, *op. cit.*, pp. 195-298.
3.   Quoted by Chapman, Michael. *CSNNews.com* Managing Editor, July 31, 2007.
4.   Oppenheimer, Andrés, *Castro's Final Hour*, Touchstone, New York, 1992, pp. 30-52.
5.   *Ibid*, pp. 17-30.

Appendix I

Name Changes of Congolese Cities

CURRENT NAME	NAME Ca. 1960
Kinshasa	Léopoldville
Kisangani	Stanleyville
Kalemie	Albertville
Moba	Baudouinville
Bandundu	Benningville
Bukavu	Constermansville
Ilebo	Port-Francqui
Isiro	Paulis
Kananga	Luluabourg
Likasi	Jadotville
Lubumbashi	Élisabethville
Lukutu	Élisabetha
Lusanga	Leverville
Mbandaka	Coquilhatville
Mbanza-Ngungu	Thysville
Mobaye-Mbongo	Banzyville
Mbuji-Mayi	Bakwanga
Ubundu	Pointhierville
Kindu	Port de Kindu, also Kindu-Port-Empain
Arua	Aru
Niangara	Niangana

APPENDIX II

Anti-Castro Cubans That Fought For Freedom In Congo

Pilots, Aircraft Maintenance, and Administration

Afont Rodríguez, Tomás
Alvarez, Francisco "Panchito"
Balboa Alvarado, José
Baró, César
Bartes, Francisco
Batista Fernández, Nildo (1956)[1]
Blanco, Reginaldo
Bernal Fernández, Gastón (1941)
Blázquez del Pozo, Antonio "El Pedrusco"
Bringuier, Jorge
Brito García, Orlando (1956)
Cadena, Enrique
Cantillo Huget, Amado (1957)
Carol Armand, Oscar Alfonso
Castellanos Reyes Gavilán, José Manuel "Memel" (1943)
Castillo Leyva, Rafael "Propela"
Castresana, Elpidio
Cereceda Coira, Castor
Chabau, Sosa
Cordo Lugo, Oscar
Cosme Toribio, Luis (1947)
Cross Quintana, Raúl (1948)
De la Guardia, Luis
Despaigne Pérez, Ernesto
Díaz, Manuel

Entriago Telledo, José (1955)
Fernández, Segisberto
Fernández Ardois-Anduz, Luis
Filpes, Claudio
Flaquer Carballal, Federico
García Acosta, Tristán
García Fernández, René (1948)
García Pujol, Rafael (1957)
García Tuñón, Juan (killed in action near Bunia, Congo, February 17, 1965)
Ginebra-Groero Pérez, Mario (killed near Albertville, Congo, October 1964)
Ginebra-Groero Pérez, Francisco "Chiqui"
Gómez Gómez, Fausto I. (killed in action in Bunia, Congo, December 17, 1964)
González Molina, Guillermo (1957)
González Torrecillas, Antonio (1941)
Gutiérrez, Alberto "Dr. Kildare"
Hernández Rojo, Ángel Manuel
Hernández Reyes, Héctor "Moropo"
Herrera Cabrera, Gonzalo
Herrera Pérez, Eduardo J. (1957)
Intriago, Jorge
Izquierdo Ramírez, Orlando (1955)
Landazuri, Ramiro
López Domínguez, Angel
Luaices Sotelo, César
de la Maza Barrios, Alfredo (1957)
Méndez Acosta, Santiago (1956)
Navarro Rodríguez, Jorge M. "El Puma" (1957)
Orgánvidez Domínguez, Hernán
Padrón Sánchez, Cecilio
Pedrianes, Angel
Pellón Blanco, José Leonardo
Pedroso Amores, Acelo
Pérez Menéndez, José
Pérez Sordo, Alberto (1957)
Perón Sosa, Juan C. "Titi"
Peynó Inclán, Ernesto
Piedra, Armando

Piqué Fernández-Coca, Arturo (killed in action in Congo)
Ponzoa Alvarez, Gustavo C.
Quintero, Jorge "Toto"
Ramos, Mario
Rodríguez Rendueles, Gastón
Rojas González, Ignacio M.
Roque, Luis
Salas Baró, Antonio (1956)
Seda Reyes, Leonardo (1952)
Solís Sariol, Raúl
Soto Vázquez, Antonio (1953)
Travieso Pla, René (1948)
Tuya, René
Valdéz Campanería, Fausto A.
Valliciergo, Francisco
Verdaguer, Guillermo
Varela, Joaquín "Jack"
Whitehouse Inzua, Eduardo
Yabor Justiz, Carlos

Ground Forces

Commanding Officer: Robertson, William "Rip" (Honorary Cuban exile)
Officer: U.S. Army Lt. Colonel Garza, Arthur "Art"
Officer: USAF/CIA Operative "Mitch"
Argüelles, Santiago
Benítez, Ángel
Calas, Alicio
Fernández, Alfredo "Calviño"
Fernández, Conrado
Fuentes, Félix "Felo"
García, Orlando
González Castro, José Ángel "El Chino"
Hernández, José "Juan Roque"
Lazo, Guillermo
López, Pedro
Martínez, Raimundo
Morales Navarrete, Ricardo "El Mono"
Pérez, Alberto

Rivero, Manuel "El Gallego"
Rodríguez, Jorge
Romero, Andrés
Silva Cadeba, Jorge "Fotingo"
Tamayo Cordoví, Juan "El Negro"

Lake Tanganyika Patrol

SWIFT Boat: Monty
Chávez, Ricardo
Cepero, Serapio
Alvarez, Anael
Cao, Roberto
Toledo, Félix
Arroyo, Jorge
Salcedo, Justo "Papá"

SWIFT Boat: Gitana
Arce, Remigio
Bringas, Generoso
Borges, Domingo
Sánchez. Andrés
Fernández, Luis
Reyes, Eulogio "Papo"
Ramírez, Pedro
Hernández, Gumersindo

Radio/Radar Technician: Pichardo, Roberto

Note

1.   A year within parentheses following a pilot's name indicates year of graduation from the Cuban Air Force Academy.

Appendix III

Cuban Combatants in Congo

This is a list of Cuban combatants in Congo provided in *El Sueño Africano del Che* by William Gálvez. There are significant arithmetic discrepancies with other sources. This list contains 123 names and although Gálvez states that it is incomplete, he further states that "few names are missing."[1] Several Cuban sources indicate that at one point there were as many as 200 Cuban combatants. Among these is an undated letter from Che Guevara to Fidel Castro reproduced in *El Año que Estuvimos en Ninguna Parte* by Taibo et al, presented in Chapter Ten, in which Guevara states: "And there are my 200 [men]."[2]

An additional source of incertitude is provided by Benigno.[3] In his book, Benigno stated that he was heading one of Che's companies in Congo, and he was given the war name of "Katanga." Since there was already a black Cuban soldier named Katanga, Benigno was Katanga-White[4] while the other soldier was Katanga-Black. Benigno is not included in Gálvez's list, not by his real name (or by Benigno), nor by his war name of Katanga-White. There is no mention on this list of any Katanga, black or white. There are enough inconsistencies to doubt if Benigno was in Congo, or how long he stayed there.

There are a number of Cuban combatants whose names appear in Guevara's diary, but are not enumerated in Gálvez's list. Two names have been selected, listed as 124 and 125. This reinforces the contention that there were at least 200 Cuban resident fighters in Guevara's Congo unit.

Another example of incomplete counting is the Cuban soldier Roberto Hernández Calzada, who was one of the men left behind and later rescued. His name is given in *El Año que Estuvimos en Ninguna Parte*, but he does not appear in Gálvez's list.

The number of 200 soldiers is referenced in multiple sources, and thus appears to be confirmed by default. It is possible that after Benigno defected in 1996, his name was obliterated from all Cuban official records, as may have been the names of Cuban soldiers who refused to continue fighting and were sent back to Havana in disgrace. It is also conceivable that Guevara had included some of the Congolese and Rwandan fighters in the number of men to be evacuated, but this is doubtful. Perhaps a better explanation is that there were more casualties than the seven admitted by the Cuban government. In any event, Gálvez's list follows.

Arrival-Military Rank	Name
1-Commander Moja	Víctor Dreke Cruz
2-Officer M'bili	José María Martínez Tamayo (killed in action in Bolivia in 1967)
3-Commander Tatu	Ernesto "Che" Guevara
4-First Lieutenant Inne	Norberto Pío Pichardo (killed in action at Front de Force, Congo June 29, 1965)
5-PFC Tano	Aldo García González
6-Corporal Sita	Pablo B. Ortiz
7-Corporal Saba	Pedro B. Ortiz
8-Sergeant Nane	Eduardo Torres (aka Coqui)
9-Sergeant Tiza	Julián Morejón
10-Medic Kumi	Rafael Zerquera Martín
11-PFC Ishirini	Chibás González
12-Sergeant Telathini	Víctor M. Ballester (killed in action at Front de Force, Congo June 29, 1965)
13- PFC Arobaine	Salvador J. Escudero
14-PFC Hansini	Constantino Pérez
15-PFC Sitaini	Ángel Fernández Angulo

16-PFC Rabanini — Lucio Sánchez

17-PFC Kigulo — Noelio Revé

18-Sergeant Maganga — Ramón Muñoz

19-Captain Aly — Santiago Terry Rodríguez

20-Sergeant Singida — Manuel Savigne Medina

21-PFC Sultán — Rafael Vaillant

22-Corporal Kasambala — Roberto Chaveco

23-PFC — Tom Rafael Hernández

24-PFC Wasiri — Golván Marín

25-PFC Kulula — Augusto Ramírez

26-Lieutenant Mafu — Catalino Olachea

27-Sergeant Kahama — Alberto Man Sieleman

28-PFC Tamusini — Domingo Pie Fiz

29-PFC Paulu — Emilio Mena

30-Corporal Kawawa — Wagner Moro Pérez (killed in action at Front de Force, Congo June 29, 1965)

31-Sergeant Doma — Arcadio Hernando

32-Sergeant Abdalla — Alipio del Sol

33-Captain Changa — Roberto Sánchez Bartelemy (aka Lawton)

34-Lieutenant Azi — Israel Reyes Zayas (killed in action in Bolivia in 1967)

35-PFC Aja — Andrés A. Arteaga

36-PFC Adabu — Dioscórides Romero

37-PFC Agano — Arquímides Martínez

38-PFC Ananane — Mario Thompson Vegas

39-Corporal Anzama — Arnaldo Domínguez

40-PFC Ansa — Moisés Delisle

41-PFC Au — Andrés J. Jardínes

42-PFC Alacre	Sinecio Prado
43-PFC Amia	José L. Torres
44- Corporal Anzala	Octavio Rojas
45-PFC Bahasa	Orlando Puente Mayeta (killed in action during the as sault of Che's HQ in Kilonwe, Congo October 26, 1965)
46-PFC Alau	Lorenzo Espinosa García
47-PFC Ahili	Eduardo Castillo Lora
48-PFC Andika	Vicente Yant
49- First Lieutenant Azima	Ramón Armas
50-Sergeant Almari	Argelio Zamora Torriente (killed in action in Angola in 1975)
51-PFC Akiki	Roger Pimentel
52-PFC Aga	Virgilio Jiménez Rojas
53-PFC Anchali	Sandalio Lemus
54-PFC Ansalia	Luis Monteagudo
55-PFC Arobo	Mariano García
56-PFC Afendi	Roberto Rodríguez
57-PFC Ami	Ezequiel Toledo Delgado
58-Captain Anzurune	Crisóenes
59-PFC Anga	Juan F. Aguilera
60-PFC Ahiri	José Antonio Aguiar
61-PFC Amba	Luis Díaz Primero
62-Corporal Ottu	Santiago Parada
63-Sergeant Okika	Herminio Betancourt
64-Lieutenant Kisua	Erasmo Videaux Robles
65-PFC Falka	Fernando Aldama
66-PFC Mongueso	Germán Ramírez
67-PFC Kadatasi	Arcadio Puentes
68-PFC Danhisi	Nicolás Savón

69-Sergeant Sitini-Natutu — Giraldo Padilla
70-PFC Chepua — Roberto Pérez Calzado
71-PFC Hukumu — Rodovaldo Gundín
72-PFC Isilin — Elio H. Portuondo
73-PFC Chesue — Tomás Rodríguez
74-PFC Marembo — Isidro Peralta
75-Medic Chumi — Raúl Candevat
76-Medic Hindi — Héctor Vera
77-Medic Fara — Gregorio Herrera
78-PFC Barufu — Ismael Monteagudo
79-PFC Pilau — Daniel Cruz
80-PFC Bahati — Melanio Miranda
81-PFC Chunga — Luis Hechavarría
82-Corporal Hatari — Adalberto Fernández
83-PFC Dukuduko — Santos Duquesne
84-PFC Fada Antonio — Pérez Sánchez
85-PFC Masihisano — Casiano Pons
86-PFC Nñeyñea — Luis Calzada Hernández

87-Corporal Badala — Bernardo Amelo
88-PFC Sakumu — Florentino Limindu Zulueta

89-PFC Cheni — Virgilio Montoya Muñoz

90-PFC Samani — Wilfredo de Armas
91-PFC Chembeu — Eddy Espinosa
92-Corporal Dwala — Dionisio Madera
93-PFC Hanesa — Osvaldo Izquierdo
94-Sergeant Tumaini — Carlos Coello (killed in action in Bolivia in 1967)

95-Sergeant Ngenje — Marcos A. Herrera
96-PFC Safi — Vladimir Rubio
97-Sergeant Dufu — Armando Martínez
98-PFC Changa — Domingo Pérez Hernández

99-First Lieutenant Pombo — Harry Villegas
100-PFC Zuleimán — Francisco C. Torriente (missing in

	action in Congo evacuation
101-Lieutenant Karín	José Palacio
102-PFC Mustafá	Conrado Morejón
103-PFC Abdala	Luciano Paul
104-PFC Sheik	Raumide Despaigne
105-PFC Samuel	Fidencio Semanat
106-PFC Awirino	Francisco Semanat
107-Sergeant Milton	Víctor Cañas
108-Lieutenant Ziwa	Víctor Schueg Colás
109-Captain Uta	Aldo Margolles
110-Commander Siki	Oscar Fernández Mell
111-Captain Tembo	Emilio Aragonés
112-Lieutenant Rebocate	Mario Armas
113-Medic Kasulo	Adrien Sansarique Laforet (citizen of Haiti)
114-Medic Moro Goro	Octavio de la Concepción de la Pedraza (killed in action n Bolivia in 1967)
115-Medic Fizi	Diego Lagomozino
116-Medic Kimbi	Domingo Oliva
117-Lieutenant Mauro	Justo Rumbaut
118-PFC Carlos	Florentino Nogas
119-PFC Tulio	Tomás Escadón Carvajal
120-PFC Agile	Dioscórides Meriño Castillo
121-PFC Ancine	Constantino Pérez Méndez
122-PFC Víctor	Jesús Álvarez Morejón
123-PFC Aguir	Esmérido Parada Zamora
124-PFC Maurino[5]	Julio Cabrera Jiménez (missing in action)
125-Unknown *nom de guerre*[6]	Rafael Pérez Castillo

Notes

1. Gálvez, William, *op. cit.*, pp. 361-364.
2. Taibo II, et al, p. 184.
3. Alarcón Ramírez, Dariel (aka Benigno), *op cit.*, pp. 338-339.
4. Benigno was not one of the original combatants selected for Congo, and he was white. He claims that he ended up Congo (Brazzaville) without a passport. After he obtained a new passport in Algeria, he traveled to Dar Es-Salaam, Tanzania, where Guevara asked him to stay and join the Congo operation.
5. Name appears in Guevara's diary and not on Gálvez's list.
6. Name appears in Guevara's diary and not on Gálvez's list.

Appendix IV

Interviews

All tapes and notes from the interviews are in the author's possession, unless otherwise stated.

Luis Ardois
Reginaldo Blanco
Generoso Bringas
Alicio Calas
Amado Cantillo
Oscar Carol
Lawrence R. Devlin, Congo CIA Station Chief, 1960-1967
Fausto B. Gómez, son of the late Fausto I. Gómez Gómez
Conrado Fernández
Segisberto Fernández
José Hernández "Juan Roque"
José M. Hernández, son-in-law of the late Raúl Cross Quintana
Roberto Medell
Jorge Navarro "El Puma"
Juan Perón
Gustavo Ponzoa
Eulogio Reyes "Papo"
Juan Tamayo "El Negro"
Félix Toledo
Manuel Villafaña Martínez

Timetables

Simba Rebellion Rebellion—Chapter 6

Approximate Date	Event
Late 1962	First Cuban exile pilots arrive
January 1963	Bulk of UN peacekeepers depart Congo
August 1963	Simba rebellion starts in earnest with the arrival of Mulele in the Kwilu River area
September 1963	Dissolution of Congo Parliament
October 1963	Formation of National Liberation Council (CNL)
January 21, 1964	Mobutu/Kasavubu declare state of emergency in Kwilu
May 1964	Soumialot takes Uvira and Fizi
June 1964	Soumialot takes Kalemie
June 30, 1964	Tshombé returns, becomes Prime Minister
Summer 1964	Hoare, Denard, and Schramme arrive in Congo at Tshombé's request
July 1964	Olenga and Popular Army of Liberation march north
July 19, 1964	Kabila and Massengo take Moba (north Katanga)
July 22, 1964	Rebel forces take Kindu
Late July 1964	Rebels control ½ of Congo including Great Lakes area
August 5, 1964	Kisangani is taken by rebel forces—Mulamba not present
August 6, 1964	Proclamation of Peoples Republic of Congo at Kisangani

August 6, 1964	Congolese, Belgian, and American governments commence negotiations with Simbas to end crisis
August 6, 1964	Vandewalle called to Foreign Ministry in Brussels—flies to Congo next day with Belgium's Fifth Mechanized Brigade
August 6-8, 1964	Harriman—Spaak consultations in Brussels to free hostages
August 19, 1964	Olenga attacks Bukavu—defeated by Mulamba and Makasi
August 21, 1964	Olenga orders "trial without mercy" of American diplomats
August 21, 1964	Makasi flies first B-26K combat mission in Congo
August 24, 1964	Hoare, Makasi, and ANC attack Kalemie
August 29, 1964	Dean Rusk officially recognizes Kisangani situation to be an American crisis
August 30, 1964	Kalemie taken by Col Kakuji—Hoare had retreated
Early September, 1964	Cuban exile infantrymen arrive in Congo
September 5, 1964	OAU extraordinary session—Kenya's Jomo Kenyatta to mediate and search for solution
Mid-September, 1964	Vandewalle, Hoare, Cuban exiles, Belgians, and ANC (Lima I and Lima II) start operations to retake territory
September 15, 1964	Denard and Cuban exiles take Lisala
October 14, 1964	Rebels issue new threats to foreigners in Kisangani
October 24, 1964	Hoare's Company 51 and Cuban exiles take Bumba
October 28, 1964	Rebels arrest all Americans and Belgians in Kisangani
November 1, 1964	Hoare's *Stan Column* (with Makasi support) begin drive on Kindu

November 6, 1964	Kindu taken—massacre of 100+ foreigners prevented
November 16, 1964	U.S. and Belgium agree on the logistics of a Kisangani rescue plan (if it is to take place). U.S. Joint Chiefs of Staff ordered the U.S./Belgian rescue operation
November 21, 1964	Rebels threaten to eat their prisoners
November 21, 1964	Kasavubu, Tshombé, and Mobutu authorize the Kisangani rescue operation (since in Congo territory)
November 22, 1964	*Dragon Force* arrives at Kamina air field, Katanga
Jan/Feb 1965	Cuban exile infantry departs Congo
September 1965	Cuban exile Navy arrives in Kalemie
Feb/Mar 1966	

Rescue Operations—Chapter 7

Approximate Date	**Event**
Mid-November, 1964	C-130s of Tactical Air Command from Pope AFB, NC sent to Evreux-Fauville Air Base in France
November 15, 1964	U.S. Joint Chiefs of Staff issue a warning order for the Kisangani rescue
November 16, 1964	U.S. Joint Chiefs of Staff and Belgium Supreme Armed Forces Command order the U.S./Belgian *Dragon Force* Rescue Operation
November 17, 1964	Crews told to take off for Kline Brogel Air Base in Belgium—Paratroopers & equipment picked up

November 17, 1964	Crews land at Morón de la Frontera Air Base in Spain— refueled and obtained new orders
November 18, 1964	Crews arrive in Ascension Island—told to wait
November 21, 1964	Kasavubu, Tshombé, and Mobutu authorize the rescue operation as it is to take place in Congo territory
November 22, 1964	Dragon Force arrives at Kamina Military Base, Katanga Province, Congo
November 22, 1964	Vandewalle, Hoare, and other ground forces near Kisangani, instructed to wait
November 24, 1964	05:45 Makasi strafes Kisangani Airport
November 24, 1964	06:00 Dragon Force paratroopers are dropped
November 24, 1964	07:00 runway is cleared—air landing troops begin to arrive
November 24, 1964	07:40 Belgian paratroopers reach Kisangani center and rescue hostages
November 24, 1964	07:45 Simbas open fire on hostages
November 24, 1964	07:50 Belgian paratroopers reach massacre site
November 24, 1964	10:00 Vandewalle and Hoare's forces link with paratroopers & secure city
November 24, 1964	Rip Robertson and Cuban exiles rescue missionaries at kilometer 8 mission
November 25, 1964	Cairo mob burn JFK Library
November 26, 1964	*Dragon Noir* rescue in Isiro
November 29, 1964	Dragon Force departs for Ascension Island

November 30, 1964	Dragon Force arrives in Brussels
December 1, 1964	Victory Parade in Brussels for Paratroopers
Late December 1964	Infantry Cuban exiles without injuries return to Miami
Late January 1965	Remaining Cuban exile infantrymen fly to Miami Cuban exile Navy departs Congo

Bibliography

Books on the Cold War and Castro's Export of the Cuban Revolution

Alarcón Ramírez, Dariel (Benigno), *Memorias de Un Soldado Cubano: Vida Muerte de la Revolución*. Tusquets Editores, Barcelona, 1996.

Benemelis, Juan F., *Castro, Subversión y Terrorismo en Africa*, Editorial San Martín, Madrid, 1988.

Benemelis, Juan F., *Las Guerras Secretas de Fidel Castro*, Fundación Elena Maderos, Miami, 2002.

Beruvides, Esteban M., *Cuba: Los Crímenes Impunes de Fidel Castro*, Colonial Press, Miami, 1999.

Carbonell, Néstor T., *And the Russians Stayed*, Morrow, New York, 1989.

Costa, Jaime, *El Clarín Toca al Amanecer*, Ediciones Rondas, Barcelona, 2003.

Gibbs, David N., *The Political Economy of Third World Intervention: Mines, Money and U.S. Policy in the Congo Crisis*, University of Chicago Press, 1991.

Gleijeses, Dr. Piero, *Conflicting Missions: Havana, Washington and Africa, 1959-1976*, University of North Carolina Press, Chapel Hill, 2002.

Kalb, Madeleine G., *The Congo Cables*, New York, Macmillan, 1982.

Mahoney, Richard D., *JFK: Ordeal in Africa*, Oxford University Press, 1983.

Oppenheimer, Andrés, *Castro's Final Hour*, Touchstone, New York, 1992.

Rodríguez, Félix I., and John Weisman, *Shadow Warrior*, Simon and Schuster, New York, 1989.

Schlesinger, Arthur A., *A Thousand Days—John F. Kennedy in the White House*, gh, *Cuba or The Pursuit of Freedom*, Da Capo Press, New York, 1998.

Weissman, Stephen R., *American Foreign Policy in the Congo 1960-1964*, Cornell University Press, 1974.

Books on Congo History

Ascherson, Neal, *The King Incorporated*, Granta Books, London, 1999.

Belgium Royal History & News, September 19, 2004, *http://www.royalty.nu/Europe/Belgium.html*.

Biografías Africanas, *Pierre Mulele*. October 23, 2004, *http://www.ikusks.com/Africa/Historia/biografias_mulele.htm*.

Book Rags.com *Biography of Laurent Kabila*, October 29, 2004, *http://www.bookrags.com/biography/laurent-kabila/*.

History of Belgium, September 19, 2004, *http://www.geographia.com/belgium/bxhis01.htm*.

Hochschild, Adam, *King Leopold's Ghost*, Ediciones Península, Barcelona, 1998.

Infoplease. *Tshombé, Moïse Kapenda*, October 26, 2004, *http://www.infoplease.com/ce6/people/A0849577.html*.

Kingsolver, Barbara, *The Poisonwood Bible*, Harper Torch, New York, 1998.
Lonely Planet World Guide, *Belgium History*, September 19, 2004,
    http://www.lonelyplanet.com/destinations/europe/belgium/history.htm.
Marzo, Jorge Luis and Marc Roig, eds. *Planeta Kurtz, Cien Años de "El Corazón de las Tinieblas de Joseph Conrad*, Random House Mondadori, Barcelona, 2002.
The Free Dictionary, *Moïse Tshombé*, November 13, 2004,
    http://encyclopedia.thefreedictionary.com/Moise%20Tshombe.

Books on Congo from Independence to Stanleyville Rescue

Alexander, Colonel McGill, *An African Rapid-deployment Force for Peace Operations on the African Continent*, South African Army, July 1995.
Chopra, Pushpindar Singh, William Green and Gordon Swanborough (Eds.) *Canberras in the Congo, The Indian Air Force and its Aircraft*, IAF Golden Jubilee, Decimus Books, London.
García, René, *Congo: Operación Valle del Kwilo*, Punto de Mira, Julio, 1989.
O'Brien, Conor Cruise, *To Katanga and Back: A UN Case History*, Simon and Schuster, New York, 1963.

Books on the Stanleyville Rescue

Hoare, Mike, *Congo Mercenary*, Robert Hale, London, 1967.
Hoare, Mike, *The Road to Kalamata*, Lexington books, Toronto, 1989.
Holm, Richard L., *A Close Call in Africa, Studies in Intelligence*, CIA, Vol. 42, No.3, 1998.
Hoyt, Michael P. E., *Captive in the Congo: A Consul's Return to the Heart of Darkness*, Naval Institute Press, Annapolis, Maryland, 2000.
Odom, Major Thomas P., *Dragon Operations: Hostage Rescues in Congo, 1964-1965*, Combined Arms Research Library, Fort Leavenworth, Kansas, 1988, *http://www-cgsc.army.mil/carl/resources/csi/odom/odom.asp*.
Odom, Lieutenant Colonel Thomas P., *Shaba II: The French and Belgian Intervention in Zaire in 1978*, Combined Arms Research Library, Fort Leavenworth, Kansas, 1993, *http://cgsc.leavenworth.army.mil/carl/resources/csi/odom2/odom2.asp*.
Schramme, Jean, *Le Bataillon Léopard: Souvenirs d'un Africain Blanc*, Laffont, Paris, c1969.
Vandewalle, Colonel Frédéric, *L'Ommegang: Odysée et Reconquête de Stanleyville*, Brussels, Le Livre Africain, 1970.

Books on the Role of Cubans and Cuban Exiles in Congo

Boudreau, William J., *Mobutu's Congo: A Reminiscence of the U.S. Role*, Foreign Service Life, December 9, 2004,
    http://www.unc.edu/depts/diplomatic/archives_roll/2004_10-12/boudreau.
Cahill, Thomas, *How the Irish Saved Civilization*, New York, Doubleday, 1955.
Devlin, Larry, *Chief of Station, Congo: A Memoir of 1960-67*, Public Affairs, New York, 2007.
Encinosa, Enrique, *Cuba en Guerra: Historia de la Oposición Anti-Castrista 1959-1993*, The Endowment for Cuban American Studies of the Cuban American National Foundation, Miami, 1994.
Encyclopaedia Britannica Premium Service, *Denard, Robert*, 5 December 2004, *http://www.britannica.com/eb/article?tocld=9114518*.
Gálvez, William, *Che in Africa: Che Guevara's Congo Diary*, Ocean Press, 1999.

Gálvez, William, *El Sueño Africano de Ché—¿Qué Sucedió en la Guerrilla Congolesa?* Casa de Las Américas, La Habana, 1997.

Guevara, Ernesto "Che", *The African Dream: The Diaries of the Revolutionary War in the Congo,* Grove Press, New York, 2000.

Johnson, Robert Craig, *Heart of Darkness: the Tragedy of the Congo, 1960-67.* September 17, 2004, *http://worldatwar.net/chandelle/v2/v2n3/congo.html.*

Le Bailly, Jacques, *Une Poignée de Mercenaires,* Presses de la Cité, Paris, 1967.

Leguineche, Manuel, *Yo Pondré la Guerra,* Ediciones El País, Madrid, 1998.

Price, James R. and Paul Jureidini, *Witchcraft, Sorcery, Magic, and Other Psychological Phenomena and Their Implications on Military and Paramilitary Operations in the Congo,* Special Operations Research Office, August 8, 1964.

Risquet Valdéz, Jorge, *El Segundo Frente del Che en el Congo,* Casa Editorial Abril, La Habana, 2000.

Ros, Enrique, *Cubanos Combatientes: Peleando en Distintos Frentes,* Ediciones Universal, Miami, 1998.

Ros, Enrique, *La Aventura Africana de Fidel Castro,* Ediciones Universal, Miami, 1999.

Saco, José Antonio, *Historia de la Esclavitud,* Biblioteca Júcar, Madrid, 1974.

Sanz Gadea, Joaquín, *Un Médico en el Congo,* Ediciones Temas de Hoy, Madrid, 1998.

Suchlicki, Jaime, *Cuba from Columbus to Castro,* Brassey's Inc., Washington, 1990.

Taibo II, Paco Ignacio, Froilán Escobar and Félix Guerra, *El Año que Estuvimos en Ninguna Parte,* Editorial Txalaparta, Pamplona, Spain, 1995.

World History.com, *Mike Hoare in the News,* November 27, 2004, *http://www.worldhistory.com/wiki/M/Mike-Hoare.htm.*

Index

CPSIA information can be obtained at www.ICGtesting.com
Printed in the USA
LVOW120734030312

271310LV00002B/6/P

9 781412 847667